RENT

CONTROL

RENT CONTROL

Regulation and The Rental Housing Market

W. Dennis Keating
Michael B. Teitz
Andrejs Skaburskis

CENTER FOR URBAN POLICY RESEARCH
Rutgers—The State University of New Jersey
New Brunswick, New Jersey

Published by the Center for Urban Policy Research
Civic Square • 33 Livingston Avenue • Suite 400
New Brunswick, New Jersey 08901–1982

Printed in the United States of America

Cover design: Helene Berinsky
Interior design/typesetting: Arlene Pashman

Library of Congress Cataloging-in-Publication Data

Keating, W. Dennis (William Dennis)
    Rent control : regulation and the rental housing market / edited
by W. Dennis Keating, Michael B. Teitz, Andrejs Skaburskis.
        p.   cm.
    Includes bibliographical references and index.

    ISBN 0-88285-159-4 (alk. paper)

    1. Rent control—United States. 2. Rent control—Canada.
I. Teitz, Michael B. II. Skaburskis, Andrejs.
KF6068.R3K43 1998
346.7304'344—dc21   97–26456
                                                        CIP

Contents

Preface

Rent control, the governmental regulation of the level of payment and tenure rights for rental housing, occupies a small but unique niche within the broad domain of public regulation of markets. It is, perhaps, the only form of price regulation in which the regulation occurs at the level of the individual transaction. Because every housing unit is different—at a minimum by virtue of its unique location in three-dimensional space, but in reality because of a host of subtle sources of variation—the price of housing cannot be defined on the basis of a common unit of quantity, as it can for most other goods. The price of housing cannot be regulated by establishing a single price for a given level of quality, as other commodities such as electricity and sugar have been regulated at various times. Rent regulation requires that a price level be established for each individual housing unit, which in turn implies a level of complexity in structure and oversight that is unequaled.

At the same time, rental housing occupies a very special status in the eyes of its occupants. It is costly—accounting for a third or more of most renters' budgets. It is difficult to substitute; finding a new unit requires extensive searching and involves substantial moving costs. Since any given unit is the focus of an individual's or a household's personal life, it takes on a deep psychological significance as a place of security and self-definition. That the subject of housing can evoke strong emotions should not surprise us; it touches people's most sensitive concerns—their pocketbooks and their sense of personal well-being. Regulation in such a sensitive environment cannot be simple or easy.

Nonetheless, again and again in the history of cities across the world, we find efforts to control the price of rental housing. Almost from the outset, concerns about the price and quality of rental housing have evoked movements to regulate its provision in the market. Such efforts have ranged from nonideological ad hoc attempts to soften the impact of specific pressures on rents, such as those that occur in times of shortage during war, to comprehensive efforts by socialist reformers and revolutionaries to transform the very nature of housing ownership and supply. Both the First and Second World Wars, for example, provided a substantial impetus to rent control in North America. Beyond the effects of war, housing reformers' efforts arose from the perception that without controls the market would provide rental housing for poor and working-class households only at a low level of quality, as judged by the conventional middle-class standards of the time. Furthermore, the price of such housing was perceived as burdensome, and the conditions of occupancy too often insecure or degrading. The stock figure of the grasping and heartless landlord continues to be part of the cultural heritage of the modern world, although, to be sure, that image has its roots in rural tenancy.

Residential rent control has never been universally adopted. Rather, it seems to persist stubbornly in the face of powerful forces that seek its elimination. In capitalist societies, price regulation is always a dubious enterprise, standing in opposition to free-market competition and to the forces of supply and demand. Still, despite their shortcomings, market-based capitalist societies have raised the productivity and standard of living of their members to levels unequaled in human history. Within these societies, the logic of price formation through the market is both widely recognized and supported by the web of social institutions and power relationships that constitute the societies' essential fabric. Only where market forces are clearly distorted, as in the case of natural or artificial monopolies, has regulation been widely endorsed and adopted. Certainly, among economists, who are the voice of conventional understanding of economic issues, rent control has long been anathematized as wasteful, inefficient, and inequitable. Few people of any walk of life would advocate price regulation of other commodities. Perhaps it makes more sense to ask why residential rent control is still with us.

The purpose of this book is to explain carefully and in full measure the nature of rent control as it has evolved in North America in the twentieth century. For several reasons, this is not an easy task. Rent control is one of the most frequently debated and emotionally charged issues addressed at the state and local levels in American life. The threat of its appearance evokes intense fear, opposition, and attempts to enact preventive legislation on the part of rental housing owners and their allies. Where rent control exists, the possibility of change or abolition gives rise to heated debate and intense political conflict, as evidenced in 1997 in New York City as this is being written. Inevitably, those who write about topics like rent control face the likelihood that they will be labeled as partisan toward one side or the other. Indeed, no one comes to such a subject without values that implicitly favor a particular position. Even so, walking in a minefield tends to make one especially careful of the path taken. We have attempted to traverse the field of rent control in a way that is reasoned and respectful of reality, as revealed by the best research that we can find. This book is not a tract, either for or against rent regulation.

Even if the problem of bias can be dealt with, residential rent control is still a formidably difficult subject. As a policy, it affects so many aspects of life that no single disciplinary perspective can reveal its meanings and ramifications. For this reason, the first part of this book is organized on thematic lines, drawing on research from a variety of theoretical perspectives and disciplines. We begin in chapter 1 with an overview of the evolution of rent control in North America during this century, sketching its origins and its changing character. The intent is not to provide a detailed history of what has been a very complicated evolution but rather to give a sense of the key events, the forces at work, and the issues that appear to have been central to debates over regulation of residential rents. A key aspect of rent control in the United States, for example, has been its basis in legislation at the state and local levels of government, rather than at the federal level, as is the case in most other countries where rent regulation exists. However, that state and local legislation is bounded by federal and state constitutions, and its impact has been challenged through litigation and in the courts. Chapters 2 and 3, respectively, examine rent control from the perspective, first, of legislation and administration, and second, from the perspective of the courts and litigation. Although rent control is often perceived in monolithic and simplistic terms, in fact, the state and local legislative origin of rent control regulation has resulted in a rich variety of forms and degree. The range of what is permissible has been explored, tested, and established by a combination of political conflict and accommodation in the legislative process and by litigation in state and federal courts. The peculiar nature of residential rent control—i.e., its regulation of the specific rent for each unit, though with generic permissible levels of change in rents—requires that the legislation be written in such a way as to permit a form of administration that differs substantially from that of most types of regulation. The impact and effectiveness of the regulation are in turn greatly shaped by both legislative form and administrative practice. Given the complexity of formulas and the disagreement about such basic questions as how to measure the return on investment realized by landlords or the impact of rent adjustments on tenants, both legislation and administration have been continuously subjected to litigation and court tests. These tests have turned heavily on the issue of constitutionality of rent regulation and, once it was found to be constitutional, on the rights of owners to adequate returns on their investments.

Chapters 4, 5, and 6 provide an analysis of rent control from the perspectives of economics, politics, and broad social meaning. Each chapter explores rental regulation from its particular point of view and permits us to ask very different questions about the nature and significance of this phenomenon. Traditionally, economics has dominated the written debate about rent control, though it has not necessarily determined the choice of specific legislative form or administrative structure. As noted above, economists for decades have treated rent control as an undesirable aberration, a view bolstered by the simplistic and draconian form of early permanent rent freezes. Most of the early writing on the topic tended to be argument *a priori* from simple theory, with little effort to explore the empirical reality. As noted in chapter 4, however, in the past three decades, two things have changed. First, empirical research on the economic impacts of rent control has grown in scale and quality, revealing much that was not known. Meanwhile, the growing sophistication in the understanding of housing markets has led to new insights into their character. Second, rental regulation itself has changed toward a more market-accommodating form, which has, in turn, stimulated more sophisticated theoretical analyses of the question of impact. At this point, most economists would still condemn rent control, but a significant number view it as regulation that has complex possibilities within the imperfect nature of housing markets. The basic economic issues of who benefits and who pays—and over what time frame—are beginning to be addressed both theoretically and empirically.

Chapter 5 looks at the politics of rent control, as distinguished from the specifics of legislation and administration. It explores terrain that has been little considered by researchers, even though everyone who has ever had anything to do with rent control has recognized the power of politics in rent control's formation, implementation, and transformation over time. A key question for the analysis of rent control politics is what model of political behavior is most appropriate for this particular subject. Because virtually no work has been done on the subject, we explore three possible models—based on *public interest theory*, *interest group theory*, and *principal agent theory*—and we recognize a fourth perspective in *class-based theory*. Throughout its history, most discussions of rent control have implicitly treated it purely from an interest group perspective, but little careful work has been done to test how rent control politics actually functions. This chapter should be seen as an exploration, rather than a definitive assessment, of the field.

If research on the politics of rent control is underdeveloped, examination of its broader social meaning is even less thoroughly explored. Yet rent control clearly has its roots in powerful social forces and relationships. Chapter 6 considers some of the social issues that underlie rent control, using the idea of social failure—i.e., the unraveling of critical social relationships—as its central metaphor. On this basis, concerns such as equity, equality, justice, stability, and liberty—rather than economic efficiency or political effectiveness— come to the fore. Each of these concerns has been invoked historically in support of, or in opposition to, rent control, but how they actually fit into the debate has rarely been discussed.

Each of these thematic or disciplinary perspectives on rent control gives us a unique set of insights that range from the intensely practical—e.g., administrative—to the highly abstract—e.g., those that deal with social meaning. As with any policy, such abstraction and reduction are absolutely necessary for understanding outcomes and processes that are observed. The danger, of course, lies in assuming that the insights from one perspective, such as economics, reveal all that is really important and should therefore dominate decision making. It is essential to see the interactions of the perspectives in order to avoid elementary policy errors, such as the assumption that people will have no political response to loss of economic welfare. The interactions can be seen through close examination of specific instances of regulation, which is the aim of the later chapters of the book.

Chapters 7 through 13 provide seven synoptic analyses of residential rent control in a variety of contexts. These analyses are intended to reveal the policy's range of contexts, from small to large cities, and within states. The chapters look at the varying degrees of regulatory stringency with which rent control is attempted, from strict control in Berkeley, California, to moderate rent control in Washington, D.C., Los Angeles, and New Jersey, to uniquely complex forms in New York City and Toronto. For the most part, the cases focus on conventional rental housing, but in chapter 13 we take up mobile home rental regulation, which operates within its own set of constraints and has its own legislative structure.

Together, these chapters reveal great variation and complexity, but they also suggest that there are some commonalities in the regulation of rents, and some important understandings are emerging. In particular, the case studies reveal the limits of ideological commitment in the face of market forces and political reality, whether that commitment is to make rent control stronger or to abolish it. The analyses suggest that there are many paths toward the amelioration of the consequences of rental pressure in housing markets, and that the path taken need not cause high levels of market distortion. The price, however, is that rent levels for most tenants will be close to market; this conclusion raises the issue of whether rent regulation is worth the administrative and political cost. The case studies also make plain that whatever its value to tenants, rent control is not an answer to housing people in deep poverty. The cost of acquisition and operation of housing is the key factor for maintenance and preservation of the housing stock. Although that cost may be affected by the social and political institutions under which housing is provided, it cannot be avoided simply by shifting the burden. Finally, the case studies show us that rent control is fundamentally an expression of social values and relationships, and that its adoption and continuation depend upon the presence of these social values even though, in a modest way, it helps to shape the values.

W. Dennis Keating, Michael B. Teitz,
and
Andrejs Skaburskis

Acknowledgments

Andrejs Skaburskis acknowledges the financial support of the Canadian Social Science and Humanities Research Council for his research. Michael Teitz thanks the John Simon Guggenheim Memorial Foundation for support for his research through a Guggenheim Fellowship.

The authors wish to thank Professor Robert W. Lake, editor in chief of CUPR Press; Linda S. Hayes, Anne Henoch, and Arlene Pashman, editors; and the staff of the Center for Urban Policy Research Press at Rutgers University for their support and assistance in producing this book. The authors also gratefully acknowledge the assistance of Linda Gollogly and Muriel Robinson of the staff of the Department of Urban Studies at Cleveland State University for their able assistance in producing this manuscript.

W. Dennis Keating

1

Rent Control: Its Origins, History, and Controversies

INTRODUCTION

Residential rent control, the public regulation of the rent charged to tenants for housing accommodation, occupies an anomalous position, both in housing policy and in the broader realm of regulation. As housing policy, it has been hailed and denounced. Almost universally, economists and owners of rental housing have opposed rent control since its first appearance in the United States in the early twentieth century. Tenants and their advocates have supported it, though not everywhere and not without reservations. Housing policy makers have regarded rent control with some suspicion, rarely making it a central focus of their activity. Thus, as a policy issue, rent control has stood somewhat apart from the larger housing debates in the United States and Canada. Yet, over the past eighty years, it has continued to be a matter of contention in housing policy, stubbornly refusing to disappear.

As a form of regulation, rent control occupies a similarly anomalous status. From the Progressive period in the late nineteenth century onward, Americans have wrestled with the issue of controlling the negative aspects of capitalism—especially the effects of monopolies and market failures that impose burdens on specific groups or on society in general while generating benefits for others. Regulation as a response to market failure has a

1

..ckered history, with periods of intense activity and enthusiasm, followed by reversals and deregulation. The past two decades in the United States have seen the deregulatory impulse ascendant. Nonetheless, the powerful exceptions of environmental preservation and consumer safety make it clear that the issue remains unsettled, and probably will remain so for the foreseeable future.

Over the years, price regulation has been enacted and implemented primarily at the federal and state levels of government, and has generated an immense amount of debate, study, and literature. Within that very large domain, residential rent control—which is typically implemented at the local government level—occupies only a small niche. Yet it presents an interesting case in which regulation operates directly to control prices charged by a large number of sellers to an even larger number of buyers. Because residential rent control operates within a political and organizational framework that is largely local, it rarely turns on the great issues of economic efficiency that tend to dominate the larger regulatory debates. In fact, it may be argued that residential regulation offers an example of a modern attempt to create a "just price" that hearkens back to a much older tradition of equity and social solidarity. In an era of rising inequality, that may become a key issue for regulation in the future.

This book addresses residential rent control in terms of both housing and regulatory policy, at a time when some of the conventional arguments, both for and against rent control, are showing signs of change. Hard experience and constitutional limitations have led advocates of rental regulation to modify both their expectations and their policy recommendations. "Second-generation" rent controls are very different from their predecessors. Empirical research, new theory, and a deeper understanding of housing market behavior and complexity have led some economists to revisit the original hypotheses about the nature and impact of rental regulation. Now may be the time for a reconsideration of rent control—the time to ask how it works in practice, what its real impacts are, and whether there can be a serious theoretical basis for such regulation. Our aim is not to present another polemical tract for or against regulation in this field; of those, there is no shortage. Rather, our goal is to provide a balanced view of rental regulation in the United States, with attention also to Canada. To this end, we first look at the economic, legal, and political aspects of rent control in the twentieth century, seeking to lay out the character of this form of regulation. Comparative case studies then provide examples of several types of rent control in practice and illustrate the issues discussed in the earlier chapters. The case studies are drawn from California (Berkeley and Los Angeles), New Jersey, New York City, Ontario (Toronto), and Washington, D.C.

We make no claim to be entirely unbiased. In the postmodern world, such a claim makes little sense. It will be clear from the case study chapters that the authors of this book come from varying policy positions in relation to rent control. Nonetheless, we have sought to describe the character of this policy realm as best we can, neither concealing its flaws nor falsely advertising its virtues. We leave it to our readers to judge for themselves the wisdom or the folly of enacting rent controls.

THE ORIGINS AND DEVELOPMENT OF RENT CONTROL

A product of crisis, rent controls typically have been imposed during periods of wartime housing shortages or peacetime inflation when rents increased beyond the ability of many tenants to pay without hardship. Tenant demands that government institute rent control to protect them against rents perceived as exorbitant, against further rent increases, and/or eviction have generally encountered well-organized resistance by landlords, which in turn has resulted in often vitriolic debate and intense political conflict.

The heat generated by the debate over rent control has produced little agreement about its impact on tenants, landlords, or rental housing markets. Disagreement over the social and economic impacts of rent control, whether short-term or long-standing, continues, despite numerous studies. Experts disagree over data, methodology, and the interpretation of research results. From the outset, many of the policy issues raised by rent regulation have been decided by the courts, rather than by the administrative or legislative branches of government, as those frustrated in other arenas have sought redress in legal forums.

Rent Control in the United States

Although rent control has a long history in Europe, in North America its origins date back to World War I. In the face of tenant complaints about rapidly rising rents amid a growing housing crisis, the U.S. Federal Bureau of Industrial Housing and Transportation promoted the formation of committees against rent profiteering in many localities (Drellich and Emery 1939). In England, striking munitions workers protesting landlord "profiteering" had forced the British government to enact temporary wartime rent controls (Albon and Stafford 1987, 68). Although the U.S. government never considered the imposition of federal rent controls (its main concern was the threat to industrial production posed by the shortage of affordable rental housing available to war workers), the pressures on the rental housing market led several local jurisdictions in the United States to adopt temporary emergency controls. The most notable examples were New York City (1920) and Washington, D.C. (1918) (Schaub 1920).

Landlords immediately challenged the constitutionality of rent controls, but in 1921 the United States Supreme Court upheld their legality as a temporary emergency measure. As the rental housing shortage subsided, however, emergency rent control in Washington, D.C., was invalidated by the Supreme Court in 1924 and terminated in New York City in 1929 by preemptive state legislation (Baar and Keating 1975).

Rent control reappeared as a national emergency measure in 1942, shortly after the United States was drawn into World War II. The U.S. government imposed a wartime rent freeze in designated defense rental areas, and the constitutionality of this action was again upheld by the Supreme Court as a wartime emergency measure (Baar and Keating 1975).

These federal wartime rent controls were extended temporarily after the war's end in 1945 because of the continuing housing shortage, which was exacerbated by the demobilization of the armed forces. Federal controls were later relaxed, but the outbreak of hostilities in Korea in 1950 resulted in their retightening. It wasn't until after the election of a conservative Republican president in 1952 and the subsequent Korean truce that federal rent controls were eliminated. States and municipalities, however, had the option of substituting their own controls as the federal regulations expired. Many jurisdictions briefly imposed such regulations, but by the mid 1950s rent control had disappeared entirely in the United States—with one notable exception. New York State maintained rent control in selected cities, including New York City, the largest city in the country.

Meanwhile, in the rest of the country, the postwar building boom of the 1950s eased the housing shortage considerably. Federal housing insurance and subsidy programs also made homeownership possible for millions who had hitherto been unable to afford it, especially World War II veterans.

Second-Generation Rent Controls in the United States

New York's extension of rent control remained an anomaly until the late 1960s, when a combination of rent inflation and a growing tenants' movement in the United States led to demands for rent control in "tight" rental housing markets. The movement's first success came in Massachusetts, when the state adopted local-option rent control in 1969. Tenants succeeded in enacting local rent control legislation in Boston, Brookline, and Cambridge. In contrast to wartime rent freezes, these so-called second-generation rent controls allowed for across-the-board rent increases, usually annually (see chapter 2).

Temporary federal rent controls reappeared unexpectedly with the August 14, 1971 imposition of federal price controls by President Richard Nixon. These controls, which included rent stabilization, were designed to counteract rapid inflation as the Vietnam conflict continued and energy prices soared. Nixon's peacetime rent stabilization program was terminated in January 1973, following his landslide election in November 1972.

With the lifting of the temporary federal rent control, localities, under pressure from tenants, again began to impose their own rent control. Municipal rent control mushroomed in New Jersey in the 1970s, for example (Baar 1977), and the newly authorized home rule government of the District of Columbia enacted rent control in 1975 (Diner 1983).

Berkeley, California, also enacted a renter-sponsored initiative in 1972, but this initiative was ruled unconstitutional by the California Supreme Court in 1976. In the wake of a property tax revolt in California in 1978, however, tenants—denied the promised benefits of a constitutional rollback of significant property tax increases—organized again for rent control. In short order, such major cities as Los Angeles, San Francisco, and San Jose passed moderate second-generation rent controls. The most restrictive rent controls were enacted by renter-sponsored initiatives in the cities of Berkeley and Santa Monica. In addition, many California communities enacted mobile home rent controls (Keating 1985; Baar 1992), giving the price regulation a new aspect. In these and other mobile home communities, landlords own the mobile home parks; tenants own the mobile homes and rent space in the parks.

In the 1980s and 1990s, a backlash against state and local rent controls emerged in some jurisdictions. President Ronald Reagan (former governor of California) attempted unsuccessfully to impose federal preemption of state and local rent control. In 1980, California's real estate industry conducted a statewide initiative campaign to preempt what it regarded as unduly restrictive municipal rent control. This battle continued in the California legislature for a decade and a half. Finally, in 1995, the California legislature mandated that localities with rent controls allow landlords to raise rents when rent-controlled units were vacated, beginning in 1999.

Landlords in New York City also won some concessions in the 1990s, and Massachusetts landlords launched a successful statewide referendum in November 1994 to eliminate the local rent controls that had existed in the cities of Boston, Brookline, and Cambridge for a quarter-century (Cantor 1995). The backlash was not completely successful, however. In 1995, a statewide landlord initiative designed to preempt local mobile home rent control laws was defeated by California voters.

As this brief account indicates, the political fortunes of landlords and tenants have waxed and waned as the debate over rent control has continued in the United States. By and large, the debate has taken place at the state and local levels. No federal rent control has been imposed in the United States since 1973—not even during the rampant inflation of the late 1970s. However, the U.S. Department of Housing and Urban Development (HUD) sets "fair market" rent ceilings for the privately owned rental units it subsidizes.

Rent Control in Canada

The Canadian experience with rent controls closely mirrors that of the United States. The depressed economic activity of the 1930s and the onset of World War II led to the beginning of federal government involvement in housing issues in Canada. As the war effort accelerated, the prices of goods and services, including the costs of rental accommodation in most urban centers, reached hardship levels. In response, the federal government imposed wage and price controls (including a rent freeze) as an emergency wartime measure. Through a program of selective controls, fifteen local markets saw their rental rates frozen at January 1940 levels; the market was then regulated by a local rent committee that had the power to approve rent increases and vary rent maximums, as well as set a maximum rent. By September 8, 1942, all real property, excluding farmland, was brought under rent control.

Constitutionally, regulation of property rights is a matter of provincial concern, and as a result, effective April 30, 1951, the federal government unilaterally ended rent controls. Still, most provinces felt compelled to continue controls to protect their tenants. Ontario, for example, continued controls until March 2, 1954; other provinces followed suit. By the end of the 1950s, however, only the provinces of Quebec and Newfoundland maintained some form of rent regulation.

In Ontario, calls for the reinstitution of some form of rent regulation began in the early 1970s in response to double-digit inflation, rising unemployment, record-low vacancy rates, and increasing concern about "rent gouging" in several major cities, including Toronto. Although rent control was politically unpopular, opponents of rent regulation had to concede defeat when the federal government imposed wage and price controls in October 1975 as part of its anti-inflation strategy. The federal government required the cooperation of the provincial governments in the enactment of provincial rent controls; and the government of the province of Ontario, newly elected and politically weak, succumbed to opposition party pressure and implemented temporary rent controls by the end of the year. Not unexpectedly, these "temporary" controls became a continuing feature of the Ontario rental market, until the implementation of partial decontrol in the spring of 1997.

RENT CONTROL, HOUSING MARKETS, AND HOUSING POLICY

As mentioned earlier, rent control has had an ambiguous position in housing policy. Unlike homeownership, rent subsidies, or construction of low- and moderate-income housing, rent control has rarely been adopted as a fundamental element of policy in the United States or Canada, except at the local level. Its advocates have often seen it as a step toward the realization of larger objectives, such as the proliferation of more affordable housing. Its opponents, on the other hand, have rarely viewed it simply as regulation, but rather as a profound threat. The only other aspect of housing policy to evoke similar opposition in this century is public housing, which is driven by the same perception as rent control—i.e., a belief that the market is fundamentally unable to supply moderate-priced housing of socially acceptable quality to lower-income households.

Major political and ideological battles have raged over the legitimacy and the consequences of rent control. Large numbers of tenants and landlords have been affected by its provisions. Innumerable studies and tracts have analyzed, advocated, and opposed it. To provide some understanding of rent control in the context of housing policy, the rest of this chapter will review both broad policy decisions and rent control debates.

Housing the Poor

In contrast to Western Europe, which has long had a significant stock of publicly owned, cooperative, and nonprofit housing (Ball, Harloe, and Martens 1988), almost all rental housing in the United States is privately owned by for-profit investors. The same holds true for Canada, although the province of Ontario has a significant stock of "social housing" (Dreier and Hulchanski 1993), which enjoys governmental subsidies in the form of tax and mortgage advantages but is still considered "private."

Although over the years many state and local governments in the United States have regulated the condition of rental housing to enforce health and safety standards (Friedman 1968), except for a short-lived effort to build housing for ship workers during World War I, the federal government in the United States did not intervene directly in the housing market until the Great Depression of the 1930s. Even during the Depression, the largest single focus of federal housing policy was middle-income home-ownership and support of the home-building industry through mortgage insurance and tax deductibility of mortgage interest and property taxes. That remains the focus of the government's broad policy today. However, housing policies increasingly have begun to reflect other political and so-cial goals and values, including an attempt to make housing more afford-able for low-income groups. The federal government's first major step in this direction was the enactment of the public housing program in 1937, which made federal subsidies available for the construction (but not the operation) of low-income housing to state and local governments that wished to participate. Later, with the passage of the Brooke Amendment in 1969, the federal government also began providing operating subsidies in response to the growing financial crisis in public housing as units aged and the population became increasingly poorer.

Public housing as the shelter of "last resort" has since faced recurring financial crises. As a result, HUD and the courts have taken over the opera-tion of a number of "troubled" housing authorities—in Boston, Chicago, Philadelphia, and San Francisco, for example. Except for housing for the elderly, little new public housing has been built in the United States since the 1960s.

Instead, since 1974, most federal housing assistance has been in the form of below-market-rent subsidies, provided primarily through HUD's Section 8 program and, more recently, through housing vouchers. To qualify for HUD's rental housing programs, tenants are expected to pay 30 per-cent of their income for rent. In 1989, about 4.1 million renter households out of a total of 31.6 million renter households in the United States received rental assistance through HUD's subsidy programs. These programs served only a fraction of the poor households in the country—only 28 percent of the 11.9 million very low-income renter households, for example, and only 7 percent of the 6.4 million low-income renter households (Congressional Budget Office 1994, 33).[1] The number of households needing assistance seems unlikely to shrink, since the lack of decent, affordable housing can only be exacerbated by the budget cuts suffered by HUD in 1995-1996 as the Republican-controlled Congress slashed HUD's $26 billion budget by approximately $6 billion in rescissions.

Furthermore, low- and moderate-income tenants in the United States will not be able to count on the federal government for much future relief from high rent burdens and substandard rental housing (Stone 1993). In the face of a political consensus to balance the federal budget by the year 2002, federal domestic social programs like lower-income housing assistance face the threat of further draconian cuts (DeParle 1996). With few exceptions, state and local governments have not provided major rental assistance either.

This cutback in federal support helps to explain why regulatory policies like rent control have proven to be attractive to the tenants and their advocates as a means of addressing high rents. Rent control almost always has been proposed and been politically viable in those localities where renters are a majority of the population. (In the United States as a whole, just under two-thirds of the households are homeowners [U.S. Department of Housing and Urban Development 1995, 1996]).

The Debate over Rent Control

Despite its popularity with tenants, rent control as a regulatory policy has been under attack since it was first introduced in North America. In addition to legal challenges to its constitutionality (discussed in chapter 3), rent control has been attacked as economically inefficient and counterproductive as an instrument for redistributing housing benefits (see chapter 4).

The economic arguments against rent control revolve around the following claims:

- ❑ Under rent control, landlords cannot earn a competitive return on their investment—i.e., a market-determined rate.
- ❑ As a result, landlords undermaintain their rent-controlled units, thereby reducing the quality of rental housing.
- ❑ As rent-controlled housing becomes less profitable, landlords may seek to convert it to other more profitable uses (e.g., condominiums or nonhousing commercial uses).
- ❑ The number of available rental units would thereby be further reduced, and the rental market would be further tightened.
- ❑ In extreme cases, landlords may refuse to rent any units at all and may even demolish buildings in the hope of replacing rent-controlled units with more profitable uses.
- ❑ In addition, the decrease in profitability acts as a powerful disincentive to the construction of new rental housing, even if the new housing is exempt from controls. Landlords fear the future imposition of rent control. This fear, in turn, exacerbates the very rental-housing shortage that required rent control in the first place.

These claims and the counterarguments in favor of rent control—e.g., that the displacement of tenants is minimized, that more tenant income is available for spending on other necessities, and that the alleged negative impacts either do not occur or are caused by other factors—are analyzed in detail in chapter 4.

Is Rent Control Equitable?

In theory, rent control is aimed at protecting tenants who are vulnerable to displacement from what are perceived as "extortionate" or "unfair" rent increases. But as an element of social policy, critics charge that rent control itself is inherently unfair. Certain types of rental housing are often exempted from rent control, for example. These include owner-occupied, publicly subsidized, and newly constructed units. And usually there is no income test to determine which tenants should be entitled to protection. Although rent control is generally justified as necessary to protect low- and moderate-income tenants, it usually applies to all tenants living in regulated units, regardless of their income. One practical reason for this broad-based policy is the difficulty of verification of tenant incomes when a large number of units are covered. Opponents argue that rent control is therefore misdirected because its protection is not specifically targeted to those who most need it (Tucker 1990). A corollary argument maintains that the benefits of rent control are skewed in favor of those tenants best able to take advantage of regulated housing, e.g., older and richer white tenants.

In some jurisdictions, so-called luxury units renting above a certain threshold have been exempted on the theory that only affluent tenants could afford them, and that these tenants are not in need of the protection offered by rent control. In 1993, for example, the New York State Legislature de-regulated rent-stabilized units with a monthly rent of $2,000 or more that were vacated as of October 1, 1993. The legislature mandated that even if these units were not subsequently vacated, rents could be set at market rates at the expiration of the leases of the tenant-occupants whose annual incomes exceeded $250,000. New York City estimated that only about 1,500 rent-stabilized units out of a total of approximately one million units in 1993 would be affected by this mandate (McKinley 1994). The median monthly rent for vacant units in New York City in March 1993 was $650, while the median monthly rent for occupied rent-stabilized apartments was $525 (U.S. Bureau of the Census, New York City Housing and Vacancy Survey 1994). Interestingly, this was not the first time that luxury units had been decontrolled in New York City. In 1926, all apartments renting for more than $20 per room had been decontrolled (Salins and Mildner 1992, 55).

Critics of rent control point to the fact that many low-income tenants cannot afford even regulated rents. In 1992, for example, almost half (48 percent) of rent-stabilized tenants in New York City paid more than 30 percent of their income for rent (Rent Guidelines Board 1995). To address this problem as it affects elderly tenants, New York City has introduced a unique Senior Citizen Rent Increase Exemption program, under which rent increases for low-income, elderly tenants are limited or frozen. Landlords are then reimbursed for the lost income from these tenants through tax rebates. Currently, tenants sixty-two years or older with annual incomes of $20,000 or less who are paying more than one-third of their income for rent are eligible for the program. In 1992, 17 percent of all rent-stabilized tenants were sixty-two years or older (Rent Guidelines Board 1995).

The situation of nonelderly, low-income rent-stabilized tenants, on the other hand, has been exacerbated in recent years because the Rent Guidelines Board (RGB) has granted landlords special rent increases for low-rent apartments (usually formerly rent-controlled). In June 1996, for example, the RGB authorized special rent increases of $20 monthly for those rent-stabilized apartments renting for $400 or less per month.

The overall impact of rent control on low-income elderly and minority tenants is still not clear. A 1987 study of Santa Monica's renter population under rent control compared it to the renter population of 1979, when rent control was enacted. The study concluded that rent control had protected low-income renters, especially the elderly, against displacement, but it had not slowed a longer-term trend of decline among black and Latino tenants (Levine, Grigsby, and Heskin 1990). Moreover, no disproportionate benefits for middle- and upper-income tenants were found. (The impact of rent control on different groups of tenants in Berkeley is analyzed in chapter 7.)

One other often-heard argument against rent control is that it limits tenant mobility. Since long-term rent control guarantees, in effect, a lifetime tenancy (assuming good behavior by the tenant), it is reasoned that tenants are generally reluctant to move. Reluctance becomes even more likely if little new rental housing is available or if unregulated market rates on existing housing are out of the reach of most tenants (Kristof 1970). Where there is vacancy decontrol—i.e., where landlords are allowed to increase rents (either to market levels or above the normal ceilings) upon a vacancy—the reluctance to move becomes firmly entrenched. The converse holds that rent control stabilizes neighborhoods by reducing tenant transiency.

In 1998, Cambridge reported on the impact of rent decontrol. During the study period from 1995 to 1997, median decontrolled rents rose by 54 percent (compared to an increase of 14 percent in the unregulated rental market). Forty percent of Cambridge tenants paid 30 percent or more of their income for rent. More than one-third (38 percent) of tenants in formerly rent-controlled apartments had moved since decontrol. Overall, new tenants since decontrol generally had higher incomes and were neither elderly nor families with children.

Rent control is also charged with creating a "black market" in subleases. Because vacant apartments are not made available at regulated rents, it is argued that vacating tenants and/or landlords often demand illegal rents (or "key money") from desperate tenants in search of housing or from tenants able and willing to pay a rent that is higher than the regulated amount but still below-market, particularly if such an arrangement guarantees them security of tenure. The upshot, the reasoning goes, is that landlords will discriminate in favor of better-off tenants who can afford to pay these rents. The most telling examples of immobility cited are elderly tenants occupying apartments whose size exceeds their needs but who refuse to move for fear of rent increases they cannot afford.

The counterargument to this line of reasoning is that lessened tenant mobility under rent control is a necessary trade-off for the protection of tenants who cannot afford to compete in the unregulated market. In 1993, approximately 30 percent of New York City's rent-stabilized tenants lived below the federal poverty line. Their chances for obtaining a public housing unit were exceedingly slim. New York City has a very long waiting list for public housing.

Another argument against rent control maintains that it is overly bureaucratic and inefficient. The registration of rents, the review of landlord and tenant complaints and hardship appeals, and the inspections required to assure compliance with housing code standards are all said to be cumbersome, costly, and time-consuming. However, the administrative costs of rent control are usually relatively low, and they are often either shifted from landlords to tenants through a rent surcharge or incorporated into the general rent increase as an allowable operating cost.

The results of the numerous studies on rent control have failed to convince either landlords or tenants of the correctness of their opponents' arguments. Legislative bodies have typically been more influenced by the political weight of the competing forces than the conclusions of rent control studies. The validity and acceptance of the studies have often been challenged on the basis of who commissioned and paid for them, the research methodology used, the data sources, the length of the study period, and/or the qualifications surrounding their conclusions.

The Urban Land Institute, for example, commissioned an evaluation of residential rent control by prominent real estate economist Anthony Downs, a Senior Fellow at The Brookings Institution. Downs (1988, 1989) concluded that the negative effects of rent control outweigh any short-term benefits. As it happened, the organizations that cosponsored the study were all major national organizations opposed to rent control, including the Building Owners and Managers Association International, California Housing Council, Mortgage Bankers Association, National Apartment Association, National Association of Home Builders, National Association of Realtors, National Multi-Housing Council, National Realty Committee, Rent Stabilization Association of New York City, and the U.S. League of Savings Institutions.

One of the most controversial rent control studies was conducted by conservative analyst William Tucker, who argued that homelessness is related to rent control because it exacerbates the housing shortage for low-income tenants least able to compete in a regulated market (1990). His research methodology was criticized as inadequate and his conclusions deemed insupportable by sociologists Appelbaum, Dolny, Dreier, and Gilderbloom (1992). Tucker responded (1991), as did his critics (Appelbaum et al. 1992). Their repartee illustrates the kind of heated debate that research on rent control fosters, with completely divergent approaches and conclusions.

Even the data generated in New York City by the U.S. Census Bureau for the city's periodic housing and vacancy surveys has typically resulted in much different policy interpretations by landlord and tenant groups. In 1976, for example, the city's housing agencies issued a report on the rental housing situation, based upon 1970 U.S. Census data, which concluded that increases in rents had exceeded increases in tenant incomes and that half of the city's tenants were paying rent in excess of the norm (25 percent of income) (Fried 1976). The U.S. Census study did not address landlords' operating income or return on investment, however. That same year, another study agreed with the U.S. Census findings but also pointed to increased deterioration of the rental housing stock and tax delinquencies (Sternlieb and Hughes 1976). The Rent Stabilization Association (RSA) pointed to a decline in the net operating income of regulated landlords. The RSA then used this to challenge the 1976 rent guidelines, arguing that the operating cost index compiled by the U.S. Bureau of Labor Statistics and the methodology used by the New York City Rent Guidelines Board (RGB) were invalid. In turn, the RGB issued its own study, which attacked the methodology used by the experts hired by the RSA (Keating 1987, 97).

The greatest divide in this debate, however, is not the dispute over research methodology and interpretation of data, but rather a matter of philosophy. Rent control opponents (e.g., Epstein 1988; Salins and Mildner

1992) reject the right of government, absent compensation to owners, to solve rental housing shortages or tenant distress through regulation involving price controls. Epstein characterizes this as an unconstitutional taking of private property (Epstein 1985). Rent control opponents also dispute the ability of government to resolve the low-income housing problem through regulation.

In contrast, rent control proponents see the enactment of controls as a duty, as well as a right, of government in order to correct the deficiencies of the rental housing market (e.g., Radin 1986). In their view, the general welfare (at least of those tenants protected) prevails over the property rights of those landlords whose apartments are regulated. Obviously, the self-interest of affected landlords and tenants plays a critical role in the view of the necessity for and utility of rent control.

Notes

1. HUD defines "very low income" as below 50 percent of an area's median income (for a four-person household); "low income" is defined as between 51 and 80 percent of an area's median income.

W. Dennis Keating

2

Rent Control Legislation and Administration

INTRODUCTION

Although rent control is often perceived as monolithic in character and uniform in structure, the reality is much more complex. Rent control legislation differs considerably depending upon the author of the legislation (the federal, state, or local governing body, or landlord or tenant initiatives); the setting (the type of housing to be regulated, the problems involved, and the political and social context); and the legal constraints (such as those imposed by national or state laws).

Similarly, the administration of rent control permitted by legislation varies greatly. At one end of the spectrum, professional bureaucracies administer rent control as they would any other government program. At the other end, controls are administered by legislatively empowered voluntary committees. Usually, policy is set by a government legislative body, such as a state legislature or city council, and administrators are delegated to carry out its policies. In a few instances, however, policy-setting rent control boards have been elective bodies, separate and autonomous from a general legislative entity, such as a city council.

RENT CONTROL LEGISLATION

No matter what specific form they take, laws to regulate rent levels must address some fundamental issues. Since rent regulation is a form of price control and intervenes in the most basic way with market processes, it must address both the mechanisms for stabilizing rents and the potential responses of participants in the market to regulation. Six key groups of questions are implicitly or explicitly addressed by rent control legislation:

- ☐ What rental housing is to be regulated? Over what period of time? Is there differentiation among tenants?
- ☐ On what principles are rents to be set? How are the interests of tenants and landlords to be reconciled?
- ☐ What specific standards and mechanisms will be employed to determine permissible rent levels?
- ☐ How will potential responses by market participants that could offset regulation be avoided? In particular, how will transfer of rental units into ownership status be controlled? How will rental housing quality levels be maintained in the face of strong incentives to lower them? How will new rental housing be encouraged? How will tenants' security of tenure be sustained in the face of incentives to move them out? How will black markets in rental housing be deterred?
- ☐ How will the regulatory structure be governed and administered?
- ☐ Who will pay for regulation?

Designing legislation that can respond to these questions in a way that meets the objectives of its framers while avoiding destructive impacts on the housing stock, landlords, and tenants is no easy task. Different aspects of the questions will be explored throughout this book. In this chapter, we will describe some of the actions that have been taken by rent control legislators, with selective illustrations from various jurisdictions (see generally, Baar 1983, 1987).

THE SHAPE OF RENT CONTROL LEGISLATION

The shape of rent control legislation naturally depends upon its sponsors and the political environment in which it is enacted (see chapter 5). When drafted by tenant advocates, its features are predictably more favorable to tenants, as demonstrated by the tenant-authored ballot initiatives enacted in Berkeley (see chapter 7) and in Santa Monica, California, the most notable U.S. examples. At the other end of the spectrum, the most obvious example of legislation favorable to landlords is the rent stabilization ordinance adopted by New York City in 1969. Most rent control legislation falls somewhere in between these two extremes, representing a compromise between competing tenant and landlord interests.

Like other regulatory legislation, rent control laws can be drafted very broadly, granting an administrative agency the power to determine the amount of annual across-the-board adjustments, for example, and/or individual rent adjustments. Or the legislation can be written to include far greater detail, specifying allowable increases, for example, and fair return standards, thus leaving much less interpretative discretion to the agencies designated to implement the legislation. Whichever the approach, since rent regulation must be justified as an exercise of governmental "police power," the basis for controlling rents must be specified in the statement of purpose or preamble. Typically, a housing shortage is the basis for the legislation, and the grounds for it include rapidly escalating rents, very low rental vacancy rates, high rent-to-income ratios for tenants (in excess of 25-30 percent), or widespread actual or threatened displacement of tenants due to escalating rents. Some laws propose protecting tenants in general, while others specifically state the need to protect low-income tenants.

Since U.S. rent controls have never been designed to be permanent, they generally contain "sunset" clauses, which require their periodic renewal by municipal and/or state legislative bodies. In some legislation, termination is mandated if the rental vacancy rate rises to what is considered to be a normal market rate (e.g., 5 percent in the case of New York's enabling legislation). Exceptions are the voter initiatives enacted in some California municipalities; they can be terminated only by another initiative repealing rent control. The state legislature can pass preemptive legislation, however, as it did when it passed a law allowing landlords to go out of business and, more recently, when it imposed mandatory vacancy decontrol.

Rent control legislation may not necessarily cover all tenants. Although rent control has not been means-tested, certain classes of rental housing have often been exempted from regulation. The reasons given for exemption are either that tenants residing in these types of housing do not need or deserve regulation, or that allowing exemptions provides an incentive to landlords to increase or maintain the supply of rental housing. Two categories of units are usually exempted: owner-occupied units, at least in buildings with four units or less; and nonprofit and government-owned and -assisted housing units (whose rents are already regulated). Also often exempted are single-family dwellings and newly constructed or substantially rehabilitated units. To encourage new construction following the enactment of rent control, newly constructed apartments are either designated permanently exempt or the initial rent, at least, is exempt and allowed to be set at a market rate. Occasionally, so-called luxury housing is also exempt. Instead of being based on the income of the occupant, however, this exemption is based upon rent levels.

One controversial exemption involves vacated units. Typically, landlords are allowed to charge the new occupants of vacated units what amounts to a market rent, under the designation of "vacancy decontrol." The decontrol is usually not permanent; all future rent increases for the "sitting" tenant are subject to regulation. Nonetheless, vacancy decontrol has caused a great stir in cities like Boston and New York, and in the state of California. Interestingly, New Jersey rent control ordinances have long included vacancy decontrol without occasioning great debate.

The prospect of permanent decontrol, of course, ignites even more controversy, because it amounts to the phasing out of rent control through attrition, as tenants move. Proponents of permanent decontrol see this as the best course of action, because "sitting" tenants remain protected, while landlords are able to increase their revenue through the market rates charged to new tenants. Opponents of permanent decontrol, however, view the process as haphazard—one that gives landlords a strong incentive to try to force tenants to move as soon as possible. The opponents also claim that, given the rental housing shortages that led to the original rent regulation, market rents on vacated units will likely be higher than the market would otherwise justify, further skewing rent differentials and discouraging tenants from moving.

A milder form of vacancy decontrol allows landlords a vacancy bonus. When a unit is vacated, the landlord is allowed to charge the new tenant an initial rent above the existing rent guidelines. New York City's original rent control system, for example, allowed landlords a 15 percent vacancy bonus; the city's more recent rent stabilization system allows landlords to charge a vacancy bonus in varying amounts. Once the new rent is set, subsequent rent increases are subject to rent guidelines.

DEFINING RENT LEVELS

Vacancy decontrol notwithstanding, usually the single most contentious issue in rent control legislation is the setting of controlled rent levels. With the enactment of rent control, a "base date" rent must be selected; all subsequent rent increases are calculated from that base date. In the face of escalating rents, the base date often involves a rent rollback, but except in wartime, long-term rent freezes have been rare. The second-generation rent control laws that have been enacted in the United States generally allow for annual or periodic rent adjustments for all landlords.

What the term "rent" specifically covers is defined either in the statute or in an administrative regulation. Rent is usually defined broadly in order to prevent attempts by landlords to circumvent rent control by imposing additional charges for services. Likewise, "landlord" is defined precisely in the legislation in order to prevent tenants who sublease their controlled units from charging their tenants additional rents or fees. Rent increase allowances can be set by legislation or at the discretion of an administrative agency, an appointed board, or, at least in the case of Berkeley, an elected board.

Not surprisingly, landlord and tenant advocates usually differ as to how rent increases are to be set. The simplest standard is an across-the-board percentage increase, often linked to a cost-of-living index, such as the Consumer Price Index (CPI) in the United States. In recognition that landlords' mortgage costs may be relatively fixed and may not vary much annually, rents may be tied to increased operating and maintenance costs, exclusive of mortgage financing. These costs can be estimated simply as a percentage of a cost-of-living index, or they can be documented annually. An annual survey of landlord operating and maintenance costs has been the method used in Berkeley and New York City under the rent stabilization system. New York City's Rent Guidelines Board surveys the following costs: administrative, contractor services, fuel, insurance, labor, parts and supplies, replacement, and taxes (Rent Guidelines Board 1995). Surcharges may also be added, e.g., in the form of administrative fees or additional rents for historically low-rent units.

Although rent increases are normally obtainable across the board on an annual basis, under some mobile home rent control laws, an individual landlord petition for each tenant is required. In this setting, the landlords are the owners of mobile home parks, each with a sizable number of tenants. A Berkeley tenant initiative requiring individual landlord petitions for each and every unit slated to receive a rent increase, without explicitly authorizing consolidation on a building-wide basis, was also enacted in Berkeley in 1972. In 1976, the California Supreme Court held this provision to be so unconstitutionally cumbersome as to deny landlords a fair return. However, the California Supreme Court has not required annual general adjustments for mobile home rent control.

Rent control in the United States must recognize that private rental housing is an investment. The U.S. courts have required that rent control legislation must permit landlords to receive a "fair return" on their investment if the market allows, as a matter of constitutional law (see chapter 3).

TABLE 2.1

Fair Return Standards

---

1. *Cash flow*
   Gross rent = operating expenses + mortgage payments

1a. *Return on gross rent* (a variant of the cash flow standard)
   Gross rent = x (operating expenses + mortgage payments)

2. *Return on equity*
   Gross rent = operating expenses + mortgage payments + x (cash investment)

3. *Return on value*
   Gross rent = operating expenses + x (value)

4. *Percentage net operating income*
   Gross rent = x (operating expenses)

5. *Maintenance of net operating income*
   Gross rent = base-date gross rent + x (current operating expenses minus base-date operating expenses)

Source: Baar 1983

What constitutes a "fair return" has, of course, occasioned a great debate and numerous lawsuits. Minimally, however, it is agreed that rents must be periodically adjusted to enable landlords to cover their increased operating and maintenance costs without unduly long delays or lags in such rent increases.

In providing for a fair return, several different standards have been proposed and used in different jurisdictions. The most commonly used fair return standards are cash flow, return on gross rent, return on equity, return on value, percentage net operating income (NOI), and maintenance of NOI. Baar (1983, 784–85) illustrates these standards (table 2.1) and the variables that they consider (table 2.2) below.

Arguments can be made for and against each standard. Under the cash flow standard, for example, a landlord is entitled to rents that are sufficient to cover operating expenses and mortgage payments. What constitutes a fair rent is largely determined by the owner's mortgage financing. The fair return on gross rent standard is a variation of the cash flow standard. It, however, guarantees that the regulated rent will yield a cash flow equal to a specified percentage of operating expenses and mortgage payments.

The return on equity standard goes beyond the cash flow and return on gross rent standards to provide for a return on the owner's cash investment. This standard is usually specified as a designated percentage return

TABLE 2.2

Variables Considered in Fair Return Formulas

	Operating Expenses	Mortgage Interest	Value	Cash Investment	Base-Date Gross Income	Base-Date Operating Expenses
Cash flow	x	x				
Return on gross rent	x	x				
Return on equity	x	x		x		
Return on value	x		x			
Percentage NOI	x					
Maintenance of NOI	x				x	x

Source: Baar 1983

on the owner's "equity" (cash investment) and may exceed the rate of return on government-guaranteed securities. The owner's equity, therefore, becomes an important variable in determining the fair return. In some jurisdictions, equity (as defined) must be adjusted for subsequent inflation.

Under the return on value standard, the landlord is entitled to rents adequate to cover operating expenses and yield a specified return on the "value" of the building. Mortgage interest is not considered an expense since the rate of return is calculated on the full value of the rental property rather than on the owner's equity. Determining that "value," however, poses a major problem. If a market value is used, the whole purpose of rent control may be defeated, because presumably rents would have to rise well above the regulated rent levels. Using assessed value is equally problematic, since assessed value is usually determined through comparable sales. Landlords could argue that the sale value of regulated properties does not reflect their true value; any lag time in assessments may add to the problem. Furthermore, calculation of the replacement value of regulated properties cannot be used as a proxy, since the replacement value often far exceeds the current value.

Under the percentage NOI standard, landlords are entitled to a specified percentage of gross rental income. If the ratio is not met, rents must be increased. This approach avoids the "circularity" problem of the return on value standard and the problem of taking the owner's purchase price, equity investment, or mortgage finance arrangements into account. It has the disadvantage of imposing a uniform standard ratio on all properties despite differences affected by the age, location, and size of buildings and their management.

Under the maintenance of the NOI standard, landlords can obtain rent increases necessary to cover increases in operating expenses. Fair NOI is considered to be that which the landlord earned during the "base" period when rents were first regulated. Using this standard avoids the problem posed by the percentage NOI standard, because each landlord is treated individually. It also avoids the problems associated with return on value and cash flow standards. Owners must cover their mortgage expenses from the income left after operating expenses are paid. Almost all maintenance of NOI standards index the base period NOI for subsequent inflation. The courts have ruled that freezing NOI indefinitely is confiscatory.

Baar (1983) explains in detail the differences among these formulas and their impact on landlords, as well as the problems of administering them. As mentioned in several of the case studies in this book, the courts have regularly addressed the complicated issues surrounding fair return (see chapter 3).

One other way owners can affect the real return on their investments is by reducing the quality of housing supplied by a given unit. Landlords might, for example, stop providing services such as security, or lower the quality of everyday maintenance (e.g., by painting less frequently, or not responding to tenant complaints). Landlords might also defer major capital replacements (e.g., they may repair roof leaks rather than replace the roof). In order to sustain a constant-quality rent level, rent control laws must find ways to inhibit such behavior. Direct regulation of quality is the obvious answer but also the most difficult to enforce. How quality decline should be measured, and who should identify whether it has occurred, are bound to be contentious issues. As New York City's requirement for painting units every three years demonstrates, regulating maintenance does not ensure quality. The paint landlords use may be cheap or thinned, and its application may be slapdash. Or owners may simply ignore the law. Maintenance regulation requires either a costly inspection system or a process that is tenant initiated, with all its attendant problems of verification. A more subtle approach to maintaining quality would be to attempt to sustain rent levels that are high enough to encourage vacancy and turnover, so that owners have a stronger incentive to keep existing tenants. But that approach may compromise the very objectives of rent control. Most ordinances make clear that quality may not be diminished without explicit rent adjustment, but the inability to regulate quality is a constant source of friction.

Further friction arises when landlords seek rent increases to cover specific cost increases—for instance, when landlords try to recoup their costs for capital improvements. Generally, rent increases for major capital improvements (e.g., a new roof, or a new heating and cooling system) are amortized over the life of the improvement. The costs of minor improvements (e.g., safety locks, fire alarms, energy conservation equipment) are not eligible for such special rent increases, however, unless a surcharge is added to general rent adjustments.

Capital improvements are, in many respects, a larger-scale parallel to the maintenance issue. Because they involve substantial expenditures that cannot be absorbed easily by owners, some form of pass-through—as well as some form of landlord-tenant dispute—is inevitable. Controversy also arises because capital improvements offer landlords potential opportunities to increase their returns through a variety of means, ranging from the legitimate to the illegal. Additionally, where capital improvements require major reconstruction, as in seismic retrofitting, tenants can be forced to move. In Los Angeles, a city with a moderate level of regulation and little evidence of serious maintenance issues, capital improvements amendments were among the most frequent and heavily debated issues in rent stabilization.

Finally, rent regulation covers not only rent levels but also evictions. Protection against eviction is often written into legislation to prevent landlords from circumventing rent control by evicting upon termination of the lease any tenant who complains about landlord violations of rent control. But this restriction has the effect of converting periodic leases into statutory tenancy. As long as the tenants pay the controlled rent, they can be evicted only for a specified cause, such as creating a nuisance, illegally subletting, or violating occupancy standards. Owners are usually allowed to evict a tenant in order to occupy one of their own units, however. In New York City, there is a long history of landlords trying to reclaim rent-controlled apartments from tenants who they claim are no longer in residency and have illegally sublet their units.

GOVERNANCE AND ADMINISTRATION OF RENT CONTROL

The legislation that enables rent control also specifies how it is to be governed and administered, leaving here, too, much room for variation. Most rent control legislation in North America is passed by local governing bodies, either city councils or county boards of supervisors, which remain responsible for overseeing the regulatory systems that are established. In some instances in California, the enabling legislation has been initiated by citizen initiatives at the municipal level, and in some of those cases governance is vested in an independent, elected board.

Where rent controls are municipal, states can always override (preempt) and impose statewide standards. In 1971, for example, the New York state legislature mandated that in the future New York City could pass no rent regulation stricter than what was already in existence. As previously noted, the California legislature has twice preempted municipal rent control. In 1983, New York State reassumed the administration of rent control from New York City. In 1994, Massachusetts voters abolished by statewide referendum municipal local-option rent control.

In some states, the adoption of municipal rent control requires state authorization. For example, in 1979, a Baltimore, Maryland, rent control referendum passed by the city's voters was ruled invalid for this reason. In contrast, municipal rent controls exist in the states of California and New Jersey without state enabling legislation. California voters twice defeated landlord efforts to enact statewide preemptive standards to weaken existing local rent controls, in 1980 and again in 1995. In Canada, municipal rent regulations are dependent upon provincial authorization.

A number of considerations affect rent control administration. The political context, for example, is likely to affect the extent to which administrators see themselves as personally committed to the goals of the program, as opposed to merely civil servants executing the will of the legislature. The political context is particularly relevant in the realm of tenant appeals and tenant-landlord disputes, especially where rent control systems generate high degrees of conflict. The scale of the program also affects the extent to which administrative roles must become specialized and expertise developed, whether in generating information for rent settings or in managing heavy flows of registrations or fee payments. Like most other municipal activities, rent control involves both routine, day-to-day activities and intermittent, frequently unforeseeable policy problems. In both areas, the administrative skills of those in charge can make a huge difference to the effectiveness of the program. The source of funding, too, affects administrative style. Programs that are self-financing through registration fees—and where the fees are easily collectible—face the fewest difficulties in meeting their administrative objectives. Where resources are insufficient, perhaps because of landlord resistance to fees, administering rent control effectively becomes very difficult.

At times, rent regulation has been administered by volunteer boards without paid staff. This was the case in wartime, at least for a while, and continues to be the case today in some U.S. jurisdictions—e.g., in California and New Jersey, especially in the governance of mobile homes. But volunteer boards can work effectively only if the number of units regulated is relatively small, the guidelines are simple, individual petitions are rare, and landlords are cooperative. In most cities of any size, these circumstances are not all present, and a paid staff is required to administer rent control.

Rent control is usually administered by a separate and identifiable municipal agency. Sometimes an existing housing agency takes on this additional role, usually creating a new internal division, as was the case in the city of Los Angeles and in the state of New York. Assuming that the law requires the registration of regulated units, the administrative agency takes over the registration task and maintains data on regulated units. Ontario, Canada, for example, established a rent registry to track rents. The administrative agency also handles any complaints of violations (mostly filed by tenants) as well as petitions for rent increases, filed by landlords. In most instances, the agency is responsible for the development and implementation of rent increase guidelines. A notable exception is New York City. Since 1969, a separate body called the Rent Guidelines Board has met annually to determine annual rent guidelines for rent-stabilized units; that is its sole purpose. Where there are a large number of regulated units, special petitions are generally handled by hearing examiners (often attorneys).

Absent an appointed body, the decision of the agency staff or a hearing examiner is final, with appeals of their decisions directed to the courts. If there is an appointed board (or an elected board, as currently exists in Berkeley, California), staff decisions, including those of hearing examiners, may be appealable to the full board or a board-delegated panel.

In the absence of long-term political controversy over rent control and assuming adequate staff and budget, a rent control agency can function as efficiently as any other municipal agency, as was the case in Los Angeles and many other cities. However, if there is divisive controversy, a rent control agency may find itself in a political cross fire and unable to easily administer the law. In Berkeley, many landlords initially refused to register their rents and pay registration fees. As control of the elected board went back and forth between landlord and tenant factions, and as the law was amended and challenged regularly in court, the task of obtaining full landlord compliance became difficult. Establishing the legal rent for units not initially registered proved particularly troublesome.

New York City, which has by far the longest experience with rent controls in the United States, has also experienced the most administrative problems, ranging from lengthy waiting periods for decisions on petitions, to the inability of landlords to obtain code-enforcement compliance to meet the standards of the Maximum Base Rent (MBR) system established in 1970, to a backlog of tens of thousands of tenant complaints, triggered by reform legislation in 1974 and 1983. New York City also has the most complicated set of rent regulations, which must be explained to a landlord group that has a wide range of holdings, a wide range of financial and managerial capacity, and that comes from diverse backgrounds. In addition, rent regulation agencies in many cities have had to explain their rules to tenants and landlords of many different nationalities and languages. Without the cooperation of landlords and tenants, the administration of rent control can be very difficult.

Despite these problems, the cost of rent control administration has rarely been a major issue—only in those jurisdictions (e.g., California) with large per-unit fees have administrative costs sparked public controversy. Rent control can be funded directly by a state or local government, or landlords can be charged a fee. The fee is generally passed on to tenants either as part of their annual rent increases or as a special surcharge added to general rent adjustments.

CONCLUSION

Rent control legislation and administration in the United States and Canada have emerged through a complex process of trial and error, initiative and challenge, innovation and marginal change. As will be seen in later chapters, rent control laws have always been subject to legal challenge, as well as to the twists and turns of the economy and politics. The essential issues that rental regulation must address are quite clear, but the legislative resolution of the issues can result in very different systems and regulatory practices. In this sense, the legislation can be seen as both an outcome and an input to the regulatory process. It represents the outcome of great political struggle, but it is, simultaneously, the warp upon which the complex patterns of legal challenge, regulatory policy, and administrative practice are woven. Understanding that pattern requires a careful look at the courts, the economy, and at politics.

W. DENNIS KEATING

3

The Courts and Rent Control

INTRODUCTION

From its inception in the United States following World War I, the legality of rent control has been regularly challenged in the courts. The constitutional right of government in the United States to control prices, including rents, has been ruled invalid in some important respects. Rent control procedures have also been subject to judicial review. Therefore, it is important to understand the legal bases for the regulation of rents and judicially imposed limits to governmental exercise of this power.

PRICE REGULATION AND RENT CONTROL

Prior to the Great Depression of the 1930s, the United States Supreme Court interpreted the federal constitution to allow the states to regulate prices only of those businesses "affected with a public interest" or during a temporary "emergency" (Baar and Keating 1975). When laissez-faire economic and political theories prevailed, these two situations were considered to be exceptions to the norm, in which the private market rather than the government sets prices.

When rent control was first enacted in 1919 in Washington, D.C., and in 1920 in New York City to deal with rental housing shortages and escalating rents, the United States Supreme Court invoked both exceptions. In *Block v. Hirsh* (1921), a bare majority (5–4) upheld temporary rent control. The majority characterized rental housing as a necessity, being affected with a public interest. Justice Holmes took "judicial notice" of the shortage of rental housing caused by the influx of wartime workers, even though World War I had actually ended prior to the imposition of rent control. Holmes declared that the temporary emergency caused by the housing shortage was undeniable. Under these conditions, the majority rejected the argument that the government could not constitutionally override preexisting contracts (leases), holding that the public welfare superseded the rights of private landlords, at least temporarily.

However, the courts reserved the right to determine whether such an emergency actually existed, notwithstanding a legislative declaration of a housing emergency or its extension (*Chastleton v. Sinclair* 1924). In 1925, the federal courts decided that there was no longer a housing shortage in the District of Columbia sufficient to justify the continuation of rent control. This decision ended that initial experiment in municipal rent control (Baar and Keating 1975).

The decision of the United States Supreme Court to uphold the constitutionality of rent control ran contrary to a long line of decisions invalidating price regulations. Very conservative courts had regularly invoked the doctrine of "substantive due process," under which they ruled that price regulations constituted arbitrary governmental action that deprived private businesses of their constitutionally protected rights to contract, liberty, and due process. In a further shift, the United States Supreme Court in 1934 adopted a position of judicial deference to legislative judgment in the area of economic regulation, absent any "taking" of private property.

This turnabout amid controversy over the constitutionality of New Deal economic emergency measures was not directly applied to rent control by the courts until the 1970s (Baar and Keating 1975). World War II federal rent controls to address rental housing shortages, for example, were upheld as constitutional under the wartime powers of the federal government during an emergency, the existence of which was uncontested (*Bowles v. Willingham* 1944).

Federal rent controls were gradually terminated after World War II and the Korean conflict and have only reappeared once, as part of the short-lived federal price stabilization program of 1971-1973 during the Vietnam War era. Federal appellate courts have rejected challenges to state and local rent controls based upon the substantive due process and taking doctrines (Drobak 1986).

REGULATION OF PRIVATE LANDLORDS

Under American law, which evolved from the English common law, the landlord–tenant relationship is embodied in the lease. The basis of land-lord–tenant leases derives from feudal conditions in Europe in which land rather than an apartment unit was the focus. The lease sets the terms of the rental agreement, and the lease has been assumed to be the result of free bargaining in the market. The landlord's contractual rights are defined by state laws and constitutionally protected under the due process and con-tract clauses.

The law only gradually took notice of greatly changed conditions af-fecting modern urban rental housing markets. In the late nineteenth and early twentieth centuries, the courts upheld the imposition of basic health and safety standards by state and local governments, even though these imposed added costs to landlords, and incorporated them into existing leases (Friedman 1968). Taking judicial notice of unsanitary and substan-dard conditions in slum housing, the courts upheld the right of state and local governments to impose housing and building codes on private rental housing, to prevent harm not only to affected tenants but also to the public at large.

It was not until the 1960s, however, that U.S. courts began to recognize an "implied warranty of habitability" in residential leases. Regardless of the terms of the lease, the courts concluded that tenants were entitled to the protection of the minimal standards of the municipal housing codes and could withhold rent and defend against eviction actions for nonpay-ment of rent, based upon proven landlord violations of these housing codes. As a corollary, retaliatory evictions against tenants who report landlords to code enforcement agencies for violations were made illegal, to protect ten-ants who exercise their constitutionally protected right of free speech to demand decent housing and code compliance (Rabin 1984).

Within a relatively short period beginning in 1970, a majority of states reformed their landlord–tenant legislation and greatly expanded tenant rights. Given this trend (and the reluctance of the courts to overturn price regulations), the state courts were more inclined to uphold the legality of "second-generation" rent controls than they might have been prior to the transformation of landlord–tenant law. It should be noted, however, that the United States Supreme Court, in reviewing a challenge to Oregon's landlord–tenant law preventing tenant rent-withholding based on hous-ing code violations in an eviction action, declared that decent housing was not a constitutionally protected fundamental right under the Fourteenth Amendment of the U.S. Constitution (*Lindsey v. Normet* 1972).

THE CONSTITUTIONALITY OF RENT CONTROL

State and local governments in the United States are able to enact rent control under the authority of the "police power" inherent in government to protect the general welfare. The government derives its constitutional power to regulate private property and its owners from this police power. Judicial views of the reach of police power and its appropriate application have varied, depending upon the era and the political and economic, as well as legal, perspectives of the courts that have reviewed the enactment and implementation of rent control.

The constitutionality of rent control has been challenged by landlords on a variety of grounds, including due process, equal protection, and takings. Due process issues arise when landlords claim that rent control administrators or policy-making boards are unreasonable or arbitrary in their decisions. Procedural due process standards require that landlords (and tenants) receive adequate notice of regulations and decisions that affect them, be afforded an opportunity to make their views known in public hearings prior to the adoption and implementation of the regulations, and be treated fairly in decision making. Equal protection claims arise when landlords claim that the exemption of some classes of rental units from coverage, different rent allowances for different types of units, and other differential policies unreasonably discriminate.

The Fair Return and Taking Doctrines

The most serious constitutional challenge raised against rent control has been the claim that it constitutes a taking of property, based on a denial of a fair return. Challengers have sought invalidation of the taking or payment of compensation to landlords. Although the taking of private property without just compensation by government is unconstitutional, the United States Supreme Court has yet to issue a uniform definition of what constitutes a taking. Instead, through a long series of cases, mostly involving land-use disputes, the courts have defined various bases for finding a taking. These include denial of all reasonable use of the owner's property; confiscation of all value; physical invasion and permanent occupation by government of the property or its equivalent through regulation; denial of investment-backed expectations; and the absence of a legitimate public purpose justifying regulation. These standards have been applied on a case-by-case basis by often divided courts, both federal and state.

Landlords who claim that rent control constitutes a taking argue that rent ceilings have had a substantial negative impact on either their return on investment or their net operating income. The impact differs according to legislative and administrative formulas for rent increases and provision of a fair return for landlords. Some formulas provide for annual rent increases, others for only occasional rent increases. Some formulas index allowable rent increases to inflation (fully or partially), while others do not.

The United States Supreme Court has agreed to hear only two rent control cases involving taking claims under second-generation municipal rent control ordinances. In *Pennell v. City of San Jose* (1988), the Court's majority ruled that peacetime rent controls did not constitute a "taking" on their face. In fact, San Jose's ordinance was quite generous to landlords. Addressing the potential application of an unusual tenant hardship provision, the Court upheld this against a taking claim. In *Yee v. City of Escondido* (1992), a majority of the United States Supreme Court rejected a claim, previously accepted by two federal appellate courts, that municipal mobile home rent control constituted a regulatory taking because it amounted to a governmentally mandated permanent physical occupation of the mobile home park owner's property by mobile home tenants (see chapter 13). In neither case did the Court address the issue of fair return.

While property owners are not constitutionally entitled to the highest possible return on their investment, rent control statutes do provide a fair return. The formulas vary (see chapter 2), but those owners who claim that their rents do not provide a fair return can apply for special hardship rent increases. Many rent control systems impose a ceiling on special rent increases. If higher rent increases are required to provide a fair return, the amount in excess of the ceiling is phased in incrementally beyond a single year. Landlord applications for hardship rent increases are reviewed through hearings on individual rental units or apartment building rent adjustment petitions, with affected tenants having the right to oppose them. After review by hearing examiners, the rent increases are appealable to a rent control administrator or board, and their decision is, in turn, appealable to the courts (Baar 1983).

Landlords have attacked the constitutionality of fair return formulas both as enacted (i.e., "on their face") and also as applied to individual landlords and their property. The courts presume the validity of municipal price regulation. Landlords, therefore, have a heavy burden of proof, which requires convincing evidence that rent control has had a very deleterious effect on their return on investment (as measured by net operating income or cash flow).

Fair Return Case Law

The thorny problem of what constitutes a "fair return" on investment in the housing market is at the heart of the judicial dilemma in dealing with rent control takings. To determine what constitutes a fair return on investment, the extent of the "investment" must be determined first. In addition to the landlord's original cash investment (equity), subsequent investments (e.g., major capital improvements financed by the owner) can be added. But if a historical return on investment formula is to be used, landlords argue that their original investment must be adjusted for inflation throughout their period of ownership, unless rent increases have been fully adjusted for inflation.

Another definition of "investment" is market value. Normally, in the absence of rent control, this is measured as a multiplier of the rent roll. However, once rents are frozen or rolled back to a "base date," the multiplier formula does not work. Landlords have argued in favor of using the market value prior to the imposition of rent control as a proxy for "investment." But if the rents reflecting market value were considered excessive and led to rent control, continuing to use them as a basis for future rents would defeat the purpose of rent control.

Another basis for determining market value is assessed value, which can be determined in a variety of ways. However, due to problems associated with assessment standards and methodology, assessed value often is not representative of current market value (Baar 1984).

Rate of Return

Whichever definition of investment is chosen, the next hurdle to be addressed is what the rate of return should be. Courts have generally said that the rate should be competitive. However, landlords argue that, given the risk associated with real estate investment, the rate should be higher than, for example, the prime commercial bank rate. Tenants, on the other hand, argue that risk is inherent in real estate investment and rent regulators should not guarantee what the private market does not.

Tenants have also argued that, since landlords have benefited from such tax incentives as accelerated depreciation and deferred capital gains, the rate of return should include consideration of such benefits to landlords and be lowered accordingly. Landlords have countered that such incentives vary in their economic value and do not accrue to all landlords. Administratively, it would be difficult to develop a fair return formula that would be generally applicable to all ownership investment patterns.

Adjustment for Inflation

Whatever rate of return is selected, landlords argue that rents must be fully adjusted for inflation lest their actual rate of return be deflated. Many annual rent adjustment guidelines take inflation into account. However, not all allow for a full inflation adjustment. One common reason is that not all landlord costs increase annually. For example, if the landlord has a fixed-rate mortgage, the cost does not rise unless the mortgage is refinanced. Furthermore, some operating costs may not rise as much as the overall rate of inflation. On the other hand, over the long term no cost can be exempt from inflation altogether, including the cost of borrowed capital.

Some courts (e.g., *Searle v. Berkeley Rent Stabilization Board* Cal. 1990) have declared that, without at least periodic adjustments for inflation, the value of regulated rents, and therefore the rate of return, will steadily erode, and eventually rent control will become unconstitutionally confiscatory. The most extreme example would be a long-term rent freeze without any adjustments for operating cost increases or inflation. Only a wartime emergency such as World War II has justified such a draconian policy. In reviewing second-generation peacetime rent control, the courts have accepted the validity of partial inflation indexing. Judicial rulings in California (Mitgang 1995) and New Jersey are reviewed next.

RENT CONTROL IN CALIFORNIA

In *Birkenfield v. City of Berkeley* (1976), the California Supreme Court, in reviewing the first rent control ordinance passed by voter initiative, upheld the validity of municipal rent control but invalidated the measure. This 1972 initiative required the review of individual petitions by landlords to determine allowable rent increases based upon enumerated factors, but there was no specific fair return formula. The court held that the initiative, lacking any provision for annual citywide rent adjustments, was too cumbersome a mechanism for the efficient review of individual unit rents and could not guarantee landlords the opportunity for rent increases sufficient to provide a fair return.

In 1980, another rent control initiative was approved by Berkeley voters (see chapter 7). It froze rents at their 1980 levels, provided for annual citywide adjustments to cover cost increases, guaranteed a fair return on investment, and provided for individual landlord rent adjustments where required to provide a fair return. An elected rent stabilization board was authorized to determine a fair return formula. Landlords also challenged this initiative, claiming that it was confiscatory on its face because it did not provide a fair return on value. The California Supreme Court agreed that inflationary adjustments over time were necessary to guarantee landlords a reasonable profit because a freeze of NOI would be confiscatory. But the Court presumed that the rent stabilization board would act constitutionally and rejected this facial challenge. It also rejected the landlords' contention that the only constitutionally permissible fair return formula was based on return on market value (*Fisher v. City of Berkeley* 1984).

The Berkeley Rent Stabilization Board, alternately dominated by tenant and landlord factions, adopted a fair net operating formula. Subsequently, its implementation was ruled to be confiscatory because rent increases were not adequately indexed for inflation (*Searle v. Berkeley Rent Stabilization Board* Cal. 1990).

RENT CONTROL IN NEW JERSEY

New Jersey, the state that has had the most municipalities with rent control, has witnessed the implementation of a variety of fair return formulas (Baar and Keating 1983). New Jersey has no state enabling legislation defining a fair return. The New Jersey Supreme Court has addressed the question of what constitutes a fair return more frequently than any other state supreme court in the United States in the era of second-generation rent control.

In three cases in 1975 (*Hutton Park Gardens v. West Orange, Brunetti v. Borough of New Milford*, and *Troy Hills Village v. Township of Parsippany-Troy Hills*), the New Jersey Supreme Court outlined the essential constitutional requirements for a fair return under municipal rent control. The court ruled that rent increases do not have to keep up absolutely with operating cost increases; landlords are not necessarily guaranteed a positive cash flow; reasonable and efficient operators are entitled to a "just and reasonable" return; and localities that have adopted rent control ordinances must have a fair return formula on which to judge landlord hardship claims (Baar 1983).

In 1978, the Court again reviewed the fair return question in *Helmsley v. Borough of Fort Lee*. In a ruling similar to one handed down by the California Supreme Court, the New Jersey court rejected the argument that a formula based upon fair market value was constitutionally mandated. Rather, it concluded that such a formula was unworkable and inappropriate because it was based on the very market rents that are regulated under rent control. The court did not point to any single fair return formula as best, although it did indicate that investment-based criteria were acceptable (Baar 1983).

In *Mayes v. Jackson Township* (1986), in reviewing a challenge to an investment-based formula, the court reaffirmed the formula's validity but ruled that the landlord's original investment must be adjusted for inflation if a taking is not to occur. The court also indicated that the maintenance of a net operating income formula was acceptable, subject to an inflation adjustment. This ruling was confirmed in *Parks v. Hazlet Township Rent Control Board* (1987). Thus, in New Jersey, localities may—and have—used different fair return formulas, the constitutionality of which has been upheld in both facial and applied challenges by landlords.

PROCEDURAL REQUIREMENTS FOR REVIEW OF LANDLORD APPLICATIONS FOR FAIR RETURN RENT ADJUSTMENTS

The courts have dealt with many procedural issues related to the standards for review of landlord petitions for rent increases that they claim are necessary to guarantee a fair return. Procedural issues include the amount of information that landlords can be required to supply, the maximum length of time allowable for final decisions on petitions, and the rights of affected tenants to be heard.

Perhaps the most critical procedural issue has been the lag time between the submission of landlord petitions and the final decisions rendered by hearing examiners and, on appeal, rent control agencies. Most rent control statutes and agency regulations include maximum time periods for this process. While courts assume that administrative agencies generally act rationally and conform to statutory and constitutional requirements, as well as their own administrative rules, courts will occasionally find an agency's behavior unacceptable. A New York trial court, for example, found that a seventeen-month delay without a final decision on a landlord's petition for a special rent increase for capital improvements was not excused by the agency's administrative backlog and staffing problems (*Clarendon Management Corp. v. State Div. of Housing & Community Renewal* 1988).

LANDLORDS' DOMINION RIGHTS

A different basis for landlord opposition to rent control is the control of property by its owners. Landlords have argued that there are limits to the government's right to interfere with their "dominion" rights to control the terms of tenant occupancy of their property (Radin 1986). Rent control not only regulates rents but it is generally accompanied by eviction control, which enumerates just causes for eviction (e.g., nonpayment of rent). Beyond the causes enumerated, a landlord's right to exclude is prohibited. Landlords have some leeway, however. The regulations typically allow a landlord (or close relative) to evict a "sitting" tenant in order to occupy a unit. Tenants claim that this "right" is often a subterfuge to allow the landlord to rerent an apartment at a higher rent to take advantage of vacancy bonus allowances.

CONDOMINIUM CONVERSION CONTROLS

Faced with rent control, many landlords have sought exemption by converting their rental units into for-sale condominiums where there is a market. The courts have generally upheld the right of state and local governments to prevent the loss of affordable units and to protect rent-controlled tenants from displacement by regulating such conversions. The resulting condominium control legislation generally provides such protection as renters' first right of purchase, extended periods before eviction can take place, required relocation payments, and replacement of converted units.

In addition, New Jersey condominium conversion legislation provided special protection to the elderly and handicapped to prevent hardship. Elderly or handicapped tenants were to be given three years' notice of eviction, comparable relocation housing, or, if this was unavailable, guaranteed occupancy up to forty years. Federal courts upheld the validity of this statute against claims that it constituted a taking and violated guarantees of equal protection and due process for landlords (*Troy v. Renna* 1984).

DEMOLITION CONTROLS

Under many local condominium conversion and rent control ordinances, landlords are not permitted to remove units from the rental market (at least not low- and moderate-income units) unless they agree to replace them. The rationale justifying such an antiremoval policy is that, once the units are destroyed, they will not be replaced in a tight housing market.

The courts have upheld the right of the government to prevent this loss of affordable housing. As long as the landlord is guaranteed a fair return under rent control, the public good is superior to the landlord's dominion rights. For example, in *Nash v. City of Santa Monica* (1984), the California Supreme Court upheld the city's strict antidemolition ordinance. Taking notice of the housing shortage and the guarantee of a fair return under rent control, the landlord's claim of a taking was rejected. The court also rejected the landlord's claim that the ordinance amounted to involuntary servitude under the Thirteenth Amendment of the U.S. Constitution, because the landlord was free to sell or withhold the units from the market and had no constitutionally protected right to go out of business. In 1985, the landlord lobby persuaded the California legislature to enact legislation preempting the authority of a municipality to deny a removal permit under these circumstances. This state preemption policy was upheld against Santa Monica's objections in *Javidzad v. City of Santa Monica* (1988).

In *Fresh Pond Shopping Center v. Callahan* (1983), the United States Supreme Court refused to review a decision of the Massachusetts Supreme Judicial Court that upheld the right of a city to protect residential rent-controlled tenants against the hardship of displacement from demolition of their apartment building for commercial development (with now Chief Justice Rehnquist alone dissenting that this amounted to a taking).

ANTIWAREHOUSING

Despite provisions for a fair return on investment under rent control, some landlords have tried to hold units off the market in the hope of converting them to other uses without having to face the opposition of resident tenants. A few cities have passed "antiwarehousing" ordinances that require landlords to rent vacant units on the ground that, otherwise, they will exacerbate the very rental housing shortage that rent control is designed to ameliorate.

In *Help Hoboken Housing v. City of Hoboken* (1986), a federal court rejected claims that the ordinance violated due process, equal protection, and antitrust requirements, or was a taking. In a case involving the preservation of single-room-occupancy (SRO) housing in New York City, a divided New York Court of Appeals held that the city's ordinance did amount to a regulatory taking. The city imposed a five-year moratorium on SRO conversions and demolition and required owners to rent vacant units, including substandard units requiring rehabilitation. Exemption was allowed, but only if owners contributed $45,000 per unit to replace each converted or demolished unit (*Seawall Associates v. City of New York* 1989).

EQUAL PROTECTION

Landlords have frequently argued that they have been denied equal protection either because their units are covered when other landlords' units are exempted or because their units are treated differently (e.g., granted lower rent increases). The constitutional test, in the absence of a claim of invidious discrimination against a protected class—which does not cover landlords—is that the government may justify differential treatment as long as it can demonstrate a rational basis for its policy. Rent control agencies have usually been able to defend legislative and administrative policy against constitutional challenges on this basis.

ANTITRUST

In *Fisher v. City of Berkeley* (1986), a majority of the United States Supreme Court ruled that Berkeley's rent control ordinance did not violate federal antitrust law. In a novel action, landlords argued that rent control amounted to a conspiracy (between tenant voters and their elected representatives) to restrain trade and represented monopolistic price-fixing by the local government that was not expressly sanctioned by the state of California, as was required then by precedents granting municipalities immunity from antitrust liability.

STATUTORY ISSUES

In addition to broad constitutional challenges, virtually every type of rent control statute in the United States—federal, state, and local—has faced other legal challenges. The outcomes have varied according to the type of challenge, the circumstances, the jurisdiction, and the remedy sought. Landlords, for example, have sought remedial orders against rent control agencies, damages, and exemptions from coverage.

EXISTENCE OF A SERIOUS HOUSING EMERGENCY

Whether courts have adhered to a strict "housing emergency" standard or a less restrictive standard of a "serious housing problem" as the prerequisite for the use of the police power to regulate rents, the courts have reserved the right to review the legislative determination that such a factual situation exists. The courts have the power under the U.S. system of the separation of powers to make this review.

Some courts have deferred to legislative declarations based upon survey data presented at public hearings. These data include such factors as rental vacancy rates, tenants' rent-to-income ratios, and rent increase patterns. These data reinforce the legal presumption of validity that courts generally accord the exercise of the police power.

While landlords have tried to counter this presumption with their own data, they have had to overcome a heavy burden of proof. Beginning in 1943, for example, and continuing into the 1980s, the New York Court of Appeals has on numerous occasions rejected landlord challenges to state and local rent control based upon their claim that a housing emergency was over (Baar and Keating 1975). New York City has conducted triennial housing and vacancy surveys to justify renewal of rent control; the New York City legislation requires that the vacancy rate remain below 5 percent (see chapter 11).

Rent control in the United States has always been temporary. Therefore, rent control legislation usually has a sunset clause, which requires periodic legislative renewal based on the finding that the housing shortage continues. No U.S. rent control law has ever been adopted on a permanent basis.

PREEMPTION

According to the "preemption" doctrine that accords supremacy to the federal government in the United States, federal law preempts conflicting state and local laws. Even in strong home-rule states, state law still preempts conflicting local laws. Landlord and tenant groups both have tried to invoke preemption when it serves their interest (see chapter 5). The courts have upheld the exemption of federally subsidized and insured rental housing from municipal rent control. However, attempts by the real estate lobby during the Reagan administration to condition federal housing assistance on the termination of state and local rent control failed.

A number of states have preempted municipal rent control by a statewide ban, reserving this right to the state (the latest being Massachusetts in 1994 through a landlord-backed referendum). Other states have adopted enabling legislation, allowing municipalities to enact it by local option (e.g., Massachusetts prior to 1994). Some states have allowed local rent control but only in conformity to state-enacted guidelines (e.g., New York). In the two states with the highest number of municipal rent control ordinances—California and New Jersey—tenants fought state enabling legislation they feared would be dominated by landlords. In California, voters defeated a statewide landlord initiative in 1980 and a landlord mobile home initiative in 1995, but after years of lobbying by landlords, the California legislature enacted a preemptive vacancy decontrol law in 1995 (see chapters 7 and 9).

COVERAGE

All U.S. rent control laws have exemptions to their coverage of rental housing, which has led to litigation over whether or not certain buildings or units are covered or whether certain tenants are protected. Where certain types of buildings are exempt, such as those constructed after a base date establishing rent control, those containing only a few units, those substantially rehabilitated, or those that are owner-occupied, landlords can claim exemptions from rent control, including registration of units. This claim can require judicial review and interpretation of the legislative definition of coverage, a review of any administrative decisions on the issue, and a factual finding addressing disputed evidence. Landlords who evade registration and charge illegal rents are subject to disciplinary penalties, which the courts have generally upheld unless the landlord's behavior was found to be not willful or the penalty was found to be excessive.

The term "tenancy" is not always conclusively defined, and the lack of definition has led to litigation over whether occupants can invoke the protection of rent control or can be evicted summarily. Typical issues involve landlord claims that occupants never signed proper leases (if required); that the occupants are illegal subtenants; or that they do not meet a basic condition of tenancy (e.g., actual continuing occupancy).

RENT INCREASES

Occasionally, landlords or tenants have challenged rent increase guidelines. Where the guidelines are based on estimated landlord cost increases, those who are dissatisfied have claimed that the increases were unjustified. The courts have rarely overturned rent guidelines on this basis. Procedural challenges have also been tried.

Some localities allow landlords to increase rents only on condition that their units comply with local housing and health codes. The New Jersey Supreme Court upheld such a condition in *Orange Taxpayers Council v. City of Orange* (1980). Another typical condition is that only properly registered landlords may increase rents. This condition, too, has been upheld by the courts, resulting in rent refunds to tenants whose landlords were not properly registered but who increased rents anyway.

ADMINISTRATION

The courts have often overturned the administrative decisions of rent control agencies on procedural grounds. Landlords and tenants are entitled to due process, including proper prior notice of their rights and about public hearings, filing deadlines, and related issues. Most challenges have contested the legality of individual cases, e.g., disputed rent increases for a unit or building. The most extreme challenge to the administration of rent control was the claim of New York City landlords that the Maximum Base Rent (MBR) system instituted in 1970 was unconstitutional because of maladministration. In 1980, the New York Court of Appeals rejected this claim, noting that maladministration, even if proven, does not give rise to any judicial relief (*Benson Realty Corp. v. Beame*).

CONCLUSION

The legitimacy of rent control has been extensively challenged in the U.S. courts throughout its history. Appellate courts have upheld the constitutionality of rent control. The courts have typically deferred to the legislative body's judgment that the enactment of rent control was justified and to its formulation of the rent control system. However, rent control, as applied, has been invalidated in many cases. Given the reluctance of courts to override economic policy, they have been wary of being drawn into the debates over the wisdom of its adoption or its impact. The economic, political, and social questions surrounding rent control are addressed in the next three chapters.

Andrejs Skaburskis and Michael B. Teitz

4

The Economics of Rent Regulation

INTRODUCTION

With few exceptions, economists have viewed rent controls as bad—very bad—for landlords, tenants, homeowners, governments, and society as a whole. No housing policy has been condemned by as large a proportion of economists. More than 93 percent of the members of the American Economics Association surveyed by Alston, Kearl, and Vaughan (1992) agreed with the statement: "A ceiling on rent reduces the quantity and quality of housing available." The economics literature is full of warnings about the deleterious effects of rent controls, and this chapter begins by presenting the traditional arguments. It goes on to describe, however, the advances in the theory of rental markets that have allowed a more precise depiction of the likely consequences of rent control policy to be developed. These recent advances explain the failures in rental markets and provide an economic rationale for considering rent regulation as a valid component in the array of housing policies governments may need to use.

THE TRADITIONAL VIEW OF RENT CONTROL

The traditional back-of-the-envelope arguments against rent controls still used by many economists start by depicting a downward sloping demand curve, an upward housing supply curve, and point to the intersection that identifies the price and quantity that brings demand and supply into equilibrium (figure 4.1). The effects of rent controls are then erroneously illustrated by the drawing of a horizontal line across the demand and supply curves below the equilibrium price level P_e. At this price ceiling the demand for housing is greater than the equilibrium supply at Q_e. The ceiling prevents landlords from covering costs and induces them to reduce the supply of housing services. A large number of other unattractive indirect consequences follow as a result of the market's inability to attain equilibrium:

1. Landlords are prevented from covering the full cost of their units and are induced to cut back on maintenance expenditures.
2. The tenants' gain as a result of the reduced rent is dissipated by the maintenance cutback that causes the dwellings to deteriorate and reduces the dwellings' value to the tenants.
3. The development industry, fearing that the new buildings that are usually exempt from controls will eventually become subject to controls, holds back on construction until rents in the uncontrolled sector rise to cover the expected losses from possible future controls.
4. As rents rise in the uncontrolled new stock and vacancies decline in the controlled stock, more households decide to become homeowners and drive up the price of houses and condominiums.
5. Apartments become harder to find, search costs increase, and landlords try to reduce operating costs by screening out less-wealthy tenants, young people, and/or households with children.
6. The pursuit of "key money" is encouraged, and stress is created in the relationships between landlords and tenants.
7. People occupying controlled dwelling units are less inclined to move when their housing needs change, and aging households stay in large apartments after their children leave home. Young families face increasing hardships as suitable housing becomes more difficult to find, due to the misallocation of the housing stock.
8. Economic growth is restricted as new employees are dissuaded from moving to the city by the high price of apartments in the uncontrolled sector and the low vacancy rates in rent regulated housing.[1]
9. Most taxpayers are made worse off as property values drop in the controlled sector and tax rates have to increase to maintain

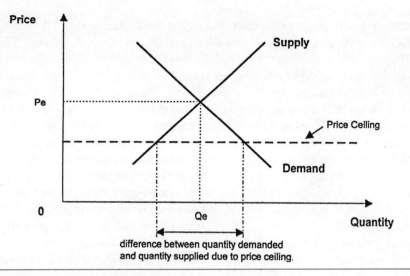

FIGURE 4.1
Demand, supply, and price ceilings

revenue levels. Landlords pay less income tax due to their reduced ability to collect higher rents. The cost of administering
the rent controls is born by taxpayers.

10. Housing quality in the controlled units continues to deteriorate,
and redistribution consequences continue to manifest themselves in an ad hoc manner.

This traditional analysis of rent controls usually ends with the procla-
mation that everyone—rich and poor, landlords and renters, firms and consumers—is eventually made worse off by the policy. New developments
in economic theory, however, challenge some of the traditional arguments
and point to market failures that provide an economic rationale for considering mild forms of rent regulation and that lead some economists to recognize that moderate rent controls can be welfare enhancing.

THE CHANGING VIEWS ON RENTAL MARKETS

Two major advances in the theory of housing markets depart from the model
depicted in figure 4.1 and help explain the consequences of rent control
policy in a more precise manner. The first identifies an error in the traditional model by recognizing that although rent controls restrict the revenue a landlord can gain from a dwelling, they do not control the price of

"housing services" (an abstract unit that is conceptually composed of the valued attributes provided by a dwelling) (Arnott 1981; Frankena 1975). The new model depicts the demand for services by the tenant of a dwelling unit and the supply of services offered by that unit as a direct function of the landlord's maintenance expenditures. The more the landlord spends on upkeep, the more services are rendered by the dwelling. At equilibrium, the cost of an extra outlay on maintenance equals the amount the tenant pays for the resulting improvement. Rent control destroys this equilibrium and prevents the landlord from recovering value in return for maintenance expenditures. As a result, the landlord cuts back on maintenance until the revenue gained from a maintenance expenditure under the controls covers the marginal cost. As the dwelling units deteriorate over time, they offer fewer "housing services" for a given rent, and the hypothetical price people pay for each of the abstract units of "housing service" increases. The market is in disequilibrium while the quality level of the dwellings stays above their equilibrium level. During this time, demand exceeds supply, and the stock misallocation consequences described earlier are expected. As the dwellings deteriorate enough to reestablish equilibrium, social welfare is also reduced, and the landlords who owned property at the time rent controls were announced suffer the loss. Eventually, renters are also made worse off, due to the reduction in the quantity of housing services available to them.

Without further elaboration of the market's characteristics or consideration of the features of second-generation controls, the conclusions drawn from these models are similar to the ones developed by using the traditional price ceiling model. This step in the evolution of theory, however, is important because it forms the basis for more realistic models of the rental market that will eventually yield different conclusions. It also provides the analytical framework for assessing the relative advantages and disadvantages of alternative forms of rent control. It points to the importance of maintenance levels and maintenance technology as determinants of the adverse welfare consequences of rent controls.

The second important advance in the economic theory of housing markets develops models of the supply adjustment process within the existing stock. Sweeney (1974a, 1974b) considers the housing stock as a commodity hierarchy chain in which submarkets are differentiated by quality levels. Housing prices are set by the demand for units of each quality level, by the cost of new construction, and by maintenance expenditures and technology. Above a certain quality and price level, new construction is feasible, and within a perfect market, rent levels in this sector will always be set by the cost of building new units. Housing inevitably deteriorates with time and drops down the quality ladder. The rate at which it filters down is a function of the landlords' maintenance expenditures which, in turn, depend on landlords' current revenues and on their expectation of future revenues when their buildings move further down the rungs of the quality ladder. If the demand for lower-quality stock increases, its price increases, and the owners of the better housing find it less advantageous to spend money trying to maintain their units at a high level. The landlords, seeking to increase current net revenues, allow their buildings to deteriorate to a lower-quality class that still yields them a good return as a result of the price increase. This process increases the supply of lower-quality, lower-priced housing. If the demand for lower-quality units were to decrease, however, or if their rent levels were to drop, perhaps because of a subsidy that increased the construction of low-priced housing, then the owners of the better stock have an incentive to keep their dwellings at the higher-quality level for a longer period of time by increasing maintenance expenditures. Consequently, filtering rates would decline. Exogenously induced price change at any quality level affects the value of all units at or above that level and therefore affects their price, their profit-maximizing maintenance schedules, and the filtering rate. Supply or demand changes at any quality level in turn affect housing prices at all levels. Rent controls affecting the price of units at any quality level affect all housing prices.

Two of Sweeney's theorems are of particular use in the study of rent regulation. His theorem 8 proves that housing prices in perfect markets with constant returns to scale are set by building costs at the quality levels that can receive new construction. The price of lower-quality housing, however, is *independent of building costs*: "At these lower levels demand changes will influence long-run equilibrium prices" (Sweeney 1974a, 308). In other words, growth in demand will, in a long-run stationary equilibrium, push some prices up and bring some down, depending on how the rates of change in demand differ across income groups. Even in a growing city and a perfect market, the equilibrium price of housing services may rise for lower-income households, while they are fixed by building costs for upper-income people. At lower levels, rent increases are not determined by changing construction costs, and they are not disciplined by cost considerations. The supply response to increases in the price of lower-income housing is through reduced maintenance at higher levels; this response is very slow in the real world and may even reverse in rapidly growing cities to make low-income households suffer major losses of income. The traditional model depicting supply adjustments in response to demand changes at lower rent levels is far-fetched.

The Sweeney model is useful, not only because it provides a framework for tracing consequences of rent controls, but also because it develops the basis for a more critical review of market adjustment processes. Buildings in North America typically depreciate at rates below one percent a year.[2] Maintenance expenditures form only a minor part of the landlord's outlays, far less than mortgage interest payments, insurance payments, and, in some jurisdictions, water charges and property taxes. Maintenance outlays, therefore, may not be a very important factor in the landlords' business plans. The economic models whose welfare conclusions depend on maintenance levels and depreciation rates should be used with caution in policy analysis. Furthermore,

> the greater part of the category of physical deterioration seems to consist of those minor incidents of wear and tear and of the elements which, summed together, form a fairly regular and substantial component of annual housing costs: flaking paint, broken windows, cracked or warped siding, leaky roofs, clogged plumbing or drains, worn-out screens, scuffed floors or linoleum, etc. The point is that with adequate maintenance the house need not depreciate in these respects. (Lowry 1970b, 365)

Which maintenance problem will the landlord ignore in response to rent control? The leaking roof and broken siding must be repaired, unless the owner plans to abandon the entire structure, an event that may occur at the very low end of the market. As Arnott (1981) illustrates, adjustments to rent control policy can eliminate serious maintenance problems. The depreciation consequence can be reduced by provisions that allow rent increases to cover rising maintenance costs or offer landlords the chance to escape rent controls once their units have reached a particular rent level.

Edgar Olsen was one of the first economists to question the traditional views on rent control by referring to Grampp's (1950, 438) observation that tenants spend their own money on maintenance. Olsen (1972, 1988) also pointed out that the design of the policy is important in determining its consequences, that penalties and rewards for upkeep can induce landlords to maintain their units:

> Despite enormous improvements . . . virtually all economists' views concerning the effect of rent control on maintenance . . . are based on incredibly simple models of housing markets and rent control ordinances and on casual empiricism. (Olsen 1988, 295)

The models are "seriously deficient" in that they ignore essential features of actual rent control ordinances. Other problems, even with the new models, are their incompleteness and their willingness to assume perfect market conditions.

THE REVISED VIEWS ON RENT CONTROL

The complexity of real housing markets has been recognized by economists who show that policies can have surprising side effects and aftereffects. Anas and Arnott (1993, 186), for example, develop a model that yields a counterintuitive conclusion showing that a reduction in construction costs due to technological improvements or due to housing subsidies can lead to higher rents, by increasing replacement construction rates that drive up land prices. As a result of the complexity of real housing markets, Anas and Arnott point out that: "We must change the 'back of the envelope' way we think about the operation of the housing market." More complex models have been developed in the 1990s to focus on the effects of imperfections in rental markets. Although these models will not develop wholehearted endorsements for stringent rent controls (they mostly justify very mild controls), their main value is to show the serious limitations imposed by the traditional economic analysis of the social welfare consequences of rent controls.

Most of the welfare rationales for regulation that are advanced by economists begin with the position that a market system that meets the requirements of competitive behavior should, for a given distribution of wealth, generate a composition of output and satisfaction on the part of consumers that cannot be exceeded by any other allocation of resources to production. At equilibrium, no consumer can be made better off without someone else becoming worse off in their own view. No resource can be used in a way that increases the aggregate satisfaction of consumers, and no resource is wasted; this is an efficient solution. It follows, then, that regulation, which intervenes in the market, can be justifiable only where the market fails to perform as stipulated by the competitive model. Market failures may take several forms and have many causes, but they have in common an element of deviation from the competitive ideal, which depends on costless transactions, perfect information, atomistic behavior of consumers and producers, and freedom from coercion. Recent models of housing markets that recognize the prevalence of market failures have been developed by Börsch-Supan (1986), Arnott (1989), Hubert (1990a), Igarashi and Arnott (1994).

THE ECONOMIC RATIONALE FOR CONSIDERING THE USE OF RENT CONTROLS

Monopoly Powers

Among the main rationales for economic regulation from a market failure perspective, the oldest and most persistent concern has been the

curbing of monopoly power. From the U.S. antitrust legislation of the late
nineteenth century to recent debates about the pricing of therapeutic drugs,
it has been argued that, if producers of commodities with few substitutes
have monopolistic control over entry and production within their markets,
they can set prices above the level that would prevail under competition.
Elementary economics demonstrates that the result should include lower
output and consumption, reduced welfare of consumers, inefficient allocation of resources as the prices of other goods and services are distorted,
and monopoly profits on the part of producers. In order to realize these
profits, certain producers may attempt to drive out all other producers and
restrict entry on the part of new firms, or the producers may collude to
restrict production and raise prices. The regulatory response to this behavior
has been antitrust legislation and the prohibition of collusion in restraint
of trade.

Most aspects of housing markets are competitive; builders and landlords tend to be small, and entry to the industry is open. In some cases,
land at the city periphery is held by a few firms that may exercise monopoly power. Toronto and Calgary may have witnessed such practices in
the past. However, Markusen and Scheffman (1978, 423) also show that
"the existence of monopoly power is not sufficient for the exercise of monopoly power and, therefore, for resource misallocation." Indeed, the mo-
nopolists' quest for development profits may accelerate land conversion
beyond the rate that would have been maintained by a competitive market.

One aspect of the monopoly power landlords hold over tenants is the
high cost of moving the occupants would incur should they have to relo-
cate. In theory, landlords could raise rents to just below the fair market
price plus the tenants' moving costs. But this aspect of monopoly power
does not in itself provide a rationale for rent controls. Although some landlords might set rents in such a manner, most give discounts to long-term
tenants (Clark and Heskin 1982; Börsch-Supan 1984; Miron 1990). Rather,
the monopoly power that provides a rationale for mild rent controls stems
from the diversity of the housing stock, the high cost of searching for a
dwelling unit, and the idiosyncratic housing preferences of consumers. The
connection between vacancy rates, search costs, and the cost of the mismatch between a dwelling's characteristics and the consumer's needs is
developed by Arnott (1989). The landlord recognizes that there are only a
few similarly priced apartments on the market at one time, that they are
somewhat different in character, and that consumers differ in their desire
for unique features. The landlord asks for an "above cost" price in the
hope of attracting the tenant who really likes the features of his or her apartment and is willing to pay a premium for its uniqueness. The exercise of

monopoly power raises rents, but due to the other premises embedded in the model, the increased vacancy rates that are generated by the quest for monopoly profits drive the landlords' profits back to normal levels. Everyone, landlord and tenant, would be better off with very mild controls that reduce the landlords' self-defeating quest for monopoly profits.

Imperfect Information

A second commonly advanced welfare justification for economic regulation recognizes the importance of accurate and sufficient information to both producers and consumers. If such information is very costly to obtain, but once known cannot be restricted or sold, then it may make sense to regulate its production to ensure its availability. A pharmaceutical manufacturer, for example, may be required to perform extensive safety testing before a new drug can be marketed. Consumers individually cannot perform this function, but without the information they may not be able to make informed choices. In this context, information about safety becomes a public good. Such goods are often produced by government directly, but in some instances it may be more efficient to produce them through a regulatory process and the enforcement of product standards. Admittedly, the line between providing information and regulating the permissible nature of goods or services to be sold is a fine one. In most instances, regulation goes beyond providing information to the prohibition of the sale of products that do not meet minimum standards. Such regulations effectively replace the notion of consumer sovereignty with the notion of a higher public welfare interest, based in part on the social costs of dealing with the results when consumers fail to gain or heed the information available to them.

In housing, the equivalent situation is recognizable by building and fire safety codes. The regulation of the production of new buildings to conform to standards of structural and functional safety ensures that consumers have the necessary information about the level of risk involved in their decision to occupy any specific building. Regulations of this type are intended to prevent people from becoming subject to risks, whether they have the information or not, since building collapse and fire inevitably have externality costs. This type of regulation and its justification are necessary parts of almost any conceivable system for rental regulation. Rent control, in itself, does not provide new forms of information to consumers, thereby allowing them to make more effective choices, but it does reduce the external costs generated by the actions of landlords and tenants who cannot at the time they make their contract determine if the other party is a bad tenant or a bad landlord.

Börsch-Supan (1986) examines the West German Tenants Protection legislation, which includes vacancy decontrol but limits rent increases during occupancy and prohibits evictions. Landlords with a vacant unit ask for a price above the one that would prevail in an unconstrained market to make up for future losses due to the constraint on rent increase. The tenant accepts the higher price, realizing that the constraint on rent increases will eventually reduce rents below the unconstrained level and he will benefit at that time. Landlords make above-normal profit in the beginning of tenancy but suffer losses in the later stage. The economic analysis shows that the constraint increases rents and reduces housing supply. However, Börsch-Supan examines the regulation as a second-best option and concludes that even though it has the expected deleterious effects, social welfare can nevertheless be increased under certain conditions. Arnott describes the underlying market failure that gives rise to the belief that rent controls can enhance what economists define as "social welfare":

> The market imperfection which derives the contract models is asymmetric information (Börsch-Supan 1986; Hubert 1990a, 1990b). In one such model, there are two groups of tenants, good and bad. A landlord discovers the identity of a tenant only after she has rented an apartment for one period. The economic environment is such that, in the absence of controls, a bad tenant moves every period, even though moving is costly, because she can get a substantially lower rent from a new landlord who does not know her identity. Each landlord realizes that by "economically evicting" his bad tenants, other landlords will be stuck with them. But since he does not pay the associated cost, he ignores it. Thus, there is a bad-tenant turnover externality—a beggar-thy-neighbor policy with respect to bad tenants. Imposing intra-tenancy rent control and prohibiting eviction eliminates the incentive for bad tenants to move, and hence the externality, and can make not only bad tenants but also good tenants better off. (Arnott 1995, 107)

Under rent regulation, tenants pay extra when they move into their dwelling in return for security from eviction. With time, good tenants are rewarded with tenure discounts, and they stay. Landlords gain some of the higher rents the tenants pay up front for having security from eviction. Both gain as a result of the controlled rent and the eviction provisions in the legislation whenever moving costs are high relative to the extra costs created by bad tenants.[3] When moving costs are low, both lose. This rationale is incomplete, however, because it does not show why landlords and tenants cannot make better contracts in the unregulated market. Hubert demonstrates that:

the publicly required provision of long-term contracts protecting the tenant against eviction may be welfare improving even though it only renders unfeasible contracts which allow for unilateral termination by the landlord. (Hubert 1991, 101)

The Prevalence of Externalities

A third broad welfare-based justification for regulation arises from another type of market failure, namely the existence of spillover or externality effects. If a firm is able to pass off some part of the full cost of production to others, then the price of its product will not reflect the true resource cost required to produce it, and misallocation will result. A common example of such a spillover is the cost of pollution by an industrial plant. Regulation through such means as the establishment and enforcement of minimum standards of performance has been the most frequent response intended to internalize these costs to the firm, or at least minimize them to others. Alternative approaches to dealing with problems of this type through taxation of pollution or marketing of permits to pollute have often been proposed but rarely accepted.

Housing has long been recognized as highly subject to externality effects, because it is fixed in space and powerfully influenced by the nature and behavior of surrounding uses. The existence of zoning may be partly explained by the desire of property owners, among whom homeowners are the most numerous, to protect the value of their houses from depreciation attributable to the location of lower-valued or incompatible activities close by.

Neighborhood effects do not provide a reason for rent regulation, but they form a basis for the belief that unconstrained markets can fail to yield socially desirable outcomes in some situations. The models that depict the supply of dwellings to low-income households and show the efficiency losses due to undermaintenance do not consider neighborhood effects. With time, houses depreciate and offer services to low-income people; with time, Beacon Hill becomes the Back Bay. But neighborhood effects can shortcut the filtering process by limiting the amount of land available for lower-priced housing. Rather than turn a stately mansion into a rooming house, it may be converted into a high-priced condominium. Neighborhood effects may retard or reverse the filtering process to remove the mechanism by which the supply of low-priced housing can adjust to changes in demand.

External consequences may also be generated by public policy. Growth controls, for example, drive up land and housing prices, and they make it difficult for developers to expand housing supply. As demand for housing grows, while the stock adjustments are impaired by policy, economic rents are generated and reaped by all property owners within the urban boundaries. Rent controls may be introduced in such situations to help reduce the extent of the redistributions created by the side effects of growth control policy. This type of rationale, however, is generally disliked by economists, who see its use as a justification of ever increasing interference by governments into market processes.

Redistribution of Economic Rents

An economic rationale for regulation is sometimes called "rent control," though it is not specifically related to housing, but refers instead to the existence of *economic rents*. In this sense, rent refers broadly to the benefit that accrues to any firm that is able to produce a commodity at a cost that is below the going market price and sustain that advantage against competing firms. For example, a mineral producer owning a deposit that is well located, rich, and easily worked will have a cost advantage against other producers with inferior deposits, and will therefore be able to gain "above normal" profits. If increasing demand for the product bids up the price for all producers, then the low-cost firm will garner economic rent in addition to its "normal" profit.[4] Strictly speaking, within the argument of neoclassical economics, there is no justification for regulating such rents. They may be arbitrary, depending upon the good fortune of the producer, or they may be attributable to superior business or technical acumen.[5] But in either case, the economic rents do not affect the efficiency of the resulting pattern of production. Indeed, any attempt to control them may give rise to resource misallocation that prevents the market from moving in a way that will eliminate them if it is technologically possible. Nonetheless, the unearned character of such rents and their appearance at times of scarcity and rapidly rising prices of commodities that are considered to be necessities do create unavoidable issues of distributional equity that have been resolved by means of controls for millennia.

> The medieval notion of the "just price" was developed by the early Church in opposition to the Roman law notion of "natural price" that had come from Stoic philosophy. The "natural price" doctrine justified any willing exchange; "just price" recognized the implicit coercion of exchange that could arise under difficult economic circumstances, e.g., famine. Unjust enrichment was forbidden under "just price," which was to be determined by what was customary. Glaeser (1957, 196) notes that political and economic instability contributed to the adoption of the "just price" doctrine by the later Roman Empire. Seeking to discourage revolution, Emperor

> Diocletian set maximum prices for about eight hundred articles. In spite
> of Diocletian's motives in installing it, the "just price" doctrine implied
> the existence of a justification for interference by the state in private eco-
> nomic activities. This doctrine continued in the scholasticism of medieval
> philosophers like St. Thomas Aquinas, who identified the "just price" as
> that which will reimburse production costs, viewed broadly. (Mitnick 1980,
> 244)

Thus, while there is little social concern about the economic rent garnered by holders of Van Gogh paintings during boom times in the art market, the same type of rent gained by food suppliers in times of famine almost universally leads to calls for either regulation of prices, or rationing
of food, or usually both. In the United States, the principal examples of
rent control regulation, in this sense, have been found in the oil and gas
industries during times of rising prices in world markets (Breyer 1982).
Most of that rent, however, has not been subject to regulation since it has
accrued to foreign oil producers. Furthermore, in the oil and gas industry,
the element of rent is confounded with the impact of cartelization and
monopoly profit, offshoots of OPEC.

Housing seems to be especially subject to the phenomenon of economic
rent. Housing units are locationally fixed, costly, and time-consuming to
produce, and they are, therefore, subject to delays in market supply response to changing conditions of demand. If demand suddenly expands,
as might be the case when large-scale in-migration to an area occurs, housing prices rise sharply, at least in the short term. Since housing constitutes
the largest single expenditure for most households, a rapid increase in its
price generates immediate and substantial pain. Seeing no improvement
in the quantity or quality of housing services being supplied, people tend
to respond with indignation and anger, and they look to the political system for redress.

Regulation of economic rent in housing is neither inevitable nor
uniform. Where rapid price increases occur for housing that is owner-
occupied, demand for regulation is rare, because inflation raises the owner's
equity and wealth. Indeed, gains from price inflation have come to be
regarded as a virtual entitlement of homeownership. The benefits to the
recipients of the rent, namely those who already own houses and the
producers of new housing, greatly outweigh the benefits to the new entrants
to the market, who bear the principal burden of the price increase. But the
new entrants gain what is usually perceived as a "really good investment
opportunity." Many homeowners will sell a house at an inflated price before
buying an even bigger one to accrue even greater capital gains in the future.

The benefits of price increases in the homeownership market are widespread and palpable. At most, there may be calls for subsidies for first-time home buyers to give them entry into the market.

In rental housing markets, however, the situation is very different, since the occupant's well-being is reduced by rent increases. Landlords may have some incentive to put back part of the economic rent into their buildings, in order to attract higher-income tenants or enhance marketability for sale, but this new investment only further alienates those tenants in place who see rising rentals threatening their occupancy. There is a perception both of the existence of an economic rent (though people will not call it that), and of a concentrated benefit for a few property owners. That politics comes into play should scarcely surprise us.

Furthermore, the rise in rents does not necessarily stimulate rental construction. Land prices are inflated by the capitalized value of the expected future growth in house prices. The expectation of continued price inflation may be more optimistic for homeowners than for professional landlords, which causes the residual value of land in the nonrental market to rise well above that in the rental market. In such markets, rental construction ceases as condominium developers outbid everyone for the available land. The market failure is created by the false optimism of home buyers and their tendency to base expectations on past trends rather than on a view of future conditions. Adaptive rather than rational expectations drive the homeownership market (Muth 1986). The ownership market is inefficient, because prices often continue to rise moderately after demand has ceased to expand (Case and Shiller 1985; Evans 1995; Abraham and Hendershott 1996). The failures in the homeownership market that create price bubbles inflate land values to the extent that residential construction is no longer feasible by building condominiums.

This rationale, more than any other, might constitute an underpinning for a theory of regulation of rental housing based on welfare and market failure criteria. Such a rationale is not without problems, however, especially the fact that it relies not on the argument that regulation leads to a closer approximation of the outcome of a competitive market, but rather on a distributive criterion. Thus, economic rent might be more appropriately seen as a version of the social failure criterion that will be discussed in chapter 6.

Market Adjustment Rates

A fifth argument relates to the speed of market adjustment and the virtual lack of a supply response to increasing demand by lower-income renters in rapidly growing cities. The slowness of market response has justified government support in the building of railways across the continent. The lack of market institutions provided the rationale for governments in the United States and Canada to create secondary mortgage markets. New housing takes time to build, and over the short run—perhaps five to ten years—construction costs can rise considerably in a metropolitan area and stay well above long-run equilibrium levels. The "used" housing that lower-income households rely on is even slower to expand, since it requires a filtering process that may even be reversed in rapidly expanding cities. For filtering to work, deLeeuw and Struyk (1975) show that city residents must be experiencing rapid growth in wealth and must have an income elasticity well above zero. The decline in the price of a dwelling unit due to the decrease in the services it offers can be entirely offset by rapid city growth rates (deLeeuw and Struyk 1975). Rechlis and Yezer (1985, 162) find that housing prices appreciated more quickly in neighborhoods built before 1939 than they did in newer neighborhoods after accounting for distance to the city center and a set of house characteristics. Muth (1975) shows that rental prices rise with growth in income and in city size.

Figure 4.2 illustrates the differences in the rents per room by age of building, using Canadian Census data for 1971, 1981, 1986, and 1991. The estimates are developed by using simple regressions that control for location, building type, and unit size.[6] The estimates show that rents drop for the first fifty or fifty-five years of a building's life, and then increase slightly. Buildings that are not demolished at the end of their usual life span are most likely renovated and serve higher-income people. The profiles for the four census years are very similar, with the only difference being the flattening of the gradient since the 1976 introduction of rent controls in Canada. In 1991 and in 1986, the average rent declined by about 17 percent over a fifty-year period. Since the average rent in new apartments was $680 in 1991, the rent would be expected to decline by $112 over fifty years. Using 33 percent as the acceptable household rent/income ratio, the decline in rents over fifty years would bring the once-new housing stock to households earning about $3,686 a year below that of the households for whom the building was initially built. It is hard to become overly concerned about the side effects of policies that may impede this adjustment process.

The slowness of filtering rates raises a number of issues. It is unlikely that profit-maximizing landlords, even when facing a riskless future with perfect foresight, will behave like the Sweeney model landlords and adjust their current maintenance schedules in light of what may happen fifty years from now.[7]

> Our knowledge of the factors which will govern the field of an invest-
> ment some years hence is usually very slight and often negligible. If we
> speak frankly, we have to admit that our basis of knowledge for estimat-
> ing the yield ten years hence of . . . a building . . . amounts to little and
> sometimes to nothing. (Keynes 1965)

CONCLUSION

Housing markets are far from perfect markets. Demand may change
abruptly, but supply is slow to respond to price signals, and production
costs can increase tremendously as home buyers' overly optimistic expectations inflate land prices to preclude the expansion of the rental stock.
Landlords may be able to exercise monopoly power due to the thinness of
the market and the heterogeneity of product characteristics and consumer
tastes. Furthermore, many renters do not have the option of leaving the
rental market to become homeowners when rents rise. The very existence
of tenure preferences is attributed to market failures:

> In a perfectly competitive world with complete markets, perfect knowl-
> edge, divisible assets, zero transaction costs, and neutral taxes, households
> would be indifferent with respect to their mode of housing tenure (Arnott
> 1987). Thus, theories of tenure choice must be rooted in specific uncer-
> tainties or imperfections that are of sufficient importance to households
> to create tenure preferences. (Jones 1989, 18)

The market failures in housing are significant to policymakers at municipal and state/province levels because housing forms the single largest
expenditure for most people. Its value to the consumer grows with time as
the external benefits gained from neighborhood develop. Housing availability affects household formation by influencing marital decisions, di-
vorce options, and the inclination to work outside the home. Rent levels
are determinants of the demographic structure of cities (Börsch-Supan 1986;
Haurin, Hendershott, and Kim 1990; Skaburskis 1994). Housing decisions
not only reflect and shape the composition of a population but they are
linked to the way we see ourselves (Cooper 1976). One's self-esteem may
be affected by a forced move. One's place on the housing-quality ladder is
related to one's place in society and to the ability to access urban resources
(Rex and Moore 1967; Pahl 1969). Changes in the location of subpopula-
tions reflect changes in the social and political order of a city. Important
also is the connection between house and home. Tognoli (1987) describes
aspects of "home"—its centrality as a place of human existence; its offer of
privacy, territoriality, and personal space; its offer of context, unity, order,

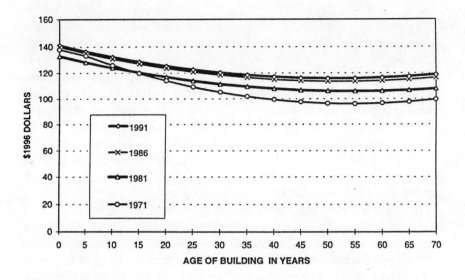

FIGURE 4.2

Rent-per-room ratios by age, using Canadian census microdata files

Source: Canadian Census Public Use Microdata Files for 1991

and continuity of life; its privacy, refuge, security; its source of self-identity; and its context of social and family relations (Murray 1990, 16). Even Heidegger (1968) uses the house/home distinction to examine *What Is a Thing?* Rent increases that threaten the occupant's security of tenure violate the United Nations' standard for basic housing.[8] The importance of housing makes large rent increases a matter for policy concern. At the very least, the importance of housing obviates the valor in calls to leave runaway markets unfettered.

The most important reason for rent regulation is created by the large swings in demand that take place in many housing markets over relatively short periods of time, in contrast to the length of the process by which competitive markets increase the supply of low-priced housing.[9] The high cost of finding new accommodation, the municipal restrictions on development and on minimum unit sizes, and the multidimensional attributes of the housing service that make it particularly important to consumers may justify the regulation of rent cycles.

This brief review of economic theory shows how recent advances have made contemporary economists recognize the value of mild second-generation rent controls. Today, most sensible people, including economists and planners, would not advocate first-generation controls that keep controlled rents falling ever further below the long-run equilibrium rents. Second-generation controls aim to stabilize the rental market and improve the tenants' security of tenure. Moderate controls may moderate the rates of change in rents and reduce cycles. In the longer term, cities must adjust to new conditions, and eventually some people will have to move. Rent regulation can moderate the pace of change and thereby significantly reduce the adjustment costs. At the same time, rent regulations reduce landlords' ability to exact scarcity rent when other real estate prices are being driven by false optimism or inflated by the market's inability to adjust rapidly to changing conditions. The relevant question for policy, therefore, is how bad the side effects of mild rent controls are relative to their benefits.

The undermaintenance problem can be reduced through designs that allow the landlord to leave the controlled stock as his or her dwelling's controlled price reaches a ceiling. Changes in maintenance costs can be factored into the allowable rent increases. Tenants must also maintain their units. Nevertheless, earlier demolition of old stock is to be expected as replacement construction becomes a relatively more attractive option. The developers of new rental housing will be discouraged by rent controls and may hold back until rents rise enough to compensate for the possible costs of future controls. Perhaps they will even be daunted and prices will rise, but this is not inevitable. Mild controls offer developers and landlords the advantage of a stable market within which discontent does not grow enough to generate the political demands for more stringent controls. The possibility of controls being enacted in cities currently without controls exists regardless of the city's particular history, and developers everywhere can consider the threat of future controls. The repeal of current controls will not change expectations of future controls.

Those who do not recognize the benefits of having a stable market will see themselves as losing out as a result of mild controls. The transfers of income during the overheating part of a price cycle are pure economic rents that do little to generate the new supply of rental housing. Second-generation controls aim to prevent the transfer of income from tenants to landlords for a period of time to ease the market's adjustment to new conditions. Nevertheless, while the rent controls are binding, landlords will be making less money than they could in the short run without the controls, and therefore they have an incentive to try to reap the windfalls.

Will the controls keep the market from allocating the dwelling units to those most willing to pay for them, and thereby generate the economic efficiency losses due to the misallocation of housing units? Yes, to an extent, and that is in part the purpose of the controls—to increase the security of tenure for the present renters and to reduce transaction costs. The controls prevent an optimal allocation of units, but so does an overheated housing market. When vacancy rates drop below one percent, prospective immigrants may have second thoughts about moving to the city; sitting tenants may not look for a more suitable dwelling; landlords will screen out costly tenants; and some forms of key money may be paid to landlords or agents. Binding rent controls contribute to these problems. But they also prevent social problems due to the exploitation by some landlords; they moderate the transfer of income from tenants to landlords; they increase security of tenure and peace of mind, and thereby change the meaning a tenant attaches to his or her home. They increase the value that can be derived from the rental stock. Whether the benefits are worth the cost is precisely the question here, as in all regulatory policy.

Notes

1. According to a series of articles by Tucker (1987, 1989), homelessness increases. These articles were thoroughly discredited by Quigley (1990).

2. Kain and Quigley (1970) estimate a 0.4 percent depreciation rate for rental housing. Weston (1972) finds a rate three times this size; Leigh (1979) has a 1.3 percent depreciation rate for renters; Margolis (1981) estimates a 0.4 percent depreciation rate; and Follain and Malpezzi (1979) show a 0.8 percent drop in the value of dwellings. The Malpezzi, Ozanne, and Thibodeau (1987) article provides city-specific estimates of depreciation rates for rental buildings of different ages: Atlanta, Baltimore, Buffalo, Chicago, Cincinnati, Columbus, Houston, Miami, Rochester, and San Francisco have rates well below the 0.5 percent level for ten-year-old structures. Even if deferred maintenance doubled the depreciation rates, the rental buildings would still have life expectancies of more than a hundred years. Furthermore, the depreciation rate appears to decline with the age of the building and thereby extends the life expectancy (Goodman and Thibodeau [1995]; Lowry [1970b]). Chinloy (1979, 1980) estimates depreciation rates below one percent.

3. The high transaction costs associated with moving support the conclusion of Anas and Cho (1988, 201): "If, however, current [Swedish] institutions such as the rationing of dwellings result in sufficiently lower transaction costs for households relative to the free market, then deregulation is not Pareto preferred."

4. Given the Sweeney (1974a, b) conclusion that the price of housing services is set by the structure of demand, not by construction costs, the economic rent may be defined as the difference between the long-run equilibrium rent that would be generated by a competitive market and the

prevailing rent. Constraints due to industry capacity, land-use policy, and approvals processes may raise prices above their long-run equilibrium level. The exercise of monopoly power generates an economic rent.

5. Arnott refers to Fallis (1988) to explain that the higher prevalence of rent control in Europe may be due to differences in the notion of fairness. North Americans are more concerned with *ex ante* equality—equality of opportunity—while Europeans are more concerned with *ex post* equality— equality of result. Accordingly, Europeans are more likely to favor rent control to prevent unexpected demand-induced increases in rents, which entail fortuitous and, therefore, undeserved redistributions (Arnott 1995, 109).

6. The parameters for the age and age-squared variables were estimated using regressions that included as control variables the room counts, rooms squared, building type, occupancy more than five years, and categorical variables identifying Toronto, Montreal, and four regions. The number of cases in the regressions were well over 100,000 except for 1971, yielding estimates with low standard errors.

7. Wallace Smith (1968) casually observed that "owners of new buildings typically consider their structure to have fifty-year life spans, and owners of twenty-five-year-old buildings typically consider the structures to have fifty-year life spans; owners of 100-year old buildings typically consider their buildings to have fifty-year life spans."

8. In 1987, the International Year of Shelter for the Homeless, the United Nations included in its definition of homeless, people who "did not have adequate protection from the elements, access to safe water and sanitation, affordable prices, security of tenure. . . ." (Fallis and Murray 1990, 1).

9. Peter Chinloy (1996) describes cycles in retail markets that have vacancy rates just above 10 percent. Skaburskis (1988) describes the Vancouver cycle in 1979-1981 when house prices doubled and then fell back again to their original level. Vacancy rates were below 0.1 percent. Although the rental sector was not monitored, the example illustrates the extent to which housing markets can be irrational and presents a situation in which stabilization policies would have been helpful.

Michael B. Teitz

5

The Politics of Rent Control

INTRODUCTION

R ent control is always political and almost always conflictual, and the reason is not difficult to understand. To regulate rents in a market system requires public action, which involves making political decisions from which some will gain while others lose. The regulation of rents, if it is effective, implies transfers between groups, particularly tenants and landlords, who are quite aware that substantial costs and benefits may be involved, even if they do not always understand the actual scale of those transfers.[1] As a result, organized landlord and tenant interests have faced off in legislative bodies, in electoral campaigns, before administrative agencies, and in the courts. In some jurisdictions, such as the city and state of New York, the political struggle has raged for decades. Elsewhere, it is more episodic, but always latent.

In light of the centrality of politics to rent control, it is remarkable that so little attention has been paid to the careful study of rent control politics. In comparison to the economics of the issue, explicit political analysis is rare. Malpezzi (1996) in his extensive bibliography on rent control, for example, lists hundreds of items on rent control laws, economic impacts, and policy, but only two with "politics" in their titles—Dreier (1979) and Niebanck (1985). Discussions of rent control in general are often so overtly ideological or partisan that they are only marginally interesting as studies of politics, though their content might well be useful material for a study of attitudes and values. The scarcity of research on rent control politics is even more curious when one considers the fact that the politics of regulation has been the object of enormous amounts of research and debate for decades. It is true that rent control is something of an odd fish in the sea of regulation. Its scope is small compared to other areas of regulation, such as public utilities; and its focus is local, not national. Nonetheless, an adequate understanding of the subject requires that the nature of rent control politics be explained.

It is a difficult task. The very absence of serious research on the subject constrains what can be said. In consequence, part of this chapter will be devoted to constructing a usable framework for talking about the politics of rent control and filling it in with the evidence that is available.

CONCEPTUAL BASES FOR THE POLITICS OF REGULATION

Why governments should intervene in the market—and how they should do it—has been the subject of investigation by political scientists, economists, and sociologists for at least a hundred years. Although no generally accepted conclusion has been reached, a number of approaches to the issue have evolved and constitute conceptual frameworks within which specific issues are debated.

From the perspective of political systems within market-oriented societies, we can identify three broad theoretical positions on how regulatory politics may be understood. A fourth position stands outside the market, but has its own powerful tradition. Roger Noll (1989) identifies the first three positions as *public interest theory, interest group theory,* and *principal agent theory,* each of which seeks to understand the ramifications of the politics of regulation in the context of the market. To these, we add *class theory,* which introduces a politics that substitutes an alternative structure for the market itself. In the case of rent control, this is historically an important political thread.

RATIONALES FOR PUBLIC INTERVENTION

Before discussing these theoretical positions, it is necessary to consider briefly why governments should intervene at all in markets—i.e., the basic rationales behind regulatory politics. Noll (1989) cites five rationales for regulation, all based on the idea that market failure leads to inefficiencies in economic activity, with a resultant loss of welfare. The three most common and accepted rationales among economists are, first, the existence of monopoly, which gives rise to monopoly profit and "deadweight" loss; second, imperfect information, which leads to erroneous decisions and efficiency losses; and, third, the presence of external effects or public goods, which prevent producers and consumers from taking account of the full economic consequences of their actions. To these, Noll adds two more rationales for regulation that he sees as politically common, but economically less defensible. The first is the existence of "destructive competition," an argument made during the Depression that an industry might not be a natural monopoly, but may still be unable to arrive at a stable equilibrium. The second is the existence of "scarcity rent"—i.e., the producer's surplus that occurs in markets with rising industry supply curves, such as the markets for natural resources or urban locations. In such markets, low-cost producers gain windfall profits. The argument for regulation in these situations can be based either on the effect of scarcity rents[2] on income distribution—i.e., distributive justice—or on the creation of externalities—when rising rents lead to evictions and forced relocations, for example, and include costs that are not counted in the market. Although arguments have been made that residential rent control is justified by *de facto* cartelization of local rental housing markets (Gilderbloom and Appelbaum 1988), the scarcity rent justification is by far the most widely used argument, fitting as it does those crisis situations in which rent control is often adopted.

Another very different kind of justification is based in Marxian class theory. It is no accident that in socialist revolutions, one of the first policies to be adopted, typically, is the imposition of draconian rent control, often with confiscation of "excess" housing. From St. Petersburg in 1917, to Cairo in 1954, to Havana in 1959, this pattern has been repeated and has been a key element of revolution—the ultimate political act—stemming from the belief that housing should not be subject to the market. According to this theory, state-provided housing should eliminate slums and reduce inequality in shelter. While it may seem far-fetched in the American context, the underlying theory that a property-owning class should not control a basic need such as housing has resonated in attempts to remove rental housing from the market altogether. In fact, removing rental housing from the market was an explicit goal of both early utopian communities and radical advocates of rent control in Berkeley, California, in the 1970s. It lives on, albeit in a mutant form, in advocacy for a protected, nonprofit, or public housing sector for the poor, as a means of ensuring that they enjoy housing of a socially acceptable and affordable standard.

APPROACHES TO REGULATORY POLITICS

Leaving aside for the moment the nonmarket justification for rent control, let us consider the three broad approaches to regulation identified by Noll (1989). *Public interest theory* asserts that regulation is essentially a political response to market failure. As Noll (1989) points out, this view requires that there be a positive theory about the conditions under which market failure occurs (as described above), together with a normative theory that government ought to act to improve market efficiency, and a positive theory that if market failures do occur, governments will address them through regulation. Such was the logic of intervention in the United States in the Progressive era, when regulation of monopolies was established.

For governmental regulation to be the most desirable means of addressing market failure requires violation of the Coase theorem, i.e., that imperfect information and transaction costs prevent parties affected by market failure from reaching private agreements to solve the problem. Sophisticated public interest theory explores the conditions relating to transaction costs and imperfect information that should give rise to efficiency-enhancing regulation. Even though self-interested groups participate, they still have a common interest in minimizing inefficiency. With competition among groups for the attention of politicians, there is an incentive for the latter, in turn, to seek efficiency also, since it generates wealth for allocation among the parties. The principal problems with this approach are, first, that efficiency-maximizing regulations may not be effective as conditions change, because transaction costs prevent their modification; and, second, the assumption in the literature that institutional arrangements themselves are not particularly significant.

From the perspective of residential rent control, therefore, public interest theory, with its emphasis on economic efficiency, may not be the most useful model for analyzing political action. As we saw above, although a market failure justification for rent control may be made, justification is far more likely to be grounded in the idea of scarcity rent. Thus, an approach that takes explicit account of rent-seeking behavior may be more desirable.

Interest group theory sees regulatory processes as the outcomes of the interactions between groups that are affected by change in particular economic and social realms and governmental entities that might affect those outcomes. Such a view may be placed within a larger perspective in democratic politics that sees a continuing struggle among competing interest groups in a society (Dahl and Lindblom 1953; Downs 1957; Truman 1960; Dahl 1967). In its simplest form, this argument contends that in a responsive political system, the group with the largest stake should be able to dominate political discourse and decision making on a particular concern. However, this view does not take into account the transaction costs of political intervention, which have been recognized as very powerful in modern political analysis. If transaction costs are substantial in relation to benefits received, then large groups, within which individuals either bear low costs or enjoy very small gains, may have much more difficulty mobilizing politically than smaller groups for which the individual gains or costs are substantial. Writers such as Olson (1965) have pointed to this argument to explain the difficulty of mobilizing consumers—who are many and whose expenditures on a particular item are likely to be small in relation to income, in contrast to producers, whose entire incomes and survival may depend on a single product—even though the aggregate benefit to consumers may be very large. Thus, even though regulations may be adopted in a surge of public interest at a specific time, the deeper interest of those who are regulated has led in many instances to the political "capture" of the regulatory process. In some instances, producers have even embraced and advocated regulation, either to stave off more hostile regulation, or to control the market and reduce competition (Kolko 1965; Weiss 1987). In either event, the objective is to capture or maintain economic rent.

Interest group theory is attractive as a basis for the analysis of rent control politics. The polarized struggle between landlords and tenants looks like a simple two-interest-group case. The absence of rent control in most residential markets can be explained by a combination of efficient markets and the imbalance of relative benefits between a broad group, tenants, and a narrow one, landlords. The appearance of rent control at critical moments would seem to be explained by the fact that since a large proportion of a renter's income is typically spent on housing, a sudden increase in that component of expenditure may be enough to stimulate collective action. Once rent control is in place, however, maintenance of the collective action may take many forms.

This theory presents some complications, however. Most analyses of interest group regulatory politics have been carried out in the context of the traditional logic of regulation—for example, the control of monopoly, in which regulatory capture actually sustains rents, and deregulation implies the loss of rents for producers, especially for labor (Noll 1989). In these scenarios, deregulation favors consumers over producers. Clearly, this is an unlikely situation in residential rent control. Yet, there is a class of consumers, a latent group, who might benefit by deregulation—namely, those who would enter the housing market if supply were increased, but they have no voice. Although regularly invoked by both sides in the debate, the interests of this group are central to neither side. In addition, once residential rent control is in place, it requires a political structure for its governance and an organizational structure to operate and maintain it. The introduction of these political structures suggests yet another framework for analysis of rent control politics.

Agency (principal agent or state-centric) theory has emerged in the analysis of regulatory politics as a response to the observation that regulatory agencies themselves may have interests that are different from those of their principals, whether executive or legislative (Moe 1984; Noll 1989). This argument is based on agencies' superior information, their ability to change policies in subtle ways that are difficult to observe, and the high transaction costs to legislatures of monitoring agency behavior or changing de facto policies. Noll (1989) points especially to "shirking," i.e., the reluctance of an agency to pursue the policy objectives of elected political leaders. Despite the apparent risk, agencies may "shirk" in order to avoid conflict with those who are regulated, or to pursue their own political or personal agendas. Noll (1989) argues that there are substantial reasons why agencies will not stray far from the direction of their principals over the long term. Moe (1984) points out that politicians may also have a direct interest in moving some allocative decisions away from the market into the political realm, where they may exert power through favors, exceptions, and so on. Moving decisions into the political realm makes the agency problem even more complex, since the degree of administrative discretion may be written directly into law as part of an initial compromise that reflects expectations of agent behavior. Still, in whatever way it may be manifest, such behavior is sufficiently common in regulation that it should be considered.

For residential rent control, the problems of agency have scarcely been examined, but there is evidence of situations in which they come into play. To the extent that rent control is advocated and adopted on ideological grounds as a redistributive measure, we might expect that the agencies established for its implementation will initially be made up of people committed to the policy regardless of subsequent changes in political control. Indeed, there may be efforts to remove rent control altogether from broader political control, through the creation of elected rent control boards that would presumably be tenant dominated. On the other hand, agencies formed under less overtly ideological impulses may resist subsequent efforts to move policy in a more activist direction, whether toward deregulation or intensified control. As Noll (1989) suggests, forms of control that depend heavily on individual case-by-case decisions may be more likely to drift from political control than those primarily engaged in rule making and implementation. In residential rent control, both aspects are necessary, but their balance may vary greatly.

Against the three approaches discussed above, a *class-based theory* of rent control derives from very different intellectual roots. Although other approaches are all compatible with neoclassical, marginalist economics and imply regulation, class-based theory derives from Marxian roots, with the implied structural transformation of property relations. The grounds for such transformation that exist in Marxian economic and social theory include the assertion that activities such as property rental have no socially productive value; the distinction between use-values and commodities; and the argument that housing, as a critical use-value, should not be treated as a commodity simply to be traded in the market.[3] Thus, political revolutions from the left in this century have repeatedly evoked punitive measures against landlords, both urban and rural.[4] In cities, such revolutionary change has involved a range of measures, from freezing rents at nominal levels to confiscation of rental property and enforced sharing of privately owned housing.

This case might seem to have little relevance to the North American situation in which the dominance of market relationships in housing has never been seriously challenged. Nonetheless, a strand in the politics of North American rent control connects to this tradition. The argument that housing of socially acceptable quality will not be provided for poor households by the market is one that has resonated in both North American and European housing policy debates since the latter part of the nineteenth century. This argument was the basis of the conflict in the United States between those, like Lawrence Veiller, who sought to regulate housing quality at the turn of the century, and others, like Catherine Bauer, who supported the development of public housing as an alternative. Public housing has not fared well, but the insulation of, at least, the low-income segment of housing from the rest of the housing market has continued to be a long-standing theme in housing policy, and has been echoed by a distrust of homeownership by writers on the left of the political spectrum (Marcuse 1975). When rent control re-emerged as an issue in the 1970s, its effect of reducing the market value of rental housing was advanced by its more radical advocates in some places, such as Berkeley, California, as an opportunity for subsequent purchase and transformation of the housing stock into nonprofit or limited-profit forms. In fact, although the nonprofit sector has expanded in the past two decades, relatively little of that growth has occurred through such purchases. Nonetheless, advocates of rigorous rent control still tend to reflect a more punitive stance toward for-profit owners.

In summary, among the approaches toward regulatory politics discussed above, the interest group and agency theories seem to provide the most likely avenues for analysis of residential rent control in North America. Public interest theory may be invoked for some situations. Although class theory is perhaps more important now for its contribution to ideology within an interest group situation than for its practical application, it cannot be ignored.

RENT CONTROL POLITICS

Rental regulation is a continuing process rather than a singular event. Critical moments occur, but they should be seen as part of a pattern of political events and interactions over time that involve a range of actors. There is no typical rent control political process, but there are elements common to many situations where rental regulation is adopted. In this section, we will examine those elements within a framework that uses the theoretical positions discussed above, while distinguishing between three phases of rent control politics: (1) *adoption,* (2) *implementation and operation,* and (3) *termination.* The distinctions are, in some respects, arbitrary; but they enable us to look at the actors and their behavior in light of the conceptual framework discussed earlier. In particular, the temporal framework provides a way to distinguish between actors who appear to be identical, but who may have very different objectives and behaviors at different points in the rent control process.

Adoption of Rent Control: The Question of Interest

If there is any point at which politics would seem to be critical, it is during the process of rent control adoption. Rent control requires powerful changes in property relations that usually evoke strong reactions and require legislative action. Political arguments and forces must be mobilized, and the electoral or legislative process must be carried through to its conclusion. In the United States, adoption of rent control has generally been a local political decision, bounded by constitutional constraints and state and federal legislation. Only on two occasions, during a world war and a major inflation crisis, has federal action established rent control, as part of a larger structure of price regulation. In both instances, it might be argued that a public interest rationale was at work and there was broad political agreement that the action was both necessary and prudent. However, the far more numerous instances of rent control adoption by local communities are probably best cast in terms of interest group politics.

Rent control comes about through a legislative decision, made either by an existing body, generally a city council or state legislature, or directly by the electorate. The electorate can either pass direct legislation through the initiative process or elect a council or legislature that is committed to change. In either case, the immediate or future prospect of electoral politics is critical, including all the mobilization of power, money, and interest groups that follows. Since rent control is usually controversial, for it to be enacted a precipitating factor of some magnitude is usually necessary. During the

1970s, when rental regulation expanded dramatically, the precipitating factor was rapid inflation in the general price level, which outpaced incomes, especially those of the poor and elderly. Rents, which consume a substantial proportion of the income of these groups, became a focus of concern. Because rents are product specific, perceived to be locally established and paid to specific individuals or agents, they are not viewed simply as part of the retail system at large; rather, they are seen as potentially controllable through political means. The question of how and why precipitating circumstances led to politically effective mobilization of tenants in certain areas and not in others has not been adequately researched. While major cities in California, New Jersey, Maryland, and the District of Columbia were adopting rent control, for example, those in Pennsylvania, the South, and the Northwest were not. As we explore the role of interest groups, we should be careful not to ascribe inevitability to the cases where rent control was successfully adopted.

As a process driven by interest groups, the adoption of rent control would seem fairly straightforward. Tenants as a broad group might be expected to favor it, and landlords to oppose it. However, neither group is homogeneous in its composition and political views, and each group is deeply intertwined with diverse forms of advocates. Nevertheless, for the sake of brevity, this discussion treats interest groups and their advocates simultaneously.

Although tenants differ widely in terms of age, income, social status, and political attitudes, their immediate economic interest is reflected in their ability to pay their monthly rent—which includes property taxes and utility charges—and by the rent burden they bear in proportion to their income. The higher the rent burden and the lower the income of the tenant, the greater the tenant's vulnerability to rent increases, especially in a tight rental housing market. For many tenants, the security provided by just-cause eviction protections may be just as important as the regulation of rents, particularly for the less mobile, e.g., elderly tenants on fixed incomes. This commonality of interests, however, does not guarantee that tenants will, in fact, mobilize. The poorest tenants, who might appear to have the most to gain, have historically been the most difficult to bring into political action. In contrast, the more stable middle-income or lower-income elderly tenants have constituted the core of tenant mobilizations in cities where rent control has been adopted. This was true in New York, New Jersey, and Los Angeles, where tenant interests varied greatly and the role of organized tenant advocates was critical.

New York City offers particularly striking examples of differences in political behavior among tenant groups. The city has a long history of tenant organizing; many apartment buildings and housing projects are represented by tenant organizations, both in public and private housing. Demands for improved housing conditions, beginning in the nineteenth century, have led to protest politics and rent strikes (Lipsky 1970; Lawson 1986). New York City tenants have long engaged in electoral politics, endorsing and opposing legislators based on their positions on housing policy.

The adoption of the "second-generation" rent controls in 1969, in fact, presents a good example of how rapidly a political coalition can form under the right circumstances. After a period of oversupply in the early 1960s, a hiatus in construction and consequent rent increases led to a short-term upward movement in rents in the nonregulated stock and demands for regulation of the previously nonregulated, newer sector of the rental housing stock. The affected tenants in this instance were mainly middle-income, but their complaints of "rent gouging" were taken up by tenant advocates and local legislators. Virtually no accurate information on the extent of rent increases existed. Nonetheless, the city administration, faced with a mayoral election, could not withstand the political pressure and within a matter of months compromised on a form of regulation. The regulation was heavily influenced by landlord interests and incorporated landlords directly into the process of rent setting (Moe 1984; Keating 1987).

In New Jersey, the adoption of rent control in the early 1970s was prompted not just by inflation but also by widespread tenant dissatisfaction with rent increases, combined with organized leadership and advocacy. The New Jersey Tenants Organization (NJTO), formed in 1970, is one of the longest-lived and most successful statewide tenant organizations ever formed. The NJTO operates in a context of many small, individual communities, and its large membership of individual tenants has exercised great influence over both municipal governments and the state legislature in its drive to enact local rent control ordinances. The NJTO has also campaigned to ensure that no preemptive state legislation be passed by the New Jersey state legislature (Baar 1977; Atlas and Dreier 1986, 386-387). In its efforts, the NJTO has engaged in both protest and electoral politics.

A powerful reason for the uneven adoption of rent control is that not all tenants support it. Allan Heskin, who has done extensive analysis of tenant beliefs, attitudes, and values, interviewed 133 tenant activists and several hundred tenants in the city of Santa Monica and elsewhere in Los Angeles County (1983). He found that about one-fifth of both groups identified themselves as Republicans and about one-fourth as conservatives (Heskin 1983, 215-126). There was little or no indication of tenant sentiment for the elimination of "landlordism," as proposed by more radical advocates, such as New York's Metropolitan Council on Housing (Heskin 1983, 241-245). But Heskin did find a nearly universal desire among the tenants he interviewed who were under forty years of age to own their own homes (Heskin 1983, 184-185). As a result, he concluded that many of those who supported rent control did so as a way of increasing their savings in anticipation of home purchase.

If tenants are disparate in their composition and outlook, landlords, with their narrower interest in the issue, might be expected to be more politically uniform. In fact, as an interest group, landlords are quite disparate. Real estate ownership is usually not concentrated in North America. So-called small landlords—i.e., those who own one to four units—predominate (Tucker 1990, 190). These owners are likely to be nonprofessional and highly individualistic and, as a result, difficult to organize. In some instances, they may be further differentiated by ethnic composition, which in turn tends to affect the terms in which political discourse on rent control occurs. For example, in the liberal/radical environment in Berkeley in the 1980s, African-American landlords led the movement for loosening regulation and were able to gain both publicity and political attention. In contrast, large real estate investment and management companies, who are often active in the development of sizable rental projects, are usually affiliated with real estate lobbying organizations. Represented by lawyers and accountants, they routinely deal with governmental regulatory agencies. The small landlords are the ones who typically present the most fervent public opposition to rent control adoption and continuation. Their professional counterparts, while also opposed to rent regulation, often take a less ideological stance. Nevertheless, the anti-rent control views of both groups usually coalesce during electoral campaigns and legislative hearings.

Nowhere has this pattern been more evident than in New York City. In the late 1960s, the owners of rent-controlled housing became a highly visible group, calling for an end to the strict rent control of the World War II era. Their public profile was that of a small nonprofessional landlord who owned only a few units (Tucker 1990, 192ff). When rent control became a major issue in the 1969 mayoralty campaign, tenant interests were politically vocal and powerful. Liberal Republican mayor John Lindsay, who ultimately won reelection, responded to pressure from tenants in middle-income housing built after 1947 to extend rent control to cover their units, which up until then had been exempt from controls. This housing was placed under a new rent-stabilization system (the first use of this terminology) operated by the owners. These owners were very different from their rent-controlled counterparts; their holdings were large and professionally managed. Of the 358,000 registered rent-stabilized units, more than half (56 percent) were owned by 975 members (5 percent) of the Rent Stabilization Association (RSA) (Keating 1987, 100). In contrast to rent-controlled owners, who were represented by a group known as the Community Housing

Improvement Association (CHIP), the RSA did not vigorously oppose rent regulation. Instead, it successfully lobbied for a rent control system more to its liking. After adoption, the RSA was able to exercise great influence over the implementation of the program (Keating 1987).

A similar divergence of interests occurred both in the city and the county of Los Angeles. During the political battles over the adoption of rent stabilization by the city in the late 1970s, landlord interests generally stood clearly in opposition. However, the interests and behavior of large and small owners diverged in many respects during the final negotiations over the legislation. The divergence was particularly dramatic in the 1980s, when an effort was undertaken to simultaneously incorporate and adopt rent control in West Hollywood, a community that contained a large number of older rental units. Although many rental units were destined to come under quite stringent control, large owners in the remainder of the county did little or nothing. Their lack of action stemmed from the fact that they owned many newer units, occupied by younger households with less political interest in the issue. West Hollywood not only had many renters in the categories most likely to organize, it also had an extraordinary level of advocacy. Separating West Hollywood from the county helped to reduce the likelihood that anything more than nominal rent control would be imposed on owners elsewhere.

The adoption of rent control, then, turns on the ability of the critical interest groups to influence the electoral process. Wherever tenant organizations have formed and advocated rent control, landlord organizations have actively opposed them. Although outnumbered by tenants, landlord organizations have formidable weapons to employ. Together with their allies in the real estate industry, landlords have been able to raise large sums to influence electoral politics. They have contributed significantly to politicians at all levels of government. In initiative and referendum campaigns over rent control, landlords have generally outspent tenant groups. Their financial advantage has given them greater access to elected officials and regulatory bodies.

Nevertheless, tenants have often been able to prevail in the electoral process. In addition to the advantage of numbers, they have been helped by a remarkably long-lasting tradition of advocacy by people convinced that low-income housing and rent control are politically important issues (Kann 1986). Politicians are reluctant to alienate tenants, especially in close campaigns, and the tenant advocates have staunchly put forward the tenants' position. To avoid tenant pressure, legislators, influenced by landlords, have sometimes adopted milder reforms in order to forestall strict controls, as happened in San Francisco in 1979 (Hartman 1984). But no matter what specific form of regulation emerges, the battle of adoption is only the beginning of a long and arduous campaign for implementation.

IMPLEMENTATION AND OPERATION: THE STRUGGLE FOR CONTROL

If electoral politics are the key to adoption, the politics that follow are, in many ways, more complex. Implementation of rent control implies the establishment of a regulatory structure, with an appropriate administrative apparatus. Experience of regulation in other spheres suggests that the design, staffing, and operation of the rent control apparatus will not be free of political conflict. Furthermore, the fact of legislative passage does not end the electoral politics of rent control. Opponents will seek to reverse the decision or modify its provisions to their advantage. Supporters will try to extend the scope of regulation and ensure that operation of the system supports their objectives. In short, during its existence, rent control is likely to be subject simultaneously to a political process that is a continuation of electoral politics and to a form of politics that is best described by the principal agent model, in which control of the system's behavior is the central issue. Each of these forces will be examined in turn.

In the eyes of its advocates and opponents, after the passage of rent control, the immediate issue is the design and implementation of a regulatory and administrative structure, together with selection of staff. The regulatory structure—i.e., the formal rules and organization that define the operations of the rent control system—typically reflects the political outcome of the adoption process. It may be more or less overtly political in content and style; and that characteristic is likely to be reinforced by the staffing process. The system may overtly reflect the interests of a single group, e.g., tenants, or it may express a compromise position by adopting a "professional" or managerial stance. In the case of traditional rent control in New York City as well as the newer ordinances in Berkeley and Santa Monica, tenant interests initially dominated the system, both in the formation of regulations and in the propensities of the staff. In New York City's Rent Stabilization Program, however, landlords had the upper hand in administration, albeit with strong tenant advocate opposition. In Los Angeles, a more neutral, administrative style predominated as the managers sought to evade control by either side.

The broader electoral form of politics continues to dominate the first stages of implementation, as the principal interest groups strive to extend or overturn the system. How strongly and continuously such activity occurs appears to vary with local political cultures and with the strength of the legislation. This process tends to alternate between periods of relative quiescence and periods in which the conflict is renewed. A stable, long-term regulatory regime appears to be quite rare in North American cases, though it has certainly been maintained for long periods in Europe and elsewhere. In the United States, much appears to depend on the extent to which contending groups are organized and their ideological positions. The most effective interest groups present a continuing voice for their positions and bring rent control issues forward at every opportunity or threat.

In New York City, for example, the Metropolitan Council on Housing (Met Council) initially represented a left-wing radical viewpoint, promoting public housing and housing "in the public domain" (Hawley 1978; Schwartz 1986, 165-172). Many of its leaders and activists came from a labor union background, and they engaged primarily in protest politics, eschewing more pragmatic tactics as futile in reaching their ideological goals. In the 1960s and later, the Met Council took the position that rent control must remain strictly enforced and become permanent. As times changed and the concept of rent control gave way to the concept of rent stabilization, the organization had to find ways to deal with the change. In 1972, the Met Council's "old left" leadership purged many of the "new left" leaders (Lawson 1986, 217). Many of the latter then became prominent in a new organization—the New York State Tenants Legislative Coalition—formed in 1973. The new group came to represent a more middle-class tenant constituency together with tenant groups beyond New York City. Later renamed the New York State Tenants and Neighbors Coalition (NYSTNC), it led efforts to involve tenants and tenant groups in lobbying legislative bodies and engaging in electoral politics to promote housing reforms.

A similar shift took place on the owners' side. Small landlords are typically not highly organized; they tend instead to have a few very vocal and visible advocates among them. In New York, however, both large and small owners are organized and have continued to play a major role. In 1974, the placement of much of the original rent-controlled stock under the rent stabilization system precipitated a power struggle between the two groups of landlords. CHIP, the small landlord group, promoted a more confrontational policy than had previously been adopted. In 1978, a CHIP-endorsed slate took control of the board of the Rent Stabilization Association. The result was a heightened level of conflict between the RSA and tenant groups, including landlord challenges to the annual rent adjustment guidelines (Keating 1987, 99-100).

In contrast, moderate rent control cities tend to exhibit more intermittent and lower levels of conflict. Although skirmishes over a specific owner's behavior or minor policy shifts occur, the issue of rent control tends to be virtually ignored for substantial periods of time. In Los Angeles, where the city council has generally been averse to addressing the issue, partly because no side could command the necessary eight-vote majority and partly because no side wanted to run the risk of alienating important political groups once rent control was put on the table, rent control reforms have been debated only after periodic studies of the system. The changes that have been made have been relatively modest.

The operation of a rent control system produces another form of politics—one that is embedded in the relationship between the principals and agents and consists basically of a struggle for control of the system itself. In most business regulatory structures in the United States, the key issue is "capture" of the system by those who are the targets of regulation. Interestingly, rent control systems appear to have been less subject to "capture" than others, perhaps because they have often been created locally, by committed groups who watch them carefully. A more critical question for rent control is the relationship between legislative bodies and the administrators and staff of the system. Although the interests and concerns of the two may be in tandem at the outset, electoral change in the legislative body can lead to substantial conflict. In Berkeley, for example, tenant groups sought to avoid the possibility of conflict by campaigning successfully to detach rent control from the control of the city council and place it under an independent, elected board. Expectations of tenant control of the board, however, were rudely shaken when a landlord slate was elected in 1990 and proceeded to drastically increase permissible rent adjustments. The ensuing struggle saw the board attempt to wrest control from the staff, who remained substantially tenant-oriented, and were protected by their civil service status. The board succeeded in making inroads only where it could mandate a specific change in policy or staff. Subsequently, a pro-tenant majority was returned to the board, which produced yet another round of tensions.

Even in moderate rent control regimes, a similar phenomenon may occur, in part because the legislative body effectively relinquishes control to administrators and staff. The administrators' continuous attention to the issue and their expertise give them substantial power in their interactions with legislators. In a political system with a weak chief executive and strong civil service tenure, such as that in Los Angeles, managers can effectively determine much of the rent control agenda. In Los Angeles, the managers were somewhat divided among themselves, but there was nevertheless an evident desire to maintain a "functioning rental housing market" while remaining responsive to tenants. As a result, the managers tended to be tenant-oriented in specific instances, such as dealing with "problem landlords," but maintained a more landlord-responsive posture on systemic issues such as vacancy decontrol and permissible rent increases. In general, the system managers in Los Angeles tended to see themselves as the guardians of moderation and sought to temper the politically driven desires of legislators by reminding them of the larger consequences for the housing market of specific proposals that offered certain short-term advantages. In an interesting inversion, the Los Angeles case suggests that the agents may effectively "control" their principals over a long period of time, although they have a clear recognition of the ultimate political control under which they work.

RENT CONTROL REFORM AND TERMINATION

The tension between interest groups breaks out from time to time in major conflicts over rent control reform or termination of rental regulation. That such conflict occurs is not surprising, considering the attitudes and expectations of the groups involved. From the perspective of tenant activists (e.g., Atlas and Dreier 1986), rent control represents a movement for greater empowerment of tenants, an enhancement of their ability to demand better housing and fairer rents without fear of arbitrary retaliation by landlords (e.g., rent increases, reduction of maintenance, or eviction), and the promise of stability for tenants and the neighborhoods in which they live. From this viewpoint, it is imperative that rent control be accompanied not only by eviction control but also by governmental regulations to protect tenants from displacement—condominium conversion controls, for example. Such controls are usually temporary, but in some instances they have become long-term policies. Attempts to extend the reach of rent control in this way have evoked strong opposition.

Tenant organizers also see landlord opposition to rent control as dominated by ideological opposition to governmental regulation, combined with a desire for profit maximization without regard to tenant concerns. Landlords and the real estate industry are viewed as powerful political forces able to influence the government, the media, and public opinion, largely through their ability to raise money.

In contrast, landlords see rent control as a destructive and counterproductive policy forced on them by tenant activists bent on expanding government influence over housing policy (Tucker 1990). Conservative analysts (Tucker 1990; Salins and Mildner 1992) see landlords as much less politically powerful than supposed by tenants; their holdings are viewed as much less profitable than commonly alleged. Rather than a help to poor tenants, rent control is seen as a benefit to middle-income and even upper-income tenants, regardless of need and at landlords' expense.

With such a gulf, it is not surprising that attempts have often been made to modify or terminate regulation. Rarely has either side won a complete political victory in the United States. Landlords have won complete repeal of rent control in only a few instances, such as in Massachusetts in 1994–95. Landlords have succeeded, however, in having many states enact preemptive legislation, even where the prospect of passage of rent control legislation is remote. Tenants have also been unable to win permanent rent control in any area. They have come closest in California, by enacting local initiative legislation that can be repealed only by another initiative vote, or overridden by the state legislature, as occurred in 1995.

What landlords have won politically in Boston, in much of New Jersey, in such California cities as Los Angeles and San Francisco, and throughout the state of California after 1995 is vacancy decontrol. New York State landlords were also granted vacancy decontrol through state legislation in 1971, but lost it again in 1974. Vacancy decontrol in its most extreme form—that is, the permanent removal of vacant units from all rental regulation—gradually eliminates rent control by attrition. In its lesser form—i.e., when applied only to the first rent on vacant units, leaving them thereafter subject to control—the effect is a weakening of the economic impact of control on rent levels for much of the stock over time.

Although either termination or permanence is politically difficult to achieve, the benefits to the interest groups involved are so great that their efforts are likely to continue. Endemic, low-level conflict, interspersed with episodes of heightened political activity, would seem to be the norm.

CONCLUSION

Despite the lack of studies on rent control politics, it is clear that regulation of rents is subject to powerful and complex political forces. The politics of rent control have been most volatile where tenants have been best organized and able to influence electoral politics—in New York City, Berkeley, and Santa Monica, for example. As a result, rental regulation is more stringent in these places, and politics are more ideologically driven. If the real estate stakes are very high, as in New York and San Francisco, the tendencies are also reinforced, though the fact that San Francisco has moderate rent control illustrates that the mere existence of these conditions is not necessarily sufficient for strong rent control to be adopted (Hartman 1984).

Where rent controls have been moderate in their economic impact on owners, where tenant advocates are pragmatic rather than ideological, and where a political consensus has emerged on the legitimacy of regulation, rent control politics are likely to be more subdued, as in Los Angeles or

Washington, D.C. Everywhere that rent control is adopted, administrative politics come into play; they shape the formation of regulatory systems and day-to-day operations. In some instances, this level of politics may be as influential as electoral politics in the evolution of the rent control system. Whatever their nature, rent control politics seem to be predictable, but subject always to the unexpected.

Notes

1. In Los Angeles, for example, tenants have consistently given subjective estimates of the rentable values of their apartments well above estimates based on market comparisons. (See chapter 9.)

2. It should be understood that "rent" in this context may refer either to the payment for accommodation made by a tenant to a property owner, or the economic concept of "scarcity rent," which refers to the gain that accrues to the owner of a resource for which the supply cost is less than the equilibrium market price The latter rent is usually accepted as simply part of the economic system, as, for example, in the case of the windfall received by the owner of property on which low-cost oil is discovered. However, if the rent is created as a result of economic change—following a sudden surge in demand, for example, that pushes up the rent for all owners of low-cost oil—then the rent may be challenged politically on distributional grounds.

3. Neoclassical economics could also be compatible with political intervention for income redistribution on the ground of equity as opposed to efficiency. However, such an argument would imply a milder form of intervention, such as housing vouchers.

4. Such treatment appears to be related to the context, particularly the degree of urbanization in the society and the political base of the revolutionary regime. Thus, in China, rural landlords were the primary target; the issue was ownership of agricultural land by the peasant base of the revolution. In Russia, on the other hand, not until the revolution was well established was rural transformation attempted, while urban ownership of rental property was immediately attacked, in pursuit of urban workers' support as well as ideological objectives.

MICHAEL B. TEITZ

6

A Social Perspective on Rent Control

INTRODUCTION

Is there an even broader theoretical basis for discussion of rental regulation than those developed in the previous chapters? Rent control has
emerged out of real political and economic conflicts in many different places
at many different times. Can social theory contribute anything more to the
discussion? If we are to seriously examine the nature of this form of regulation, the question should be addressed. Policies may be created on the
basis of raw political or economic power, but history suggests that without
solid foundations, they are likely to do more harm than good. Indeed, this
charge has been made against rent control for at least seventy-five years, if
not longer. Yet, the practice of rental regulation has not disappeared, despite its ups and downs in popularity. Clearly, something has enabled rent
control to persist, and we are unlikely to understand the reason if we cannot conceptualize why rent control has apparently made social and political sense in widely varying circumstances. This is not to argue that rental
regulation is inevitably a desirable or even a tolerable policy. Rather, it suggests that there may be factors at work beneath the surface struggle for
pecuniary advantage between landlords and tenants.

Among the questions we might ask are the following: Can deeper reasons
be identified for the presence of rent control in a society characterized by a

market economy? What values might encourage or deter regulation? What are the philosophical and ideological underpinnings of such regulation? To ask such questions places this inquiry firmly within a long tradition of analysis of regulation, especially in relation to societies with capitalist, market economies. The fact that rental regulation is not a "normal" case of regulation in almost any ordinary sense means it may be all the more fruitful to try to clarify why and how regulation in this sphere occurs.

This chapter begins where the economics chapter ended, with the issues of market failure. However, its aim is to look at regulation from a societal perspective, taking into account social values that may explain regulation in a larger way.

SOCIAL ARGUMENTS ON RENT CONTROL

The concept of market failure is firmly grounded in neoclassical economic theory and is widely accepted. It provides a convincing rationale for the existence of regulation, but it scarcely touches the depth of feeling and the fierceness of conviction that can be observed in debates about rent control. The notion of "social failure" does not have similar currency. Yet it may be useful to represent a body of ideas and argument that exists in parallel with those of economics. Social failure occurs when a society generates, at a significant scale, phenomena that are profoundly at odds with its broadly held values. Clearly, the parallel with economics and market failure is limited. No model exists that gives us a social optimum under a certain set of assumptions, nor, in all likelihood, will such a model ever exist. Nonetheless, a perception of breakdown in social order and awareness of stress on social values are not at all uncommon in dynamic societies. A social failure is likely to stimulate some form of collective political or social response, although not necessarily through government.

The notion of social failure, as it will be developed here, is closely related to equity, i.e., the sense of fairness in social relations and outcomes. There can be no doubt that the concept of distribution—the question of who gets what—is a powerful one in the world at large, both in theory and in practice. Socialist and Marxist thought over the past century have contributed much to the development of the welfare state in European social democracies. Even where such ideological foundations were ignored or explicitly rejected, as in Germany in the late nineteenth century or in the United States since the Great Depression, questions about the distribution of income and wealth have been prominent on the national agendas of major capitalist nations (Wilensky 1965). Whether intended or not to create a new ideal society, social norms for acceptable economic and social levels of welfare have been established for individuals and groups. By no means have these norms or standards been realized; aspiration continually outruns performance. At times, under financial stress, they may have been revised downward or transformed, as we now see in many welfare states. Nevertheless, some norms have been put forward as appropriate for a society that is considered to be civilized and worthy of emulation. When those norms are violated in wealthy societies, there is a sense of something wrong, even a feeling of shame. Such has been the reaction to homelessness in the United States during the past decade, even though the shame has been mingled with frustration and hostility. Situations such as homelessness can be labeled as examples of social failure.

Still, we are lacking a conceptual framework within which it is possible to unambiguously define and identify social failure. When, in fact, is a distribution of income or wealth unacceptable? Very different perspectives may be used to address the question. For Marx the issue was not one of degree, but rather one of kind. In a Marxist framework, class relations determine the distribution of a society's product. To change the distribution requires the transformation of the position of classes and their control over social wealth. Revolution is the only means whereby this can occur, leading to dominance by the working class and public ownership of the means of production. Marxist revolutions, however, have not brought about the desired results, and the experience of recent years has not been encouraging for Marxist thought.

The history of social democracy suggests that another path is conceivable. It illustrates that transformation of both opportunity and claims to social product can occur through an evolutionary process that combines the establishment of new social norms with the regulation of social and economic behavior in order to achieve them. In countries that might be called "high welfare states," such as Sweden, a process of this kind has been underway for more than fifty years. Given the high levels of income, productivity, and welfare that these countries have achieved, it is difficult to argue that the effect has been disastrous market failure or economic inefficiency due to distortions. Distortions do occur, and in a more competitive environment the countries are now finding it difficult to support the cost of their structures. Nonetheless, these countries clearly have very different patterns of public and private expenditures from those in less-regulated societies.

Our purpose is not to advocate the system underpinning these societies, but rather to illustrate the idea that a coherent and explicit notion of a practical social order is possible. All social systems embody such a notion of order more or less explicitly, but for the idea of social failure to be concrete, some generally accepted and visible concepts and standards must exist, against which failure can be identified and tested. Where order seems to come into question, problems arise.[1] One organizing principle is the market itself. If the market is conceived as the basis of the social order, we can see when it fails, whether or not we can do anything in response. But virtually no society treats the market as the only criterion of social functioning. Other standards are always applied; rarely does a coherent structure exist for assessing their attainment.

The problem of conceiving and describing a formal social model to exist in parallel with, or as an alternative to, the market has proved intractable. One way out of the dilemma has been to convey all these considerations to the realm of politics—asserting that political decisions are the manifestation of both economic and noneconomic values. Although this approach leads in useful directions (discussed below), it does not yield a welfare-based approach to regulation. Still, we know that much distributional regulation has been instituted in the public interest, even though it is not supportable within the neoclassical economics framework. Are there some other broad social values that might underpin regulatory impulses of this kind?

One obvious possibility is *equity*, the concern for fairness in treatment, which is a virtually universal aspiration in modern societies. Together with its cousin *equality*, the concern for equal opportunity or outcome, equity may be found in almost every argument for public intervention, though their implications differ for housing policy.

To determine whether equity is an appropriate welfare criterion for society, it may be easiest to consider what is implied by inequity in social arrangements. No society treats all its members equally, or even fairly. Nevertheless, a widespread sense that a regime or situation is inequitable can be the catalyst for the loss of legitimacy of a government and, ultimately, the loss of power itself. Especially in circumstances where sacrifices need to be made, equitable allocation of burdens has long been recognized as necessary for social mobilization, and even civic order. From the imposition of draft lotteries, rationing, and price control during wars, to the treatment of victims of natural disasters, governments have struggled to create at least the appearance of equity in situations where its absence could lead to unrest or even civil disorder.[2] The social need for equity in these situations seems to transcend the routine acceptance of inequities and inequalities in everyday life.

However, even in normal circumstances, governments often presume or aspire to equity or equality as a goal. For example, the U.S. Constitution commits the justice system to equal treatment under the law for every individual. Similarly, the logic of bureaucratic procedures, from hospital waiting rooms to social insurance claims, is imbued with the notion of equitable, if impersonal, processing. Regulation reinforces these procedures. Virtually everyone is expected to stop at traffic lights, for example. And few cities have special traffic lanes reserved for particular groups.[3] Equal or equitable treatment in this context may be viewed as a benefit of social order or, alternately, seen as the imposition of a higher logic of discipline and loss of freedom (Foucault 1977). Prisoners are among the most equal of beings, and the rules for their treatment are, at least in theory, laid out on equitable principles. Like much else in modern society, equity and equality may be mixed blessings, but it is hard to deny their role in the organization of social life.

Issues of equity and equality are also present in housing policy. Early justifications for intervention to improve slum housing argued not only that slums injured the remainder of the population by breeding disease or crime, but also that it was inherently unfair that any person should live in such conditions in a rich society (Friedman 1968). A similar theme has pervaded debates over homelessness. As a result, housing advocates have been seen as reformers, for the voice of reform is also the voice of equity. Radical advocates have gone further, calling for equality of outcomes in housing and the redistribution of housing resources. Revolutions in the past century from Russia to Cuba have been followed by redistribution of housing on some basis other than ability to pay. A somewhat different strain of concern for equality is to be found in the efforts to ensure nondiscrimination in housing over the past forty years. However, in housing, as elsewhere, equality of treatment may not be equitable. For example, regulating permissible building materials in order to prevent fire is justifiable on grounds of economic externalities, but the application of that regulation also reflects a belief in equal distribution of the burden. Much the same could be said for zoning and building regulation of density, lot coverage, materials, design, and occupancy. However, such an equal distribution may be inequitable in terms of the relative cost burden on poorer households, even to the point of excluding them from living in a community altogether.

Like other housing policies, rent control also exhibits a strong element of equity-seeking in its rationale. The economic efficiency argument for redistribution of economic rent is only modest at best; it pertains to situations where supply cannot respond to increases in effective demand. If such redistribution delays or inhibits a supply response, then the redistribution may itself have a strongly negative effect on efficiency and welfare. Thus, this justification for rent control requires the additional ground of equity, especially if it is invoked during a time of great stress or uncertainty. That people who have lived somewhere for many years should suddenly be required to pay much more for housing or be displaced from their homes seems inherently inequitable. The imposition of rent control during wars or crises, when solidarity is most valued, is evidence of the important role of equity.

Yet, as we seek equity in order to offset the redistribution consequences generated by the desire for efficiency, the search may generate more inequity in its turn. Who is to say how much of any potential gain in rent should be distributed to the tenant, and how much to the landlord over the long term? The existence of economic rent implies a structure of rules and practices that legitimizes its allocation. In the United States and most Western countries, the structure inheres in the system of property rights to land and its associated claims to revenue. Property rights are not easily overturned or redefined, although reformulation occurs continuously in subtle ways. No simple and clear principle tells us when regulation should be invoked under the social welfare criterion and when it should not. In practice, governments have had to determine when the police power should be used, and they, in turn, have responded primarily to political pressure from specific groups.

Much of what we have already said about equity and equality could also be advanced in a discussion of the notion of *justice* in relation to social failure. Societies are not inherently just or unjust, and there is no general agreement as to what constitutes a just or unjust society (Rawls 1971). Nonetheless, the perception of injustice has frequently been followed by delegitimation of regimes and with social change in the name of human rights. From the American Revolution to the struggle for civil rights, U.S. history is replete with instances in which the cry of injustice has accompanied important legal and institutional changes. In many cases, these changes involved regulation—in the enforcement of desegregation and voting rights in the South, for example. In both of these instances, the issue was also one of equality, but still linked indissolubly to justice.

Instances of economic regulation in the name of justice are harder to find, even though discrimination and segregation surely have economic implications and the efforts to oppose them took on economic objectives. Perhaps the clearest case of regulation in the name of justice can be found in the sphere of labor relations, where the relative bargaining power of an employer compared to an individual worker has been seen as constituting an unjust relation that facilitates exploitation. Permitting unions and regulating their interactions with employers offsets the imbalance. It is no accident that the history of union organization includes a call for justice as often or even more often than a call for equality. To the extent that a just social system balances power among unequals in the name of deeper human rights, we might expect regulation that supports these objectives.

In housing policy, the idea of justice has not been a dominant one. Even in the areas of discrimination and segregation where housing is perhaps closest to human rights issues, the emphasis has been on equality of treatment under law. Of course, the distinction is a fine one, since the two overlap so strongly. Nonetheless, North American society has never conceded a right to housing per se, as opposed to the right to participate in the market and occupy housing for which one can pay. The closest that North American society has come has been granting the general goal of decent and affordable housing in the federal Housing Act of 1949 and affirming the right of those without the means to afford housing to participate in programs, such as welfare, that will pay for it. Progressives and radicals have advocated a housing right in the name of justice and equality of outcome, but without success. Elsewhere in the world, nations such as Sweden and the Netherlands have come much closer to the notion that not to be housed is a social failure that constitutes an injustice.

The issue of rent control, therefore, has generally not been couched in terms of justice and rights. Although being subject to the vagaries of the market might be termed unjust, little in the structure of rental regulation can be clearly identified with injustice as a dimension of social failure. There is, in the United States and Canada, no recognized fundamental right to occupy housing at a specific rent, even though legislation may create a legal "right" to do so. A landlord may deal unjustly with a tenant within the bounds of a system of rental regulation, but the injustice—as in cases of harassment—arises from general rights in the law rather than a specific right inherent in rental regulation itself. This is in sharp contrast to the issue of equitable division of economic rent discussed above.

A fourth potential dimension for assessing social failure is *stability*. If a state of affairs produces serious political and social instability, society in its current form may be threatened. How we view the threat depends on whether we see the existing structure as preferable to any alternative that might emerge. Generally speaking, we may expect conservatives to view stability as an important dimension of social functioning, whereas radicals can be expected to take the opposite position. The implications for distribution are evident. Stability implies little distributional change, or at least orderly change; instability suggests distributional shifts that may be intense and sudden. However, fear of instability may cause otherwise conservative regimes to increase equity and redistribution, as was the case in the rise of German welfare programs in the 1880s.

Economic regulation in the name of stability is nothing new. From price and quality control by medieval guilds, to regulation of insider trading in modern stock markets by the Securities and Exchange Commission, the search for economic and political stability has manifested itself in controls over the behavior of individuals and groups who might violate social norms in their desire for profit. Whether those norms are desirable in terms of the other dimensions previously discussed is not at issue here. Rather, the issue is the frequency of appearance of such forms of regulation, often despite the fact that they run counter to the precepts of regulation embodied in neoclassical economics. Perhaps the best example is the attempt to offset the "evils of competition" by regulating prices and entry during times of economic hardship (Breyer 1982). Both before and during the Depression, numerous regulatory bodies were established to prevent what was seen as destructive competition. For firms in the regulated industries, the process made eminent sense; they felt driven to the wall. For the government, the intent was to slow a downward spiral of prices and wages in the midst of deflation. The goal was stability, at a time when the very fabric of the North American capitalist system seemed in danger of collapse. That the actions taken made little economic sense appears to be irrelevant. The impending danger justified the behavior.

Housing has seen its share of stability-enhancing programs and regulatory structures. In the United States and elsewhere, the most long-lasting and powerful have been programs to enhance homeownership, which have been an explicit feature of policy in one form or another for two hundred years. Whether in the form of homesteading, or in mortgage insurance and tax deductibility of mortgage interest, the federal government has found ways to encourage the ownership of residential property. In contrast, rental tenure has often been seen as less desirable and is frequently opposed at the local level through zoning or other forms of regulation. Although rent control would seem to enhance stability, at least in the sense of making tenants less likely to move, its conflictual aspects have generally overwhelmed whatever virtue might be argued in this instance.

A final value for testing social failure is *liberty*—a topic so huge that it cannot be adequately addressed here. Housing has frequently been associated with liberty; homeownership, for example, has come to mean freedom from the grip of the landlord. Paradoxically, the concept of liberty is also the cornerstone of many arguments made by landlords to oppose rent control. They claim that liberty inherently provides them with the freedom to dispose of property as they see fit. Insofar as rent control in its extreme forms has been accompanied by confiscation of private property, the argument has a real basis. However, in the United States, the issue is much more likely to be cast as a question of when regulation becomes legally a "taking" of private property. As seen in chapter 3, this notion of "taking" has generally not been recognized in rent control. Even so, liberty is a powerful ideological and emotional symbol that pervades the question of regulation in this sphere.

CONCLUSION

Rent control, like all social policy, can be considered within a larger theoretical domain. Such consideration can generate interesting and sometimes provocative insights into what is going on beneath the surface storms of this controversial form of regulation and can encourage us to probe the deeper social ocean in which the storms occur. No model of society can provide a universal framework for assessing rent control as a social policy. But this sort of analysis can provide a kind of triangulation that permits us to locate the values that rental regulation impinges upon and the kinds of social pressures that may bring those values into play politically. Economic efficiency is not the only criterion for policy in real societies. We should not expect regulation to reflect that criterion alone.

Notes

1. The discussion over civil society in recent years provides one example of such a concern (Putnam 1993).

2. An interesting example of inequity occurred in 1989, during the aftermath of the San Francisco earthquake, when it became evident that poor and homeless people were being treated differently from the middle class by relief organizations. The resulting outcry led to a lawsuit and long-term changes by the relief organizations.

3. In the Soviet period, Moscow had special lanes reserved for high officials who were able to ignore traffic controls with impunity. In the United States, such lanes do not exist except for bicyclists (in some places), or reserved lanes for car pools and, in a few instances, for motorists who are able and willing to pay extra money to avoid congestion. The debates over the latter reflect the way in which threats to equality can provoke a response.

Stephen E. Barton

7

The Success and Failure of Strong Rent Control in the City of Berkeley, 1978 to 1995

The treatment of landlords in Berkeley is comparable to the treatment of blacks in the South . . . our rights have been massively violated and we are here to correct that injustice.

John Searle, Professor
University of California, Berkeley
Comment at Public Hearing—Berkeley Rent Stabilization Board
September 10, 1991

INTRODUCTION

On January 1, 1996, new California legislation brought an end to Berkeley's strong rent control system, a system that had been one of the city's most controversial public policies since it was introduced in November 1978.

Berkeley's rent control benefited tenants in two ways. First, like most rent control systems in the United States, it provided tenants with a sense of personal security and stability, similar to what homeowners have, by giving the tenants reasonably predictable housing costs. Tenants did not have to fear displacement from rapid rent increases, and landlords were required to have good cause for eviction. Such security, it was widely believed, gave tenants more stable personal lives and a greater stake in their communities (Barton 1985, 1997). Stability continues to be an aim under the current rent control system, which decontrols rents when a tenant moves out, allows rents to rise to market levels, and then recontrols the rent for as long as the new tenant remains in place.

Berkeley's initial strong rent control system also had a second purpose: to shield tenants as a group, and the community as a whole, from some of the economic effects of rising land values and rents. In the San Francisco Bay Area, as in other successful urban areas, land values and rents rise as the population increases; as more public investment is made in utilities, transportation, and services; and as growth continues in employment. The forces that increase land values are generally joined by restrictive land-use controls that limit additional housing supply (Dowall 1984; Fischel 1991). The restrictions increase the rents of those who do not own land and redistribute economic rent from renters to landowners. In theory, this "unearned increment" might be taxed for the benefit of society, as proposed by Henry George in 1879 (George 1992 [1879]); but when California voters passed a constitutional property tax limitation in 1978, such an approach became impossible. Permanent rent controls were an alternative way of preventing part of this redistribution from nonowners to owners.

Permanent controls were intended not only to benefit lower-income tenants economically but to provide social stability to Berkeley as a community. Rent controls were supposed to preserve the economic diversity and social fabric of the community and help very-low-income tenants remain in Berkeley and live their lives with much less stress. These tenants would otherwise be faced with the unpalatable choices of paying most of their income for rent, living in overcrowded conditions, or moving away to the economically segregated areas to which the poor are frequently consigned in American cities. Rent control was also intended to help protect Berkeley's character as an intellectual and artistic community, enabling people who spent their lives in low-paying research, writing, and other artistic pursuits to continue to pursue their dreams in Berkeley. Permanent controls were intended to eliminate much of the economic incentives to displace long-term tenants in order to get higher rents.

Berkeley's rent stabilization ordinance regulated nearly 21,000 of the 24,500 rental units in the city. When the existing system ended, about 18,700 units were registered, with 1,500 units temporarily exempt while occupied by tenants with federal Section 8 rent subsidies, and several hundred additional units temporarily exempt for various other reasons. The only units permanently exempt from registration included rental units built after 1980, pre-1980 units built with government subsidies, units in owner-occupied duplexes, and an unknown number of single-family homes rented for periods of up to nine months. Group quarters such as dormitories, student cooperative housing, fraternities, and sororities were also exempt.

By the simplest measure—slowing the escalation in rents—Berkeley's strong rent control system was highly effective. From April 1980 to April 1990, the rent component of the Bay Area Consumer Price Index increased by 106 percent, while Berkeley's rent control system allowed across-the-board increases of only 54 percent. By 1990, the average controlled rent in Berkeley was 35 to 40 percent below what it would have been without controls, not taking into account declines in quality, black-market payments, or shifts in some costs to tenants.

Critics of rent control argued, however, that rents had been controlled at severe cost—that maintenance had declined, units had been removed from the market, the tax base of the community had been eroded, and landlords had been deprived of a fair return on their investment. They argued, moreover, that the real benefits of rent control were small; that most low-income tenants in Berkeley were actually middle-class students; and that genuinely low-income tenants were being replaced by higher-income tenants. According to the critics, rent control had failed to accomplish its stated purposes.

In the November 1990 elections, the landlord-backed slate of candidates won control of Berkeley's rent board and began loosening controls, bringing rents close to market levels in 1992. In 1994, the tenant-backed slate regained control of the board; but in 1995, the state legislature passed mandatory vacancy decontrol, ensuring that there would be no return to strong rent control.

After briefly setting out the history of rent control in Berkeley, this chapter summarizes rent control evaluation reports and concludes that the primary failure of Berkeley's strong rent control system was less economic than political.

BERKELEY AND THE BAY AREA

Berkeley is a stable and largely built-out city with a 1990 population of about 103,000 people. Nearly one-quarter of the population of the city is affiliated with the University of California as students, faculty, or staff; and nearly one-third is affiliated with some institution of higher learning. Berkeley is not just a university town, however. Located next to Oakland in Alameda County, it is part of the diverse inner urban core of the ninety-eight cities and nine counties that together make up the six-million-person San Francisco–Oakland–San Jose Metropolitan Area. The city has thousands of jobs in services and manufacturing, especially in the West Berkeley industrial and warehouse district, and in the substantial, though struggling, downtown. Even so, a majority of its employed residents commute to work in other cities; Berkeley is well served by public transit and freeway connections. The residential areas are prized for their views and tree-lined streets. Several areas have popular neighborhood shopping districts.

In 1990, 56 percent of the city's 43,000 households were tenants, with a median yearly household income of $19,500; 44 percent were homeowners, with a median income of more than $50,000. Two-fifths of Berkeley's population were members of racial minorities, including many residents of the long-standing African-American community centered in South and West Berkeley, and growing numbers of Asian and Hispanic residents. Severe income disparities existed among racial groups. The 1990 Census reported a mean household income for whites of $50,323, compared to a mean African-American household income of $26,297, a mean Asian income of $31,013, and a mean Hispanic income of $31,457. About one thousand homeless people were living in parks, cars, and shelters.

The city's housing stock is a diverse mixture of about 45,800 units, of which some 26,000 typically are rented and about 19,500 are owner-occupied. In addition, an unusually large number of people live in group quarters, mostly in University of California student housing, which has 9,265 beds. Single-family homes constitute 45 percent of all housing units; another 21 percent of the units are in small apartment buildings with two to four units each; and 33 percent of the housing units are in larger apartment buildings. Small structures with one to four units provide 43 percent of all rental units, and small landlords—those who own less than ten units— own about half of Berkeley's rental housing. According to the city's Rent Stabilization Board, more than 4,400 separate rental properties are registered, as are about three thousand different owners—the majority of whom own less than five units and live in Berkeley.

ESTABLISHING RENT CONTROL IN BERKELEY, 1972–1984

Rent control in Berkeley had its beginnings in the social movements of the 1960s and, ironically, was helped along by President Richard Nixon, the target of so many of the movement's protests. On August 15, 1971, President Nixon instituted temporary national wage and price controls, including rent controls, for the first time since World War II. Controls were phased out seventeen months later in January 1973, but a group of Berkeley housing activists gathered signatures to place an initiative to continue rent stabilization on the June 6, 1972 ballot. The measure carried with 52 percent of the votes, assisted by the extension of the vote that year to eighteen-year-olds, which allowed most University of California undergraduates to vote for the first time. The hotly contested state Democratic primary—won by the antiwar candidate, George McGovern—probably drew many students to the polls.

Legal challenges delayed implementation of the rent control measure. In 1976, in a unanimous ruling (*Birkenfield v. City of Berkeley*), the California Supreme Court held the measure unconstitutional. The Rent Control Charter Amendment had allowed for rent increases only to cover increases in operating costs and had required that each increase on each unit be considered and voted on by an elected rent board. With thousands of rental properties involved, this provision was obviously unworkable; most owners could never hope to receive timely increases. The court ruled, however, that local rent controls could be constitutional if they met certain criteria.

Following the *Birkenfield* decision, landlord organizations promoted a bill in the state legislature to declare rent control a matter of exclusive state concern and to forbid California's local governments from passing rent control laws of any kind. The bill passed both the assembly and the state senate in 1976 but was vetoed by Governor Jerry Brown. State legislation that would require vacancy decontrol was introduced at nearly every legislative session thereafter but was held in committee by state senator and majority leader David Roberti, a strong rent control supporter. The legislation finally passed in 1995.

Rent control supporters in Berkeley placed a strong new rent control initiative on the April 1977 ballot, accompanied by a Tenant Union Ordinance to require landlord–tenant collective bargaining. Both measures failed by wide margins. But on June 6, 1978, the voters of California passed Proposition 13, which dramatically changed the political climate regarding rent controls in California. Proposition 13 was an initiative measure that amended the state constitution to reduce property taxes and limit future property tax increases. Its sponsors, Howard Jarvis and Paul Gann, argued during the campaign for Proposition 13 that rents would go down as a result of the lowered cost of operating rental property. Most property owners continued to increase rents in response to continued high demand and restricted supply, however. In the aftermath, many cities passed temporary rent control measures to require that the tax savings be shared with tenants. These temporary ordinances were often followed by permanent rent control ordinances.

In Berkeley, rent control supporters placed an initiative, Measure I, on the November 7, 1978 ballot. The city council proposed a compromise, Measure J, which gave renters a property tax rebate in the following year but did not control rents. The voters liked Measure I, which passed with 58 percent of the vote. Measure J received only 22 percent.

The Berkeley Renter Property Tax Relief Ordinance of 1978, Measure I, set base rents at the June 6, 1978 level; required the rebate of 80 percent of the property tax reduction to tenants in the form of a rent reduction; and froze rents until December 1979, at which time the ordinance would expire. It allowed rent increases to cover increases in operating costs, however, and relied for enforcement on direct action by tenants, authorizing rent withholding and the use of small claims court or other legal action in the event of a dispute. No rent control board or other city agency was created to administer the law, and there were no rent registration requirements. The city council extended the ordinance six months, to June 1980, to give voters a chance to decide whether to continue controls.

During the first two years of regulation, a student survey indicated that, in the absence of registration, an informal vacancy decontrol system existed. About 60 percent of the landlords provided at least partial rent rollbacks to tenants, and another 30 percent did not increase the rent of sitting tenants. But 75 percent of new tenants paid higher rents (CALPIRG 1979, 1981).

Berkeley voters passed successor legislation, the Rent Stabilization and Eviction for Good Cause Ordinance (Measure D), in June 1980. It garnered 57 percent of the vote, while a statewide landlord-sponsored initiative that would have repealed all existing local rent control laws failed. Under this new ordinance, the lawful rent in effect on May 31, 1980 was established as the "base rent," and a Rent Stabilization Board of nine members was created, one appointed by each member of the city council. The board was to set an annual across-the-board rent increase, called the annual general adjustment (AGA), which would allow rents to increase as operating costs increased. Further individual rent increases or decreases could be granted by hearing examiners, with appeal to the board, in cases where the AGA was insufficient to cover high cost increases, or where the units had been allowed to deteriorate. All covered rental units were required to register their rents and pay registration fees that, in turn, were to pay for the operation of the rent stabilization program. Tenants could be evicted for specified reasons only, which included nonpayment of rent, damage to the unit, or proposed occupancy by the owner or a member of the owner's family.

The program ran up against immediate legal, economic, and administrative difficulties. Landlords sued, arguing that the ordinance was unconstitutional; but this time the courts refused to set aside the ordinance while it was being litigated. In December 1984, in *Fisher v. City of Berkeley*, the California Supreme Court upheld the legality of the ordinance. While litigation continued, landlords who owned thousands of units refused to comply with the program's registration requirements. Their refusal so reduced the program's income that loans from the city council were required to maintain operations. Registration began on September 2, 1980, and by the end of the year, registration fees had been paid for only 40 percent of covered units, while base rent information had been filed for only 26 percent (CALPIRG 1981, 30-32). Rent program files contain hundreds of registration forms for 1980 typed with a standard refusal to cooperate on the grounds that the program violated the landlord's constitutional rights.

A more conservative city council majority was elected in 1981; the rent board they appointed set a 9 percent rent increase for 1982. Tenant activists responded by collecting signatures for a June 1982 initiative, known as Measure G—the Tenants Rights Amendments Act of 1982. The measure won 56 percent of the vote and set stiff penalty fees for late registration or failure to register. It also extended controls to about one thousand units in owner-occupied three- and four-unit properties, leaving only owner-occupied duplexes exempt. The new measure also required six, rather than five, votes from the nine-member rent board to increase rents by more than 45 percent of the increase in the Consumer Price Index, and made it more difficult for landlords to evict tenants for owner occupancy if other units were available in the same property. This measure was followed by another successful initiative on the November 1982 ballot that required direct election of the rent board.

With passage of Measure G, landlord resistance to registration dwindled to a small number of holdouts. By September 1, 1982, less than three months after the election, the rent stabilization program had received annual registration payments for 15,744 units, more than twice as many as the year before (City of Berkeley 1983, 8).

WHO BENEFITED FROM RENT CONTROL?

Berkeley's rent control system was established at a time of rapid rent increases. Bay Area rents turned sharply upward in the 1980s, increasing 23 percent from 1980 to 1990 in constant dollars, whereas renter incomes increased only 11 percent. Meanwhile, incomes at the very bottom actually declined, as public assistance payments, unemployment insurance payments, and the pay scale for low-wage jobs failed to keep up with inflation.

From 1980 to 1990, the number of lower-rent units decreased drastically throughout the Bay Area (table 7.1). In 1980, the number of units with gross rents below $250—and thus affordable to tenants with an annual income of $10,000—was more than double the number of comparable units in 1990

TABLE 7.1

Units with Gross Rent under $250 in 1980 and under $400 in 1990[1]

Area	1980 (# of units)	1990 (# of units)	Change (%)
Nine-County Bay Area	288,831	140,318	– 51
Alameda County	87,447	41,916	– 52
Berkeley	14,717	10,885	– 26

Note: 1. Includes units with no cash rent.
Source: U.S. Census, 1980, 1990

(i.e., those with gross rents below $400 and affordable to people with annual incomes of $16,000).

The effect on the Bay Area was staggering. Whereas in 1980 there had been rough parity between the number of low-rent units and the number of very-low-income tenants, by 1990 there were almost twice as many very-low-income tenants as there were low-rent units. Berkeley also suffered a substantial decline in low-rent units, even with rent control; but the decline was half the rate of the Bay Area as a whole, and half the rate of Alameda County.

It is worth noting that substantial evidence points to the fact that the rent control discount in Berkeley was quite real, and that "under-the-table" payments or side agreements by tenants to provide free maintenance or other benefits to landlords that would add to the effective rent were quite rare. A 1988 tenant survey found that only 4 percent of tenants reported paying any finder's fee, and the majority of these paid less than $100 (Bay Area Economics 1988, 89). Nesslein (1992) notes that the actual capitalization value of the rent differential of an apartment with rents between $100 and $200 a month below market would be $12,000 to $24,000. But there is not the slightest hint of payments in that range ever being made.

During the 1980s, critics of rent controls pointed to the many students living in Berkeley and argued that rent control was benefiting people who were only temporarily poor (Devine 1986). But in 1988, a survey of tenants in rent-controlled units conducted by Bay Area Economics (BAE) disproved this criticism. It showed that 46 percent of Berkeley's rent-controlled housing was occupied by low-income and nonstudent tenants; 22 percent by student households; and the remaining 32 percent by moderate- and above moderate-income nonstudent households. The survey showed that low-income, nonstudent tenants occupied the largest share of units renting for less than $400 a month.

Other critics claimed that landlords would still prefer to rent to higher-income tenants and that poor tenants could lose out. The 1988 Berkeley tenant survey revealed, however, that most tenants learned of the availability of their apartment from either the former tenant, the landlord, or through some other form of word of mouth, indicating that rent-controlled units were generally rented by tenants in the same social circle as the people who originally occupied them (Bay Area Economics 1988, 87). As a result, tenant incomes in Berkeley in 1990 were distributed in much the same way that they were when rent stabilization was passed by the voters in 1980.

Even though rent control benefited tenants in general, including the poor, it is still important to recognize that rent control alone was not a sufficient means of assisting poor tenants. Even with rent control at its strongest in 1988, more than 70 percent of the 5,600 very-low-income nonstudent tenant households in Berkeley shouldered rent burdens of more than 30 percent of their income, and about two thousand of these households had rent burdens that were more than half their income. These households included a greater number of African-American households, and a somewhat greater number of households headed by single parents, than tenant households in general. But rather than recognizing the problem and fighting for subsidies to supplement below-market rents, Berkeley's tenant activists concentrated on keeping rents as low as possible.

Rent control was also intended to benefit Berkeley through increased community stability, and the evidence shows that it was successful on this score. In 1990, 33 percent of Berkeley tenants had been in place for six years or more, up from 20 percent in 1980. Meanwhile, the number of tenants who had been in their apartments less than fifteen months had fallen from 44 percent to 31 percent.

Critics claimed that this pattern demonstrated that rent control had reduced mobility and made the housing market less efficient, stability and mobility being two sides of the same phenomenon. However, the argument here is not about the effects of rent control, but rather the significance of those effects. On the one hand, tenants should be able to move when they want and to find a place that is larger or smaller when changes occur in the family, for example. On the other hand, tenants should also be able to have stability in their lives so that they do not fear that they will be forced to move when they don't want to.

Most people's idea of a good community in which to live is "civic" rather than "market" based—i.e., a neighborhood that is stable, where people develop a commitment to the quality of life in the neighborhood they live in, not one with high mobility. People working in real estate often say that, as neighbors, homeowners are preferable to tenants because they are less transient. At the same time, economists often criticize rent control for reducing tenant mobility. The economic, market-centered perspective focuses on the rental market as a whole and on tenants' ability to move to new housing within the marketplace, whereas the sociological, citizen-centered perspective focuses on tenants' current quality of life and the social fabric of the neighborhood.

Rent control gives tenants a level of stability closer to that of homeowners and provides some incentives to remain rather than move to a new apartment that is likely to have higher rent—just as homeownership provides incentives to remain rather than to absorb the high costs of a real estate transaction and, in California, a likely increase in property taxes.

FORMS OF LANDLORD RESISTANCE

Conversion of Units from Rental to Owner Occupancy

Landlord resistance to rent control takes many forms. In addition to political and legal efforts to change the law or refusal to cooperate with it, landlords can also try to withdraw units from the rental market and shift them to more profitable uses, usually through conversion to owner-occupancy status. Or they can simply hold units off the market, or reduce services provided to tenants through lower maintenance.

The U.S. Census reported that the number of units rented in Berkeley declined from 27,821 in 1980 to 24,512 in 1990, a loss of 3,309 units. This loss resulted primarily from (1) conversion of rental units to owner occupancy, (2) the removal of units from the housing stock through a merger into larger single-family homes, and (3) an increase in vacant units in buildings that owners wanted to convert to owner occupancy. It is ironic, given the widely held view within the real estate industry that homeownership is preferable to renting, that rent control's role in encouraging conversions was widely cited as a negative rather than a beneficial side effect of rent controls.

In the early months of rent control, the city council became concerned that landlords would respond to the regulation by converting multifamily rental property to condominiums. In November 1979, the council adopted an ordinance to prohibit the conversion of existing rental units to condominiums, stock cooperatives, or community apartments unless the rental housing vacancy rate rose to 5 percent. But this ordinance did not apply to single-family houses.

Berkeley has many single-family rentals. According to Census data, in 1980 there were 4,900 rented single-family dwellings. By 1990, however, there were only 3,613, a 26 percent reduction. Conversion of these single-family homes to owner occupancy accounted for more than one-third of the total reduction in rental units.

Nearly a quarter of all rental units in Berkeley have traditionally been in buildings with four or fewer units, and the town has a long history of shared ownership and owner occupancy of two- and three-unit buildings. Such owner-occupied units were commonly called TICs because the co-owners held them as "tenants-in-common." During the 1980s, tenants resisted TIC conversion through ballot initiatives and in the courts, but their efforts were unsuccessful. For example, an initiative measure to increase the ownership requirement for owner-occupancy evictions from 50 to 51 percent, so that no more than one tenant in a building could be evicted for purposes of owner occupancy, failed in November 1986; other similar measures failed in 1988. Two California Court of Appeals decisions in 1986 and 1988 held that TICs were not illegal subdivisions because the agreement between the owners, even when formalized and written, was a contract that was separate from the property itself.

After the 1986 decision, a network of real estate investors, agents, lawyers, and lending institutions rapidly developed to support creation of TICs. They developed sources of financing, drew up standard agreements for use among buyers, and actively publicized the TIC option to owners, encouraging them to sell their units when tenants moved out, even encouraging them to persuade tenants to leave in order to clear buildings for TIC sales. With the necessary institutional framework in place, the size of the buildings being converted to TICs increased; some buildings sold as TICs had as many as nine units. At its peak, in 1989, the rate of conversion reached 150 units a year. A total of about seven hundred rental units had been converted by 1992, when the city council banned further TIC conversion of rental units in properties with four or more units.

Other forms of conversion of rental units also took place. The available data indicate that the city lost approximately 1,050 units, virtually all rentals, from its existing housing stock between April 1980 and April 1990. The largest single portion of the loss resulted from the removal of four hundred residential hotel rooms during the 1980s, mostly in the downtown area. The difficulties faced by the owners of residential hotels, however, were not the result of rent controls. Rather, they reflected the difficulties of trying to make a profit while serving the very poor, as well as the greater profitability of commercial hotels and office space.

The second-largest part of the loss of units took place in single-family neighborhoods where secondary units, often illegal, were reabsorbed into existing homes. With the increase in housing prices and the rise of two-income families, many of these homes are now owned by high-income professionals and managers who are typically more interested in using the extra space as a home office than generating extra income by renting the space to students at the university. This reabsorption has also occurred in neighboring cities, but not as extensively as in Berkeley. Although second units were specifically exempted from rent control, homeowners may have felt heightened concern over renting in a city in which tenants are understood to have more rights and to be more demanding than in other places.

Multiple units were also converted for use by a single family. A substantial number of rental properties in Berkeley were formerly large single-family homes, so reconverting them to one large unit was not difficult.

The rate of conversion of multifamily rental property to owner occupancy in Berkeley stemmed from several interacting factors. First, there was a high unmet demand for ownership housing as a result of Berkeley's reluctance to allow new construction that could change existing neighborhood character. Second, rent control had reduced the profitability of rental housing and thus increased the comparative profitability of conversion to owner occupancy. Third, despite the ban on condominium conversion, landlords were allowed to convert units to owner occupancy through tenancy in common until 1992.

Berkeley could have reduced conversion of rentals to owner occupancy between 1980 and 1990 by changing any of these three influences. Among the available alternatives to weakening rent controls, Berkeley could have increased supply by loosening zoning protections that discouraged the construction of new condominium apartments and town houses. Berkeley could also have made it much more difficult to convert multifamily properties.

In the area of single-family housing, Berkeley did not have the same range of alternatives. There was probably no other way to increase rentals besides loosening rent controls, since Berkeley does not have the space to construct new single-family detached houses. However, it is not immediately obvious whether it is better for a community to have more single-family rentals with higher rents or more owner-occupied single-family homes with lower rents for the remaining rental units.

Holding Units Vacant

In theory, with rent control holding rents to below-market levels, the vacancy rate in Berkeley should have gone down rather than up during the 1980s. But Census data show an increase of 652 vacant housing units in Berkeley during the decade, from 1,630 vacant units in 1980 to 2,282 units in 1990. The overall vacancy rate also increased from 3.5 percent in 1980 to 4.98 percent in 1990. The vacancy rate was particularly high in smaller properties.

There are several possible reasons for this high level of vacancies. Owners may simply have held units off the market, waiting for rent controls to end—a course that is less costly with smaller properties. Indeed, the number of boarded-up units in Berkeley increased by fifty between 1980 and 1990. In one case, the owner of a building with four units took it off the market at the time Berkeley passed its first rent control ordinance and actually kept it vacant for the next twenty years before finally selling it. Another owner of a five-unit property emptied the building after the 1979 rent control ordinance passed and kept it vacant until 1994, when it was finally sold to a nonprofit housing corporation.

Some other owners held units vacant in an attempt to attract tenants who were receiving rental assistance under the federal Section 8 program because the program paid an "approximation" of market rent rather than the amount of the controlled rent. This bonus made it much easier for Section 8 tenants to find apartments in Berkeley during the strong rent control period.

Owners also held units off the market in order to have a vacant building to sell to potential owner-occupants. Units in smaller buildings are generally more attractive to owner-occupants, and with condominium conversion banned, the complexities of owner occupancy through tenancy in common were more easily dealt with in smaller properties.

Still, the increase in the vacancy rate is not the result of rent control as such. Nesslein (1992) found that vacancy rates declined in the rent-controlled census tracts he studied in Santa Monica during the same period. However, due to the prevalence of larger apartment buildings and the existence of an ordinance allowing condominium conversion, TICs were rare in Santa Monica. The most likely reason for the increase in the vacancy rate in Berkeley is that owners were holding units vacant in preparation for sale as TICs.

Reduced Maintenance

It is widely assumed that building maintenance will be reduced under rent controls and that the reductions are sometimes so severe that rental units are destroyed by the resulting undermaintenance. A widely quoted sentiment is that "Next to bombing, rent control seems in many cases to be the most efficient technique so far known for destroying cities" (Lindbeck 1971, cited by Kiefer 1980).

Visitors to Berkeley, however, will not see the areas of abandonment and severe deterioration that characterize so many other American cities without any form of rent controls. Housing abandonment is primarily the result of tenant incomes that are so low the tenants cannot pay rents high enough to cover the operating costs of the building. Other secondary causes of undermaintenance are institutional racism, which results in waves of disinvestment as minorities move into new areas, and "milking"—the process by which landlords try to recoup their investment and profit quickly by ceasing maintenance and operating functions, other than rent collection, leaving their mortgage lenders with uninhabitable buildings (Bartelt and Lawson 1982a, b; Devine 1973; HUD 1973; Marcuse 1981).

Rent controls may have subtle effects on maintenance. It is plausible that landlords whose rents are low enough to attract tenants without difficulty will reduce expenditures on appearances; they may cut back on such services as exterior painting and landscaping that are normally intended to increase the appeal of their property. During the 1980s, critics of rent control frequently asserted that Berkeley "looked like a slum" due to decreased maintenance. Other longtime Berkeley residents, however, maintained that rental property in Berkeley always looked bad, pointing out that before rent control the blame was placed on the large, transient student population that supposedly did not care about the appearance or conditions of the buildings they lived in for such a short period of time.

The usual economic model of landlord behavior is a simple one: If rents are held below market, the landlord will reduce maintenance until the value of the unit being rented has been reduced to the level of the controlled rent. Thus, if controlled rents are 70 percent of uncontrolled rents, maintenance should be reduced until the housing services provided by the rental units are reduced in value by 30 percent (Kiefer 1980; Murray et al. 1991). Since rents in the Bay Area are substantially above a "free market" level because of restrictive land-use regulations, it is not logical to assume that further regulation, in the form of rent control, would necessarily lead to reduced maintenance.

This "typical" model is based on an inaccurate description of rental property and the role of the landlord. Any economic model of rental housing must include the dual nature of rental property, in which the landlord provides both housing—a product requiring ongoing operating expenditures and maintenance—and land, the value and usefulness of which depend on what the public and private sectors do outside the boundaries of individual parcels of land. This second aspect is what economists sometimes call "pure economic rent," to distinguish land rent and other forms of rent from the normal profits based on the production of goods or services

(Friedman 1984). Because Berkeley has a central location within the San Francisco–Oakland metropolitan area, and because governments have poured billions of dollars into the creation and maintenance of such public facilities as the University of California at Berkeley, the Bay Area Rapid Transit system, and the freeways, land in Berkeley is very desirable.

There is broad agreement in the economic literature that land rent, in theory, can be taxed or otherwise redistributed without impact on the production of goods and services. To the extent that rent controls simply hold rents below the extraordinarily high levels reached in certain areas due to high land values, there need not be any reduction in maintenance. However, rent reductions beyond the level of land rent will necessarily cut into operating costs and the normal profit for providing housing services, and a reduction in housing services will be the result.

If rent controls reduce only land rent and do not affect the profit from provision of housing services, in other words, they may have no effect whatever on maintenance. Such an outcome requires that property under rent controls maintain the same rent differential between units of different quality that exists without controls (Mayer 1978, 1981, 1984). As long as the economic impact on the landlord from diminished quality remains the same, so that a certain reduction in maintenance results in a reduction in the amount of rent that tenants will pay, then the economic incentive for maintenance remains the same whether or not there is rent control. If a premium for high-quality maintenance is added to a lower "base rent" under rent control, the effect should be no different than it would be in a region with generally lower land values and correspondingly lower rents.

For different reasons, rent controls can both sustain and reduce such a differential. Rent controls, for example, accompanied as they typically are by protections against eviction for anything other than specified good causes, can enable tenants to exercise their rights to a warranty of habitability and to the removal of code violations. However, tenants may be more willing to overlook code violations if they think they are receiving a bargain on their rent, or they may make the repairs themselves.

The only objective data on maintenance comes from a 1994 Berkeley Community Development Department study, which examined building permit data for rental properties in adjoining census tracts in Berkeley and the neighboring cities of Albany and Oakland. This study found no significant decrease in maintenance expenditures in Berkeley after rent control began in 1979, but it found an increase in maintenance expenditures in the same period in Albany and a decrease in Oakland, coupled with major increases in rents in both cities. In the two years after the 1992 rent increases, however, the Berkeley permit data do show an increase in maintenance expenditures at the same time that such expenditures declined in the neighboring cities, probably reflecting the statewide recession. These data suggest that major maintenance remained relatively constant under rent control when the tenant population also remained relatively constant, but may increase in response to the opportunity to bring in a new, higher-income tenant population.

UNDOING RENT CONTROL: THE FAIRNESS ISSUE, 1984–1994

Once a permanent ordinance with registration requirements was passed in 1980, the rent program staff hoped to complete and verify all rent records for 1978 and 1979, but it was never provided the resources and staff to do so. Problems stemming from insufficient staff plagued the system from the beginning. The rent board did not hire adequate staff to get program records in order until 1984, when the staff was nearly doubled in order to deal with unpaid registration fees. Even then, because registration and payments of fees were the rent stabilization program's top priority, program staff were never able to find the time necessary to bring all owners into a roughly equal degree of compliance.

As previously noted, during the first two years the system operated without registration, which allowed landlords whose tenants did not ac-tively enforce the ordinance to practice an informal vacancy decontrol. As a result, once registration was required, there was no easy way to deter-mine the correct information for units where the original tenants had moved out. Rent stabilization program staff tried to correct unwarranted rent pay-ments when tenants complained, but only about 10 percent of controlled units had their base rents corrected, and a large majority of units kept base rents that were probably not in full compliance with the ordinance. Under the regulations, if a rent increase was found to be illegal, all subsequent rent increases were invalidated. Owners then became liable to reimburse their tenants for every dollar of rent paid over the amount of the 1978 monthly base rent.

As a result, any application for an Individual Rent Adjustment became hazardous for the landlord. An effort to get an increase to cover the costs of a capital improvement, for example, could result in the discovery of past illegal rents being charged; it could trigger a major rent reduction and re-funds to tenants that might amount to thousands of dollars per unit. Simi-larly, an effort to evict a tenant could result in the tenant's attorney, or a tenant advocate, uncovering illegal rent payments, which in turn could become a defense against eviction. Potential buyers, moreover, could not gain assurance that current rents were legal, since at any time a new con-troversy could erupt.

In 1986, the state legislature responded to landlord lobbying by passing a bill, effective January 1, 1987, that required the rent board to certify base rents once and for all. Rent stabilization program staff made a last effort to obtain correct rents by mailing announcements of the 1980 base rents to tenants and informing them of their right to protest the base rent. The board then "certified" its rents, making it no longer possible to change the 1980 base rent.

By 1987, the rent stabilization program contained base rents that varied widely among similar units. One explanation for this disparity was simply that landlords typically charge somewhat different rents, depending on their judgment of the market and personal preferences, and these differences were frozen in place by rent control. Probably most important, however, was that many landlords did not fully comply with the initial 1978 rent rollback; they started with their 1980 base rent at a higher level than others who either cooperated fully with the system or had been unlucky enough to get caught. The landlords who had fully complied with the ordinance and who had charged their tenants lower rents were stuck with significantly lower rents than the majority of landlords who had avoided compliance. Supportive landlords who complied with the law were important political allies for the system, but they received no reward and instead were in effect punished for obeying the law.

On November 6, 1990, Berkeley voters saw the first landlord effort at changing the rent control system since 1982—an initiative called the Historically Low Rent and Single Family Home Amendments of 1990. "Historically low rents" referred to rents that had been unusually low in 1978, when rent control began, and thus had stayed low due to rent control. The issue was strongly promoted by the Black Property Owners Association, whose ability to publicize the problems of minority, working-class landlords provided a far more appealing image than that of the Berkeley Property Owners Association. The Black Property Owners Association argued that many of their members were not professional landlords and that they had often set rents at very low levels. Since rent control had frozen these low rents permanently into place, minority landlords were forced to sell out to nonminority landlords who would not rent to minority tenants. These arguments, made by minority landlords who owned small numbers of units, won a great deal of public sympathy from both homeowners and tenants.

Opponents of an increase for "historically low rents" argued that most very low rents were, in fact, the market rents of the time, reflecting the condition of the units and the desirability of the neighborhoods in which they were located. Many of these units were occupied by poor tenants who could not afford rent increases. In 1989 and 1990, the five pro-tenant members of the nine-member board failed to agree on an effective response. As a result, in November 1990, although the voters were sufficiently supportive of rent control to narrowly defeat the landlords' initiative, the uncompromising tenant-majority on the board was also defeated and a pro-landlord slate gained control of the rent board for the first time since it became an elected body. In 1991, the new board majority passed a "Historically Low Rent" regulation that set minimum rents for all units at a level that increased the lowest quarter of all rents.

The "Historically Low Rent" increases were only a beginning. The main line of legal challenges to Berkeley's rent stabilization ordinance centered on the way the ordinance allowed rent increases only for increases in operating expenses and not for landlords' profit. The detailed data on costs collected by the rent board over the years allowed reconstruction of the profitability of an "average" rental property in Berkeley. An analysis conducted by the city's Community Development Department showed that a typical Berkeley rental property purchased in 1978 and sold in 1991 had received an average annual pretax rate of return of 9 percent. To many landlords, this rate of return was not considered competitive. The calculation of this rate of return, moreover, depended on the odd fact that during the strong rent control period, rental properties in Berkeley continued to sell at the same average gross rent multiplier, even though this multiplier became increasingly unrealistic as expenses became a larger part—and net operating income a smaller part—of the total rent. In effect, profitability was sustained only to the extent that new buyers were either willing to speculate on the future diminution or elimination of rent control, or they simply did not understand what they were getting into (City of Berkeley 1994).

Most original owners had difficulty selling their buildings for what they considered an "appropriate" price—one that would give them a clear profit on their investment. Many felt trapped by the rent control system. With a realistic sales price based on the long-term continuation of strong rent controls, the Community Development Department analysis showed the typical owner's rate of return was reduced to 6 percent, only slightly higher than the rate of inflation. Furthermore, the analysis showed that after taxes and transaction costs, the owner would receive slightly less money for the building than he had originally paid for it or had invested in it in 1978. Since the owner had received an income stream during the years he owned the building, he would not actually have lost money, but it undoubtedly would feel like a loss to most owners. They would be acutely aware that they would have done better putting their money in the bank.

By contrast, the analysis showed that if Berkeley had not had rent control, and rents had increased by the same amount as in the rest of the Bay

Area, the average Berkeley landlord would have received a 20 percent annual rate of return. Since landlords in neighboring communities were undoubtedly receiving similar rates of return, a sharp contrast was created between Berkeley and other Bay Area cities.

In December 1984, in *Fisher v. City of Berkeley*, the California Supreme Court upheld the law, allowing the rent stabilization program to continue, but required that the board make provisions to allow rent increases so that profits as well as operating costs could increase with inflation. In 1987, after several years of debate about how to respond to the additional requirements of the *Fisher* decision, the rent board amended its regulations and allowed landlords to file for individual rent adjustments to receive an increase in their net operating income equal to 40 percent of the increase in the Consumer Price Index. Net operating income was defined as that part of "rent" left after operating expenses; it is used to make mortgage payments and provide cash flow to the owner.

Landlords again filed suit against the ordinance, arguing in *Searle v. City of Berkeley Rent Stabilization Board et al.* that this regulation was not an adequate response. In July 1990, their argument was upheld by the California Court of Appeals. The Court held that the board had failed to adequately justify the 40 percent figure, and that the adjustment should be general, for all landlords, since all landlords' profits were diminished by inflation and it was not practical to expect that all landlords could have individual rent adjustments processed by the rent board.

The new pro-landlord majority that had gained control of the rent board in the November 1990 election responded to this decision with the so-called Searle increase—an across-the-board rent increase on all rental units, averaging 28 percent—that provided an inflation increase for average net operating income. The board also required that landlords phase in this increase in three annual installments for low-income tenants who requested it. The board then set a further 5 percent annual general increase, which meant that most rents increased by one-third in January 1992.

The city council and tenant organizations filed suit against the rent increase, arguing that only the part of net operating income that measured average cash flow should be considered profit to the landlord and thereby subject to an inflation adjustment. The other part of NOI, the 50 to 60 percent that typically went for mortgage payments, the critics argued, was normally a fixed cost or, if adjustable, had actually declined since the beginning of rent control and should not receive an increase. The courts upheld the board's action as within its discretion, whether or not it was necessary. Tenant organizations gathered signatures to put partial repeal of the increase on the June 1992 ballot. The repeal measure accepted the "Historically Low Rent" increases but proposed reducing the retroactive Searle increase from 28 percent to 9 percent. The repeal measure failed, garnering only 46 percent of the vote. The tenant groups tried once more in November 1992 with an identical measure but failed again, this time winning just 48 percent of the vote.

With these major rent increases in place, the number of units renting for less than $400 in Berkeley was reduced by two-thirds. In 1994, only 3,100 controlled units had legal rent ceilings under $400 a month, less than one-third of the previous total. The average rent discount was reduced to about 15 percent; Berkeley had caught up with the rest of the Bay Area. In 1996, the California legislature required phase-in of vacancy decontrol and allowed for an initial 15 percent rent increase when a unit was vacated. By June 1996, only half of the new post-vacancy rents filed with the rent board took the full 15 percent increase, however. Some landlords, with rent ceilings already above the market, did not even bother to file for an increase.

ALTERNATIVES TO RENT CONTROL

There are two major alternatives to rent control as a means of protecting lower-income people—social housing and housing allowances (Barton 1996). Some proponents of rent control in Berkeley had never expected it to last as long as it did and had hoped the city would move toward conversion of rental housing to social ownership by limited-equity cooperatives and nonprofit housing corporations. In 1991, with major across-the-board rent increases likely, the city council approved a Rental Housing Acquisition Program. But by 1996, just over one hundred units had been acquired by local nonprofit organizations, far too few to make much difference to tenants experiencing major rent increases. Other communities with far less radical reputations had far larger nonprofit housing sectors by then. Why was Berkeley behind, say, prosaic Hayward in southern Alameda County?

First, in Berkeley, the progressive ideal had been the limited-equity cooperative—a complex form of ownership that is nearly impossible for tenants to create without extensive assistance. Few tenants, secure in their below-market rent-controlled units, were interested in investing years of effort in the creation of permanently affordable housing. Few tenants in the 1980s would have predicted the demise of rent control in a town with a tenant majority. Some owners offered to sell their buildings to their tenants, only to find that they were not interested. Second, the debate over rent control had radicalized Berkeley landlords; they responded to any effort to promote purchase of rent-controlled housing by tenants or nonprofit organizations as a form of confiscation. In response, progressive council members backed off from social housing programs, gave them little financial support, and denied any intention to move beyond rent control. Only with the demise of rent control did both progressive and moderate elected officials in Berkeley come to accept nonprofit housing developers as providers of a valuable social service.

Meanwhile, property owners and political moderates consistently argued that rent control placed an unfair burden on one sector of the community and that deserving low-income tenants should be assisted through housing allowances, such as the Section 8 program. Repeated promises were made that if rent control were loosened, property owners and other citizens would support local taxes to create a fair and equitable program. With the elimination of rent control, however, all need for compromise was ended, and no such program has ever been seriously proposed. The tenant activists vehemently opposed creation of a locally funded subsidy program as a giveaway to landlords, never seeing it as a necessary supplement to a rent control system that could not possibly reduce rents to the level needed by the very poor. Instead, they tried to hold rents to unrealistically low levels and undermined public support for rent control.

At its peak, in 1991, the Berkeley rent control system held rents down by $45 million a year, meaning that landlords were forgoing an income stream with a capitalized value of half a billion dollars. By way of comparison, the city budget that year was $140 million. With so much money at stake, it is no wonder that Berkeley landlords spent hundreds of thousands of dollars in initiative campaigns, rent board elections, city council elections, and court cases. Having created a local program of such immense value to tenants, however, the progressives seemed to have little sense of how to manage what was arguably the city's single most valuable public asset. Instead, rent control was taken largely for granted after the initial years of conflict, given no more staff than any other minor city department with an annual operating budget of $2 million, and avoided by most elected officials with major stature in the community because of the divisiveness and bitterness of its political conflicts. Those who ran the system showed little understanding of what was fundamental to the system and what could be compromised, until it was too late to compromise and the system was lost. It is not certain, of course, that any local compromise could have avoided statewide vacancy decontrol, but in Berkeley most of the rent discount created by rent control had already been eliminated by the locally elected rent board.

The progressives showed little awareness that a regulatory program was highly vulnerable to political change in local politics, to the courts, and to the state legislature. They made little effort to convert any substantial amount of housing to such forms of social ownership as limited-equity cooperatives or nonprofit housing corporations that would have given low-income residents the permanent constitutional protections afforded to other property owners.

Notes

The views expressed in this chapter are those of the author and do not necessarily reflect the views of the City of Berkeley.

MARGERY AUSTIN TURNER

8

Moderating Market Pressures for Washington, D.C., Rental Housing

INTRODUCTION

A dvocates often advance rent control as a panacea for problems of housing affordability, whereas opponents blame controls for the poor quality and dwindling supply of low-cost units. In the District of Columbia, a balanced system of rent control appears to have moderated housing affordability problems during periods of rapid rent pressure, although it by no means cured them. Although the profitability of rental housing would have been higher in the absence of controls, there is no convincing evidence that rent control in the District of Columbia significantly deterred investment in either maintenance or new construction. In recent years, as market pressures abated, the impacts of controls on rent levels may have diminished. Nevertheless, the District's system has been retained, serving in effect as a hedge against future periods of rapid rent inflation.

Rent control alone cannot fully protect poor households from unaffordable housing cost burdens. Other more costly interventions would be required to supplement what poor households can afford to pay toward rent, and to preserve and expand the dwindling stock of low-cost rental units. Still, evidence from the District of Columbia shows that a carefully balanced program of rent control can make a positive difference for a city's renters without serious adverse effects on either housing maintenance or new rental housing production.

THE DISTRICT OF COLUMBIA'S
RENT CONTROL PROGRAM

The District of Columbia's rent control program was established in 1975 in response to rapid inflation in rent levels during the early 1970s. The central objective of the District's rent control program was to protect tenants from excessive rents and rent increases. In the early and mid 1970s, unaffordable rents were increasingly recognized as a serious housing problem for District renters, especially those of limited means.[1] In 1974, the share of District renters paying more than 30 percent of their income for rent (27 percent) was just as high as the share living in physically deficient housing units (U.S. Department of Commerce and U.S. Department of Housing and Urban Development 1974).

The District's rent control regime is a moderate one that explicitly seeks to maintain the profitability of investment in rental housing. Like other rent control programs implemented in U.S. cities during the 1970s, the District's system provides incentives for landlords to maintain their existing rental properties and to produce new ones (Downs 1988). Investors who add to the supply of rental housing in the District of Columbia are not subject to regulatory restrictions on the rents they charge. And landlords who maintain controlled properties adequately can automatically increase rents each year.

Approximately three-quarters of the District's rental housing stock is covered by rent controls. Only five classes of rental units are entirely exempt from rent regulation:

1. units held by owners of fewer than five D.C. rental units;
2. units added to the rental stock (either through new construction or substantial rehabilitation) since 1975;
3. units in continuously vacant buildings;
4. cooperative units; and
5. publicly subsidized rental housing.

For units that are subject to controls, the District's rent control program does not hold rent levels fixed but allows owners of units that are properly registered and in compliance with the city's housing code to increase rents annually by the lower of 10 percent or the rate of increase in the Consumer Price Index. At vacancy, a unit's rent can either be increased by 12 percent or pushed up to the rent level of comparable units in the same property, whichever is higher.

In addition to these automatic adjustments, the D.C. rent control program offers several mechanisms for landlords to petition for increases in

rent levels. First, rents can be increased to reflect cost increases when owners undertake capital improvements or make changes in the services or
facilities they provide. In addition, landlords whose properties are generating less than a 12 percent cash return on equity can petition for "hardship" rent increases. And finally, property owners can negotiate voluntary
agreements with tenants to increase rents if 70 percent of tenants agree.

In 1985, after a decade of experience with this rent control program,
the D.C. city council voted to extend rent controls for another five years.
However, in response to claims that rent control was benefiting relatively
affluent renters at the expense of small property owners and that the
District's "pro-tenant" regulatory environment was discouraging investment in rental housing construction and rehabilitation, the council mandated a comprehensive study of the impacts of rent controls on the city's
rental housing stock and on the producers and consumers of rental housing in the District of Columbia. This study was conducted by the Urban
Institute, a national research and policy analysis institution, and provides
the basis for the findings presented in this chapter.[2] Since the completion
of the Urban Institute study, the District's system of rent control has twice
been extended, with relatively little debate or opposition. Most recently,
the D.C. city council voted to extend the existing system of controls to the
year 2000.

PERCEPTIONS OF RENT CONTROL AMONG
WASHINGTON, D.C., TENANTS AND LANDLORDS

District renters strongly approve of rent control. When surveyed in 1987,
sentiment ran at least three to one in favor of rent control for virtually all
segments of the renter population. Interestingly, however, many D.C. renters did not know whether their units were controlled. Almost 40 percent
either did not know or answered incorrectly when asked to identify the
control status of their units. Tenants who lived in controlled units, however, were more likely to know their control status than those living in
exempt units, and the share of households with accurate information increased systematically among those who had remained in the same unit
for several years.

The primary benefit of rent control, as perceived by residents of controlled units, is that it makes rents more affordable. Roughly 90 percent of
respondents living in controlled rental units indicated that rent control had
made their apartments more affordable. In addition to rent savings, D.C.
tenants value the sense of security provided by rent controls; about 80 percent of those who lived in controlled units said that rent control provided
them with the security to stay in their apartments if they wanted to. District

of Columbia renters also indicated that rent controls and the accompanying tenant protections enabled them to demand maintenance and repairs without fear of eviction or retaliatory rent increases.

While D.C. renters enthusiastically support rent control, landlords generally perceive it as a significant deterrent to investment in rental housing. Virtually all owners of controlled units interviewed in 1987 expressed the opinion that rent control had a major impact on their revenues. A majority also viewed the administrative costs of rent control as a significant factor in their operations. Owners of most of the District's controlled rental units (80.6 percent) reported that they did not intend to invest in D.C. rental housing in the future. The most commonly mentioned concerns were low rents (45.5 percent) and a regulatory environment that makes investments in other jurisdictions more attractive (50.2 percent).

Empirical evidence suggests that both renters and landlords in the District of Columbia may exaggerate the impacts of the District's rent control system. Findings from the Urban Institute study, which estimated the impacts of a decade of rent controls on rent levels and housing affordability and on profitability, maintenance, and rental housing production, are summarized below. These findings indicate that the D.C. rent control program indeed moderated rent increases and made housing more affordable for many renter households. However, not all households living in rent-controlled units enjoyed significant rent savings, and housing affordability remained a serious and widespread problem for low-income renters. From the landlord's perspective, the findings confirm that controls reduced the profitability of investment in rental housing. However, there is no convincing evidence that the maintenance of the existing stock suffered as a result, or that investment in new construction and substantial rehabilitation would have been significantly higher in the absence of controls.

IMPACTS OF RENT CONTROL ON RENTS AND HOUSING AFFORDABILITY

The Urban Institute study estimated that, in the absence of controls, the monthly rent for the average D.C. unit would have been at least $50 higher, and possibly as much as $200 higher, than it was in 1987. The best estimate was that 1987 monthly rents were on average $95 to $100 less than what they would have been absent controls, and that roughly three-quarters of D.C. renters would have paid higher rents in an unregulated market.

A three-step process was employed to estimate what rents would have been in 1987 had rent controls not been in effect. First, data from the 1974 American Housing Survey (AHS) were used to estimate a hedonic regression equation, which measured the contribution of various housing attributes to total rent in an unregulated market environment. Table 8.1 presents the results of this estimation. Next, the hedonic rent equation was applied to data on characteristics of the rental stock in 1987 to estimate what these units would have rented for in 1974, before the imposition of rent controls. Finally, three alternative assumptions about rent inflation in an uncontrolled market were applied to the predicted rents in order to estimate 1987 rents in the absence of controls. These assumptions were based upon patterns of rent inflation for central cities nationwide and for six uncontrolled central city rental markets in the Middle Atlantic region.

The Urban Institute's *lower bound estimate* assumed that in the absence of controls, rents in the District would have increased at an average annual rate of 8.8 percent between 1974 and 1987—half a percentage point faster than the rate for the surrounding suburbs. On average, central city rents in the United States as a whole rose 0.5 percentage points faster on an annual basis than suburban rents over this period. The *upper bound estimate* assumed rent inflation of 11 percent annually in the absence of controls— four percentage points higher than the rate of income growth among renter households. On average, U.S. central city rents rose four percentage points faster than renter incomes over this period. Finally, the Urban Institute's *best estimate* assumed that rents would have grown by 9.5 percent annually in the absence of controls, approximately the rate of rent inflation experienced by U.S. central cities generally, and specifically by six large cities in the Middle Atlantic region (table 8.2).

The estimated rent savings generated by controls in the District moderated the problems of housing affordability D.C. renters had to face in 1987. Although affordability problems in the District were still severe, a much larger number of renter households would have had excessive rent burdens in the absence of rent control. Specifically, in 1987, 43 percent of all renters in the District paid more than 30 percent of their income for housing, and about 10 percent paid more than three-quarters of their income for rent. At the "best estimates" of uncontrolled market rent levels, the share of households paying more than 30 percent of their income for rent in 1987 would have increased from 43 percent to more than 50 percent, a level typical of other central cities in the United States (figure 8.1).

The rent savings generated by controls were not evenly distributed among D.C. renters. In fact, not all households living in controlled units paid lower rents in 1987 than they would have in an uncontrolled market. About one-quarter of all D.C. renters probably paid 1987 rents as high— and perhaps higher—than the "market" rents that would have prevailed in the absence of controls. Among the rest, about one-third paid rents that were within $100 of estimated market rents; another third paid between

TABLE 8.1
Market Rent Hedonic Regression Equation: D.C. Rental Units, 1974

Unit Attributes	Coefficient	Standard Error
Intercept	6.027**	0.040
Single-family house	-0.151**	0.018
Duplex	-0.318**	0.024
3- to 4-unit building	-0.337**	0.017
5- to 9-unit building	-0.268**	0.016
10- to 19-unit building	-0.206**	0.014
20- to 49-unit building	-0.194**	-0.018
Efficiency unit	-0.609**	0.030
2-room unit	-0.484**	0.026
3-room unit	-0.306**	0.021
4-room unit	-0.198**	0.024
5-room unit	-0.081**	0.020
No complete bathroom	-0.528**	0.031
1 bathroom	-0.263**	0.030
Recent mover	0.020	0.019
Moved in 1–2 years ago	0.122**	0.012
Moved in 2–3 years ago	0.079**	0.013
Moved in 3–4 years ago	0.050**	0.015
Moved in 4–5 years ago	0.069**	0.023
Black household head	-1.22**	0.023
White household head	0.090**	0.023
R-squared	49.49	

** Significance at the 99 percent confidence level

Source: Turner 1990

$100 and $200 less; and the remaining third paid rents more than $200 below estimated market rent levels.

The households that experienced the greatest rent savings were those that remained in their controlled units for six or more years. Roughly half of those who had moved more recently paid rents as high, or higher, than they would have in the absence of controls. The findings suggest that when controlled units are vacated, landlords sometimes raise rents to levels above those that would prevail in the absence of controls, to compensate for the possibility that, if the new tenant stays for more than a year or two, rents will be constrained from rising as rapidly as they would in the absence of controls. Thus, the turnover of controlled units plays an important role in determining the level of rent savings—with units that turn over frequently much more likely to charge rents at or above market levels than units that have experienced only occasional turnover.

TABLE 8.2
Patterns of Rent Inflation in U.S. Central Cities, 1974-1983

	Average Annual Increase in Median Rent		Average Annual Increase in Median Income	
	Central City	Suburbs	Central City	Suburbs
U.S. Average	9.4%	8.9%	5.3%	5.9%
Atlanta	10.2	9.0	6.0	6.6
Baltimore	8.9	8.8	3.9	6.4
Hartford	9.0	9.3	6.9	6.6
Philadelphia	9.9	7.7	5.3	5.5
Pittsburgh	11.5	11.0	6.4	5.7
Rochester	7.5	7.5	5.4	5.5
District of Columbia	**7.8**	**8.3**	**6.1**	**6.5**

Source: Turner 1990

It is not surprising, therefore, that elderly households and families with children were the most likely to enjoy rent savings from the District's system of controls. Poor and moderate-income households, who tend to move less frequently than more affluent households, were also more likely to enjoy rent savings. Specifically, about 80 percent of poor households (incomes under $15,000) paid below-market rents in 1987, compared to 65 percent of high-income renters (incomes over $50,000). However, affluent renters, as well as young singles and groups of young adults who remained in controlled units for an extended number of years, benefited from the controls. And poor households who moved were likely to pay market rents (or higher). Thus, not all the benefits of rent control are targeted equitably or efficiently.

The Urban Institute study also showed that many D.C. renters overestimate the monetary benefits they obtain from rent control. Almost three-quarters of those surveyed believed that they would pay higher rents in the absence of controls, but the Urban Institute estimated that only about two-thirds enjoyed true rent savings. Recent movers were particularly likely to think that they were saving on rent, whereas the empirical evidence suggests that they typically paid as much or more than they would in the absence of controls.

IMPACTS OF RENT CONTROL ON PROFITABILITY AND MAINTENANCE

Because rent levels were lower in 1987 than they would have been without controls, the profitability of an investment in D.C. rental property was

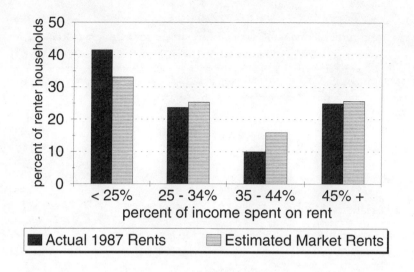

FIGURE 8.1
Rent burdens for Washington, D.C., households: controlled and estimated market rents

reduced. However, after accounting for appreciation gains and tax benefits, the profitability of investment in D.C. rental housing in 1987 still compared favorably to alternative investment opportunities. In the absence of controls, the after-tax rate of return on investment would probably have increased by only about two percentage points for small properties and by no more than five percentage points for larger properties. Moreover, although rent levels—and profits—in the District were lower, on average, than they would have been absent controls, the District's system of automatic rent adjustments appears to have compensated most landlords adequately for increases in operating costs.

The Urban Institute collected pro forma financial data for a sample of controlled rental properties from District of Columbia government records. These data were used to estimate the before- and after-tax profitability of investment in D.C. rental property as well as to estimate the impacts of rent control on profits. Because the increased rent revenues that would prevail in the absence of controls would ultimately increase property values, the impact of controls on investment in rental property is more complex than it may at first appear. The Urban Institute analysis assumed that the ratio of rent revenues to assessed property values that prevailed in 1987 would be essentially the same in the absence of controls. In other words, higher estimated revenues would translate directly into higher value estimates. The analysis also assumed that loan-to-value ratios would be roughly

TABLE 8.3

Landlord's Estimated Return on Investment for an Average Rental Unit in a D.C. Property with between 20 and 50 Units, 1987

Per Unit Values	With Controlled Rents	With "Market" Rents
Revenues	$ 4,179	$ 5,558
Value	$12,308	$16,370
Equity	$10,370	$13,792
Property Taxes	$201	$267
Interest	$384	$511
Appreciation	$567	$754
Total Expenditures	$3,601	$4,676
Net Income	$578	$882
Income/Equity	5.57%	6.40%
(Income + Appreciation)/ Equity	11.04%	11.86%
After-tax return on equity	10.25%	10.66%

Source: Turner 1990

the same in a controlled or uncontrolled environment, so that both equity and debt would increase if values were higher. Estimates of appreciation benefits were also assumed not to be affected by controls; the study applied the prevailing appreciation rates to the estimates of property values in the absence of controls. Finally, fairly conservative assumptions about the tax treatment of depreciation and long-term capital gains were applied to calculate the after-tax return on investment. Table 8.3 presents the results of these computations for a typical D.C. property with twenty to fifty units.

Based on these assumptions, the Urban Institute estimated that in the absence of controls, D.C. landlords would realize annual increases in net income ranging from about $600 per unit in small properties to about $1,350 per unit in large controlled properties. At the same time, annual appreciation gains would probably be about $100 per unit in large properties and up to $800 per unit in the smallest properties. If D.C. landlords devoted these increased revenues entirely to raising investment returns, the profitability of the average large rental property would rise by as much as five percentage points, and the profitability of smaller properties would rise by about one or two percentage points. However, the majority of controlled-housing providers in the District also stated that, if their revenues were to

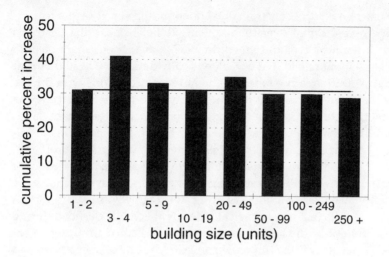

FIGURE 8.2
Estimated operating cost inflation by building size, 1981–1987

rise significantly, they would either increase maintenance expenditures or undertake property improvements. Therefore, if the typical housing provider used half of the increase in net operating revenues to expand maintenance or finance property improvements, the estimated profitability of the average large rental property would increase by only about two percentage points, and the profitability of small properties would increase by less than one percentage point on average.

Cash return on equity was relatively low for controlled rental properties in the mid-1980s, but the District's automatic rent adjustment mechanism kept pace with most increases in operating costs. Even for units continuously occupied from 1981 through 1987, allowable rent adjustments met or exceeded increases in the cost of operation for most types of rental properties. Specifically, the District's automatic rent adjustment factor resulted in a cumulative increase of 31 percent in rent levels during the 1981-87 period. The increases were not distributed evenly across all size categories, as illustrated by figure 8.2. Properties with three and four units experienced substantially higher increases—averaging about 41 percent. The above-average increase in operating costs for these properties was primarily attributable to dramatic increases in assessed values and, therefore, in property taxes and interest payments due. However, even though these properties experienced above-average cost increases and corresponding reductions in cash flow, their property values and hence, appreciation benefits, increased substantially.

Because rent control constrains revenues and profits, it seems reasonable to hypothesize that over time housing deficiencies in the District's rental stock would develop. Indeed, in 1987, a significant share of D.C. rental units—about one in five—was physically deficient. The higher rent levels that would have prevailed in the absence of controls would have increased landlords' gross rent revenues by an average of 33 percent, the Urban Institute study concluded. And, as mentioned earlier, many landlords indicated that they would have used these higher revenues to improve building maintenance or to address deferred maintenance problems. In fact, the increased revenue that would have been realized in the absence of controls would probably have been sufficient to improve maintenance substantially in at least half of the existing stock. However, the proportion of D.C. rental units that were physically deficient actually declined during the decade following the implementation of rent control, from 26 percent in 1974 to 20 percent in 1987; moreover, in 1987, the rate of deficiencies was higher among exempt units (25 percent) than among units that were subject to controls. Finally, most tenants in controlled rental units (80 percent) believed that building maintenance was as good or better than it would be in the absence of rent controls, and a substantial share (61 percent) reported that the protections offered by rent control made them more willing to insist on building repairs. Low-income households were particularly likely to name this feature as a benefit of the District's rent control program.

IMPACTS OF RENT CONTROL ON HOUSING PRODUCTION AND AVAILABILITY

During the 1970s, the total number of rental units in the District declined substantially—from 199,100 in 1970 to 170,500 in 1981. This decline, which occurred despite new rental construction averaging about 740 units per year, was attributable to the removal of at least 3,340 units from the rental stock annually. Was the newly imposed system of rent controls—and other tenant protections that accompanied it—to blame? Rent control certainly may have been a factor in the decisions of some landlords to remove properties from use or to convert them to owner occupancy, but careful analysis strongly suggests that, even in the absence of controls, the District's rental stock would have experienced a precipitous decline during the 1970s.

Many uncontrolled central cities in the United States experienced the same pattern of decline, due to widespread demographic and economic conditions (table 8.4). Specifically, the relative attractiveness of homeownership, the expansion of suburban housing opportunities for minorities, and the basic cost of rental housing production all appear to have

TABLE 8.4

Change in Rental Housing Inventory for U.S. Cities, 1974-1983

| | *Average Annual Rates* | | |
	Net Change in Rental Inventory	New Rental Construction	Rental Unit Removals
Atlanta	-0.4	2.0	2.7
Baltimore	-0.9	1.8	3.0
Hartford	-1.4	0.0	4.4
Philadelphia	-0.4	0.7	3.2
Pittsburgh	-1.4	0.0	4.0
Rochester	-0.8	2.0	5.3
District of Columbia	**-1.4**	**1.5**	**4.5**

Source: Turner 1990

undermined the rental housing stock. Units were withdrawn from central city rental inventories, and the level of new (unsubsidized) rental production was low because fewer middle- and high-income households chose to be central city renters, and because the remaining renters could no longer afford to make housing investment sufficiently profitable.

Even during the 1970s, when the rental stock was shrinking, new rental units were being built in the District. In fact, D.C. experienced a higher rate of new rental construction (1.5 percent annually on average) than many uncontrolled cities (see table 8.4). In the 1980s, as construction continued, it became clear that rent control was not the determining factor in investment decision making. Starting in the early 1980s, demand for rental housing in the District began to pick up, largely because rising interest rates, lower inflation, and reductions in marginal tax rates all contributed to make homeownership less affordable relative to rental housing. At first, the supply of rental units continued its decline, and the result was a dramatic drop in the rental vacancy rate, from 6.2 percent in 1981 to 2.5 percent in 1985. Subsequently, the District's rental stock started to grow in size, increasing by about 1,600 units between 1985 and 1987. This turnaround represented a lagged market response to renewed levels of effective demand.

It is possible that this response might have occurred more quickly in an unregulated rental market. But the responsiveness of District investors to changing demands for rental housing—and the similarity to trends in uncontrolled central city markets—suggests that rent control was not the principal factor in investment decisions, although it certainly may have been a consideration. Moreover, investors in new and substantially rehabilitated rental units (which are explicitly exempt from controls in the District) reported that they did not see rent control as a deterrent; only about one-quarter of those interviewed advocated the elimination of rent control. More cited the District's system of eviction protections as a cause for serious concern. These protections were seen to reflect a strong "pro-tenant" bias in the local regulatory environment. In addition, the cost and availability of land and structures for new construction and substantial rehabilitation, as well as the availability of long-term financing, were cited as critical constraints on the ability to build or substantially renovate housing in the District.

Still, the availability of low-cost rental housing in the District of Columbia—as in other cities throughout the country—is more sensitive to the number of units lost from the affordable stock each year than to the number of units added.[3] In this regard, rent control, along with other aspects of the local regulatory environment, may have prompted some landlords to remove properties from the rental market. During the 1970s, an average of one thousand units was removed annually from the District's housing stock; the vast majority of these units rented for less than $350 a month (in 1987 dollars). Many uncontrolled central cities also lost rental units during the 1970s (see table 8.4), but owners of D.C. units that were removed from the rental inventory between 1985 and 1987 consistently listed rent control among the reasons they had discontinued renting their properties. Their decisions were motivated by the lack of economic viability of their properties, and they suggested that if the District wanted to minimize losses from the rental stock, the local government should both make it easier to evict nonpaying and destructive tenants and approve substantial rehabilitation and hardship petitions more readily.

In fact, the units at greatest risk of being removed from the stock—those with very low rents and chronic housing code violations—qualified for hardship rent increases under the District's regulatory regime, but many landlords did not apply for them. Between 1983 and 1987, fewer than two hundred hardship petitions were filed annually in the District (Walker 1988). Thus, it appears that rent control was not the primary constraint preventing the owners of these units from raising rents and making property improvements. The primary problem was that the tenants who occupied the buildings were simply too poor to pay the rent levels required to make maintenance profitable. Admittedly, filing a hardship petition often presented an administrative and financial hurdle for these landlords. But if rent control alone constrained the rents that the landlords of distressed properties could charge, and if market rents for these units were sufficiently high to induce landlords to improve them in the absence of controls, then we would certainly have observed a much higher usage of the hardship petition process, despite the costs. Given the relatively low incidence of substantial rehabilitation, capital improvements, or hardship petition filings, it is hard to argue that rent control per se acted as a binding constraint on the economic viability of these properties.

CONCLUSION

No system of rent control can ensure the availability of decent and affordable housing for low- and moderate-income renters. To meet that goal, more direct remedies are clearly required, including programs that supplement the rents that low- and moderate-income tenants pay, programs that preserve existing low-rent properties, and other programs that induce the production of additional low- and moderate-cost units.[4] Rent control is a relatively "sloppy," or inefficient, mechanism for addressing the problem of unaffordable housing cost burdens. Higher-income renters, as well as those in genuine need, benefit from the rent savings that controls generate, and needy families who move frequently may actually pay above-market rents in a system like the District's, which permits relatively large rent increases when units turn over.

Nevertheless, moderate and balanced rent control regimes, like the District of Columbia's, can play a legitimate role in local efforts to moderate the high costs of rental housing. Empirical evidence demonstrates that the District's rent control program has significantly moderated rent increases and reduced the incidence of unaffordable rent burdens for poor families and the elderly. Despite these impacts, after-tax profits on rental housing investment in the District have remained competitive with alternative investment opportunities. During the first decade of controls, no convincing evidence surfaced to demonstrate that controls had resulted in reduced maintenance or housing production levels.

Since 1988, when the results of the Urban Institute study were released, rent control has not resurfaced as a major policy or political issue for the District of Columbia. Market rent inflation has been considerably more moderate during the late 1980s and the 1990s in the Washington metropolitan area—and other urban housing markets—than it was during the 1970s and early 1980s. Now, according to informed observers, ceiling rents for controlled units in the District of Columbia are typically as high and sometimes higher than renters are willing to pay.[5] As a result, there is relatively little pressure for the elimination of rent control in the District, and the existing system has been sustained due to widespread support among renter households.[6] Thus, during periods of weak demand and slow market rent inflation, a moderate system of rent control may have little or no impact on rent levels; the main reason it is retained is as a safeguard against future periods of market pressure.

Notes

1. For more on trends in rental housing cost burdens and other housing problems during the 1970s and 1980s, see Joint Center for Housing Studies (1989).

2. Unless otherwise indicated, results reported here are from Turner 1990.

3. Recent evidence indicates that, at least since the mid 1980s, more affordable units have been "lost" as a result of rent inflation than as a result of actual stock removals (HUD 1996; Turner and Edwards 1993). In the late 1970s, however, actual removal of low-cost units from the rental stock was a more significant factor.

4. In 1985, the District of Columbia created a demand-side housing assistance program, modeled on the federal Section 8 Certificate program, to supplement the rents that low-income households could afford to pay. However, the Tenant Assistance Program (TAP) was discontinued due to a combination of poor administration and resource constraints.

5. For example, one respondent reported that city council members no longer get outraged calls about units that are similar, but have dramatically different allowable rent levels.

6. In 1995, the Republican Congress included the elimination of rent control as one of many policy issues to be addressed in its oversight of the D.C. government. In response, the Democratic city council extended the existing system of controls to the year 2000 with very little discussion. In 1997 and 1998, the District's Control Board resurrected the issue, calling for a new study of rent control's impacts.

Michael B. Teitz

9

Rent Stabilization in Los Angeles: A Moderate Approach to Regulation

INTRODUCTION

Los Angeles presents perhaps the purest example of moderate, second-generation rent control in a very large American city.[1] The city's experience provides evidence that rental regulation can be managed in a way that does not provoke massive political confrontations or seriously impede the operations of the private rental housing market. In that sense, it is a story without great drama or conflict. At the same time, rental regulation has evolved within an environment of great social and economic change. Although the economics and politics of Los Angeles's efforts to regulate residential rents are complex and sometimes convoluted, the city has been able to steer its way through eighteen years of regulation on a fairly stable policy course.

THE DECISION TO REGULATE RENTS: 1977

As with several other California cities, the decision to adopt rental regulation in Los Angeles was, in part, an accident (Chapman 1981; Keating 1983; Teitz 1987). Although tenant groups and advocates had called for restrictions on rent increases during the housing inflation of the 1970s, the momentum for a decision of this magnitude in a city long dedicated to private enterprise grew out of the dissatisfaction of homeowners statewide with rising real estate taxes. The story of Proposition 13, a constitutional initiative to strictly limit both levels and rates of increase of property taxes, is well known. Through the 1970s, as housing prices in California rose faster than both incomes and the general price level, local property taxes based on assessed value rose dramatically. With the governor and legislature unable to agree on how to respond to widespread homeowner discontent, the stage was set for the draconian initiative that passed overwhelmingly in June 1978. Proposition 13 rolled back property taxes and assessed values and established a permanent property tax limit of 1 percent of assessed value. It also limited future increases in assessed value to generally no more than 2 percent per year. The result was a property tax windfall for all owners of real estate, which was rapidly capitalized into even higher property values.

Owners of apartment buildings across the state had campaigned vigorously for Proposition 13, arguing that rising taxes penalized tenants as well as landlords. There is disagreement about whether they also committed themselves to reduce rents if the initiative passed. *The Los Angeles Times* reported that members of the California Apartment Owners Association had agreed to a voluntary rebate equal to 50 percent of one month's rent, but the offer was later denied (Chapman 1981). There is little doubt, however, that tenants expected rent reductions, since the promoters of the initiative, Howard Jarvis and Paul Gann, had explicitly argued that reductions would be forthcoming. When, after the election, some owners in tight housing markets—such as San Francisco—actually raised rents, outrage among tenants ran high (Hartman 1984, 37). In the ensuing public debate, enthusiasm for rental regulation overcame opposition in several major cities in the state, and a range of temporary and permanent regulatory laws were readily adopted (Keating 1985).

For Los Angeles, the decision to regulate rents was not one to be taken lightly.[2] With the exception of the rent freeze mandated by President Nixon's price controls after the 1971 oil crisis, the city had not seen any rent restrictions since World War II. Although the city had a substantial number of rental tenants—about 57 percent of the city's population in 1977 lived in rental housing—Los Angeles's civic tradition was different from the political radicalism of some California cities, whether it be the old-line radicalism of Berkeley, or the more recent political activism of Santa Monica. Los Angeles had never shied away from civic action to promote business, as the creation of the port and the Owens Valley aqueduct attests. Nonetheless, the ideology of the city was distinctly in favor of the private sector, in housing as in other forms of enterprise. At the same time, the city had a historical strand of radical tradition that manifested itself in attempts to organize the tenant constituency (Davis 1992). The possibility of rent control was given a public airing by a Los Angeles councilman in 1976, and a landlord-tenant court and mediation board were established in 1977. During 1977, there were also stirrings of tenant activity in favor of controls, led by the redoubtable Tom Hayden. When the debate over rental regulation erupted, strong advocates were ready to speak on both sides.

Los Angeles's form of governance also played a role in the rise of rent control. The city historically has had a relatively weak mayor and strong city council; and any new legislation must gain the approval of at least eight members of the fifteen-member council. Nominally nonpartisan, the council members are elected by specific districts and traditionally have paid close attention to the desires of their constituents while responding to business interests. In 1978, the council members embodied a range of views from conservative to liberal, and it was clear that to secure eight votes for rental regulation would require compromise. However, a real incentive to act also existed; in the highly charged conditions of the time, voters might well have passed rent regulations themselves by initiative, which would have taken the issue out of the hands of the council altogether.

After considerable political maneuvering, therefore, Los Angeles adopted a form of rent control that it called "rent stabilization"; and the city chose not to adopt proposals for rent rollbacks and freezes. A six-month moratorium on rent increases was adopted on August 30, 1978, to go into effect in October of that year. Implementation of the freeze was rather ad hoc; both the Community Development Department and the Landlord Tenant Mediation Board (LTMB) had some responsibility. Subsequently, the debate over rent control flared up again, fueled by political movements for rent rollbacks at the state level, which ultimately came to nothing. The LTMB then recommended enactment of permanent controls. After a debate about cost and form of regulation, a one-year Rent Stabilization Ordinance was passed and signed by Mayor Bradley on March 15, 1979, to take effect on May 1, 1979. It is significant that the ordinance received precisely eight yes votes, to five no and two absent. The outcome of the process represented a compromise between advocates for control and its opponents; some relatively conservative members voted for the proposal, partly because they believed that Proposition 13 promises had been betrayed, and partly because they feared something worse would be proposed. The initial ordinance was enacted for one year, but during that year, it was first extended and then reenacted after some debate and modification. Following a substantial environmental impact review—the only such review of a rent control ordinance in California (Rydell et al. 1981)—a permanent ordinance was enacted in 1982.

THE RENT STABILIZATION ORDINANCE

With one or two exceptions, the initial rent stabilization ordinance proved to be a durable compromise. It reflected the basic features of most second-generation controls, with one or two local peculiarities. The ordinance covered all rental housing in the city, with the principal exceptions of single-family homes, "luxury" apartments, and housing constructed after October 1, 1979 (exempted in order not to discourage new apartment construction).[3] As with most second-generation ordinances, it provided for both automatic and specifically approved rent increases; these increases were intended to permit an adequate rate of return to ensure maintenance and preservation of the rental housing stock. In the first round, catch-up increases of varying amounts were permitted for apartments that had posted no rent increases in prior years. For those that had posted rent increases, an automatic annual increase of 7 percent was allowable. This increase coincided with the actual increase in the Consumer Price Index (CPI) for 1977-78 but allowed for no variation thereafter. For apartments that were voluntarily vacated or vacated for just cause, so-called vacancy decontrol applied. These units initially could be re-rented for what the market would bear, but thereafter would be subject to the annual 7 percent limit. The ordinance also contained provisions limiting evictions to just cause and laid out the permissible rent increases subsequent to capital improvements, rehabilitation, or other substantial changes. Provision was also made for an appeals process for owners who thought that their rents did not permit a "just and reasonable" rate of return, though this process would turn out to be set in motion only rarely.

The ordinance created a regulatory structure that was directed toward landlords and buildings rather than toward specific units. Landlords were required to register and pay an annual fee of $3 per unit, but there was no legal registration either of rent or quality of specific units. Thus, the onus or demonstration of noncompliance was on the tenant. Essentially, for reasons of both ideology and efficiency, this system regulated in response to complaint rather than by universal inspection and certification of rents in individual apartments. To this day, the city has no record of each specific unit covered by rent stabilization, only of the number of apartments per building. Initially, any landlord who failed to comply with the ordinance was subject to civil action and triple damages; tenants in these cases could use the ordinance as a defense against eviction. Later, failure to comply became a misdemeanor, punishable by fine or jail.

Administration of the ordinance was not simple in a city the size of Los Angeles. It was estimated that about 530,000 units would be covered by the law.[4] Control was vested in a new Rent Stabilization Division in the Los Angeles Community Development Department, under the Director of Housing. The agency geared up quickly, recruiting a staff to oversee the registration process. By July 1979, the great majority of eligible owners and buildings were believed to have been registered—57,335 applications had been received, 49,595 certificates had been mailed, and some 486,972 units were covered (Chapman 1981). By the early 1980s, a reasonably well-functioning regulatory administrative structure was in place.

At the end of the first year when the ordinance was up for renewal, and subsequently, the regulations were subjected to pressures from both landlords and tenants, who rapidly organized themselves to try to influence their proponents on the council. Owners sought to increase the permissible annual rent increases and to ease the constraints on capital improvements. Tenants worked to end vacancy decontrol and to tighten capital improvements regulations. As we shall see, neither was particularly effective. One of the interesting features of the permanent ordinance, which significantly influenced the political struggles, was a requirement that it be periodically reviewed by the city council with respect to substantial rehabilitation and relocation payments. The level of registration fees, combined with the efficiency of the regulatory system, ensured that a surplus would be built up that could be used for these reviews. As a result, three major evaluations of the system have been undertaken at different points in its evolution.[5] These provide the background information for the assessment of the Los Angeles rent control system that follows.

RENT STABILIZATION SETTLES IN: 1979–1984

An important feature of all rent control systems is the process whereby the participants come to terms with the existence of the system. In some cases, such as Berkeley, ideological differences and conflicting economic interests are so great that the participants can scarcely be said to come to terms with the system at all. In others, such as New York City, a permanent state of tension has given rise to continuous public dissension and maneuvering for advantage. Even in relatively advantageous circumstances, such as those that occurred in Los Angeles, a period of initial uncertainty exists, during which time the participants in the regulatory process seek to understand it, test its limits, and evaluate what it means for their interests. In Los Angeles, the years from 1979 to 1984 represented this period of settling in.

From its outset, rent stabilization existed in an atmosphere charged not only with some hostility and conflicts among interest groups, but also with enormous doubt about the economy and the direction that the real estate market would take. At the end of the 1970s, inflation was at a historically high level throughout the United States. In California, tenants and landlords alike were disturbed by the fact that their rents and costs seemed unpredictable and likely to grow faster than incomes. With the rollback of rents and the subsequent constraint of rent increases to no more than 7 percent per year in the rent-stabilized housing stock, some of the uncertainty disappeared, but it was soon replaced by anxiety. In the years from 1979 to 1982, the rate of inflation, as measured by the CPI, was consistently over 7 percent—in fact, it averaged about 11.5 percent annually—which meant that owners whose costs had increased with inflation were suffering. However, from 1982 to 1984, the average increase in the CPI was only 2.75 percent, implying that tenants whose rents rose by 7 percent during those years were paying increases well above inflation. For the full period, 1979 to 1982, the 7 percent rate of increase, when compounded, almost precisely matched the inflation rate, though the loading of high inflation years in the earlier portion of the time frame clearly favored tenants.

Thus, by the time the city council came to review the ordinance in 1984, both landlords and tenants had been favored at different times by the existing rent adjustment formula. More importantly, both had witnessed its flaws, and both could see that the intent of the regulation had not changed over the period. The bargain struck in 1978 had held up; dire predictions of politicization of the market or loss of benefits to tenants had not come to pass. At this point, it was possible to take stock of the costs and benefits of rent stabilization and renegotiate its terms.

BENEFITS AND COSTS OF
RENT STABILIZATION: 1978-1984

The *1984 Rental Housing Study*, conducted under the auspices of the Rent Stabilization Division of the City of Los Angeles's Community Development Department, attempted to provide a comprehensive review of the impacts of the system during the preceding five years (Hamilton et al. 1985a, 1985b; Rent Stabilization Division 1984). Using surveys of both tenants and owners, it sought to measure the benefits and costs of the system, as well as estimate the impact on the housing market as a whole, especially in terms of production of new housing and maintenance of the existing stock. The findings were quite illuminating.

For the city's 1.3 million tenants, living in about 489,000 units, it was clear that rent stabilization had done what it promised to do—that is, stabilize rent increases and provide a reasonable degree of assurance to tenants about future increases they might face. However, the study also showed that the combined effect of permissible increases and vacancy decontrol meant that the average rent had risen by about 11 percent annually, virtually the same rate of increase that had taken place in comparable noncontrolled areas outside Los Angeles. The study estimated that the net financial benefit constituted a flow from landlords to tenants ranging from $40 million to $106 million per year, amounting to roughly 0.3 percent to 0.9 percent of household income. However, some tenants clearly benefited much more than others. Those who had been in their units for some time and remained in them throughout the period received the largest gains, both because the rate of increase in their rents was restrained and because the rent differential between their units and equivalent units that had been vacated widened dramatically. Conversely, recent movers and new arrivals in the city appeared to be paying a premium for their units.

The study pointed out that the distribution of these costs and benefits across tenant groups depended upon their degree of longevity of tenure and their mobility. In general, lower-income households benefited from rent control, but it was the older, single-member, white, senior citizen households that benefited the most. In summary, rent stabilization appeared to be redistributive among tenants rather than between tenants and owners.

The corollary of this observation is that owners did not suffer greatly from rent control. However, measuring the financial position of owners of rental property is always a difficult task in rent control evaluations. In the Los Angeles study, a substantial effort to estimate the owners' outcomes was made, but it still fell short of the ideal. The problems with surveys of owners led the city to develop an innovative contract with the state Franchise Tax Board to generate from tax returns aggregate information about financial performance in the market. Measures of pretax return on investment, after-tax return, and internal rate of return all produced similar results, both for buildings within Los Angeles and for those outside the rent-controlled area. Rates of return proved to be extremely volatile from year to year, but taken over the period as a whole, they showed disadvantageous rates of return during the early years of rent stabilization, followed by higher relative rates in the later years.

On the basis of this information, it is difficult to make a case that the viability of rental housing was seriously threatened by rent stabilization, especially once inflation had been checked and owners were more confident that the new regulations would not be changed arbitrarily. Those who sold their properties immediately after the enactment of rent control lost money relative to owners in non-rent-controlled areas, but those who did not sell were able to realize advantageous returns by the end of the period. This result was consistent with the finding of the tenant analysis that the overall net gains to tenants were small. However, because operating costs accounted for a larger share of building expenses in Los Angeles than in surrounding communities, the pressure on return to investment and perhaps on maintenance may have been greater. Ironically, the most likely factor supporting owners' returns in the city and outside were the benefits from tax gains due to Proposition 13.

IMPACTS ON MAINTENANCE, REINVESTMENT, AND NEW CONSTRUCTION

Aside from rent, the two other major areas of concern about the impact of stabilization are housing quality and new construction. Conventional economic theory argues that both should be negatively affected by the imposition of regulation.

Housing quality is difficult to measure in the absolute sense, and even more problematic to measure in terms of change. In the Los Angeles study, both tenant interview data and administrative information on capital improvement were employed. Although tenants reported some indication of declining quality in rental housing, the decline could not be attributed to rent stabilization per se, since the rate of decline was faster in non-rent-controlled comparison cities. Overall, the housing stock in Los Angeles appeared to be reasonably well maintained, which is what would be expected if rates of return are competitive. Capital improvements data present a similar picture. The amount of capital improvements actually reported under the provisions of rent stabilization for compensatory rent increases was tiny, both in comparison to the number of units in the stock and in comparison to reported improvements by tenants and owners alike. Apparently, the combination of low vacancy rates, vacancy decontrol, and permissible rent increases was sufficient to encourage reinvestment. It is significant that the least-satisfied tenants, in terms of maintenance, were those who had the longest tenure. These were also the tenants receiving the highest levels of imputed monetary benefits from rent stabilization; apparently their landlords were less responsive to maintenance requests.

Is rent control a major disincentive to production of new rental housing? A careful analysis of new housing production in Los Angeles in comparison with surrounding non-rent-controlled communities revealed a sharp absolute and relative drop in new multifamily housing production during the initial years of the ordinance. This change was clearly counter to a regional cyclical upswing, and is most likely attributable to the initiation of rent control. However, just as in the case of rental housing operation between 1981 and 1984, production of new rental housing in the city exceeded that in the comparison areas. A statistical analysis of new construction, using both comparison areas and the differences in construction in Los Angeles before and after the appearance of rent control, indicates that most likely controls had a negative impact in the period immediately following passage of the rent moratorium and ordinance, but the impact was modest and diminished over time (Rent Stabilization Division 1985). This finding is entirely consistent with a "learning theory" of behavior on the part of owners, developers, and investors. If they discover that a rent control ordinance is only moderate in its impacts and is not subject to arbitrary change within the time dimension appropriate to their discount rate, then they will continue to invest, maintain, and build.

ADJUSTMENT AND CONSOLIDATION: 1985-1995

Following the initial rent control period and the first rental housing study, a city council review provided an opportunity for amendment of the ordinance and the reopening of issues by tenant and owner advocates. The result was a major change in the way in which rent adjustments were defined, followed by a long period of relative stability in the structure of the system. The environment of the system, however, was to change substantially over the years.

Adjusting the System: 1985–1986

One of the key objectives of the 1984 study was to assess the impacts of the rent adjustment mechanisms that had been part of the original design and to evaluate alternatives. The flat 7 percent adjustment figure was questioned by owners and tenants alike, though by 1985 tenants were much more vociferous in their objections. On May 30, 1985, after some debate, the city council introduced the first major change to the system since 1979 and amended the rental adjustment procedure. The new provision allowed for a maximum annual automatic rent increase equal to the average change in the regional CPI over a twelve-month period ending September 30 each year.[6] Upper and lower limits of 8 percent and 3 percent, respectively, were imposed, reflecting continuing fears on the part of tenant and owner advocates about future inflationary patterns, since actual implementation of rent increases lagged the CPI by about nine months.

This new provision marked a very significant change, but perhaps an even more important development in the evolution of rent control was that the city council avoided any general overhaul of the ordinance. Only three other lesser alterations were made to the ordinance. In 1986, relocation assistance was mandated for tenants evicted for "no-fault" reasons, including owner occupancy, major rehabilitation, or permanent removal from the housing stock. Shortly afterward, minimum room sizes and occupancy standards were adopted, and new mobile home parks were made exempt. Evidently, the council was adhering to its policy of amending the ordinance only after careful review, a key to preserving the law's credibility.

Evolution of the Impact of Rent Stabilization: 1985-1987

By 1988, it was possible to test the effects of the new amendments to the ordinance on tenants, owners, and the housing market. Since the essential structure of the ordinance had not changed, it was also possible to evaluate rent stabilization in light of the rather different market environment of the mid-1980s. Both of these aspects were addressed in the *1988 Rent Stabilization Review*, using a similar, though not identical, methodology to the one employed in 1984.

The most striking feature of the 1984–1987 period was the significant increase in benefits received by tenants under the system. Annual net tenant benefits were estimated at $137.6 million in 1987, 29 percent greater than in 1984. The increase in tenant benefits was primarily attributable to the installation of the CPI-based annual rent adjustment, which held rent increases significantly below the previous level. Evidence from vacancy decontrolled units indicated that, absent the restrictions, the market would have commanded a 7 percent annual increase in rents—in which case the benefits would have flowed to the owners. As in 1984, the controlling factor in the allocation of benefits to individual tenants was length of tenure in the rental unit. By 1987, the longest tenure under rent stabilization had increased to nine years. For tenants in this category, an average saving equal to about 5 percent of their annual income was attributable to rent stabilization. Other tendencies observable in 1984 were also reinforced. Households that gained most from stabilization tended to be older, smaller, with low to moderate incomes, and were more likely to be headed by whites. Conversely, those households that gained least were younger, with moderate incomes, small to medium in size, and equally likely to be white or nonwhite. Evidently, although the policy shift had made a difference, when regarded in tandem with changes in the larger housing market and over the longer time period rent stabilization had existed, the policy shift tended to reinforce benefit patterns that were previously in place.

For owners, the evidence from the 1988 study was more limited than in 1984, making inferences difficult. Presumably, an increase in net tenant benefits implied a corresponding cost for owners. However, the data did not confirm or deny that possibility. Owners' expenses continued to rise in relation to income, but average net operating income per unit also rose in 1986, the only year for which data were available. For other years, there was no evidence that any major shift toward unprofitability occurred.

A similar conclusion also emerged from the analyses of maintenance and reinvestment in the housing stock and the production of new rental housing. Although, overall, tenants viewed maintenance somewhat more favorably in 1988 than in 1984, those with the longest tenure were more dissatisfied than others with their apartments and with landlords' responses to their complaints. New rental housing construction actually boomed in the city during the mid-1980s, but this surge was probably due to changes in the tax code that had a short-term impact, together with other larger changes that are discussed below. Altogether, there is little to suggest that rent stabilization was having an impact any greater than it had in the prior period.

But, if the rent stabilization system was stable during the mid-1980s, the environment in which it operated showed signs of major change. The *1988 Rent Stabilization Review* (Hamilton et al. 1988) revealed several disturbing trends in Los Angeles. Both the population and the economic base of the city were beginning to shift. A remarkable burst of immigration, especially from Latin America and Asia, was altering the ethnic composition of the city. These immigrant households tended to be younger, less educated, poorer, and more frequently nonwhite than the population at large. At the same time, the economy was polarizing. The growth of federal defense expenditures in the early and mid-1980s had caused a huge expansion of high-technology, defense-related employment in the Los Angeles metropolitan area. These well-paying jobs boosted incomes and the housing market. Meanwhile, the influx of low-skilled immigrants stimulated the growth of low-wage sectors, such as apparel and shoe manufacture, providing employment opportunities for and attracting even more immigrants. In summary, by the late 1980s, Los Angeles was enjoying a remarkable boom, which in turn was reflected in rising pressure on the rental housing market. Despite rent stabilization, average rents rose faster than inflation or incomes; the overall average rent-to-income ratio also increased modestly. However, the share of income paid for rent rose very sharply for Hispanics and other minority groups, even as it fell for white and African-American households. Evidently, rent stabilization was able to exert only a limited influence on housing market outcomes in conditions of

change—a characteristic that would become even more evident in the suc-
ceeding years as Los Angeles's economic fortunes turned in the opposite
direction.

Rent Stabilization in the 1990s:
A Changing Environment for Regulation

By the early 1990s, the changes that the 1988 study had picked up were
clearly confirmed, but the overall picture had shifted once again. The most
important change was the onset of the 1990–1992 national recession and
the end of the defense boom in Los Angeles. By the time the *1994 Rental
Housing Study* was published, what had been one of the most vibrant economies in the country was in serious straits. Unemployment had risen to levels not seen since the Depression. Median household incomes, which had
shown modest increases during the decade 1980–1990, had fallen sharply,
especially among tenants in rent-stabilized housing. Reflecting the new
immigrant population, average household size in the rent-stabilized stock
rose by 25 percent between 1977 and 1990, doubling the incidence of severe overcrowding. Housing production also collapsed, from almost 25,000
new units in 1990 to less than one thousand in 1992. Finally, as an added
blow, on January 17, 1994, the city was struck by a devastating earthquake,
which rendered 19,000 housing units uninhabitable and damaged an additional 309,000 units, at a total cost of $1.6 billion.

The collapse of the economy, ironically, had a beneficial effect for tenants, as vacancy rates rose to levels not experienced in two decades. At the
end of 1993, the vacancy rate in multifamily housing was almost 9 percent,
more than three times its 1977 level. Even the earthquake losses could not
offset this gain. As a result, median real gross rents rose only slightly for
the stabilized stock, and average rents fell. Evidently, owners were unable
to garner the full permissible increases, and vacancy decontrol simply
dumped units into a very weak market. Nonetheless, whatever gains might
have accrued to tenants were more than offset by disastrous falls in income. By 1993, the median gross rent-to-income ratio for rent-stabilized
tenants had risen to 35 percent, up from 27 percent in 1987. Once again,
unaffordability loomed as a major issue in the city, especially for large,
low-income, primarily Hispanic households.

Under these extraordinary circumstances, it is not surprising that rent
stabilization benefits to tenants were reduced. The estimated average benefit, in 1993 dollars, fell from $20 per month in 1987 to about $8 per month
in 1993; total estimated real tenant benefits fell from $118 million to $43
million. Virtually all of the financial benefits accrued to tenants who had

occupied their units for nine or more years. As in previous years, many of the tenants with long tenure were in the older age groups. But interestingly, in 1993 a relatively strong rental market in South Central Los Angeles also seemed to have resulted in a small increase in benefits to African Americans, while benefits declined for all other groups. Although it cannot be rigorously demonstrated, one inference from these findings is that moderate rent control ordinances of this type seem to confer financial benefit only in circumstances of substantial pressure in the rental housing market. Otherwise, moderate rent control appears to become financially irrelevant.

In the difficult situation of the early 1990s, owners of rental housing appeared to fare little better than their tenants. For the first time since the late 1970s and early 1980s, the available data suggested that owners experienced declines in net operating income. Between 1988 and 1992, average expenses per unit, in real dollars, showed a slight increase of about 1 percent, while average gross rents fell by about 10 percent (Hamilton et al. 1994a, 46). Since financing costs fell by only 3 percent over the period, average real pretax cash flow plummeted 28 percent. Such a drop, if sustained, should certainly lead to falling maintenance expenditures. However, neither the data on expenditures nor the tenant interviews suggested any significant decrease at the time of the study.

What happened to rent stabilization in the midst of this turmoil? In the formal sense, very little. Apart from some changes in relocation policy and payments, the ordinance has not been significantly amended since the 1988 review. But rent control in Los Angeles is now almost twenty years old, and the market environment has changed radically. Some important issues have emerged.

LOS ANGELES RENT CONTROL AFTER TWO DECADES: REVIEW AND ASSESSMENT

An often overlooked feature of regulatory systems is the evolution that occurs both within them and between them and their environment as time passes; and second-generation rent controls have elements that ensure that changes will occur. One such feature is the almost universal exemption of new rental construction from regulation. If the system works and a substantial amount of housing is built, then paradoxically, seeds will be sown for later political conflict as the nonregulated part of the stock grows in relation to the regulated portion. This conflict surfaced in New York City in the late 1960s, when political pressure from non-rent-controlled tenants led to rent stabilization and sparked an immensely complex chain of events.

In Los Angeles in 1990, about 14 percent of total rental units were less than twelve years old. However, in some subareas occupied by middle-income households, as much as 25 percent of the units fall into this category. These households pay higher than average rents and in general incur higher rent-to-income ratios than those prevalent in the stabilized stock. They may well regard their situation as disadvantaged. Up to now, the low level of rental pressure in the market has generated little incentive to extend regulation. When these units are added to the 22 percent of units that are excluded from stabilization, however, as well as to the number of single-family houses that are rented, the nonstabilized part of the stock could represent a strong constituency if pressure on rents begins to increase. It is notable that the *1994 Rental Housing Study* addressed the issue of nonstabilized housing for the first time. If a movement to include the nonstabilized stock within the stabilization system were to arise, it would represent a serious challenge to the system's viability and the implicit bargain between tenants and owners that has existed since the beginning of rent stabilization.

A similar argument might be made in regard to vacancy decontrol, which also was examined in the 1994 study. This argument, however, appears to have been preempted by the passage of the Costa-Hawkins Act by the state legislature in 1995, which mandated that all local rent control ordinances include vacancy decontrol. Still, the Act was passed by virtue of Republican control of the legislature after many previous attempts failed, and there is no assurance that it will remain in place in the future. The appeal of vacancy control was altered significantly by a key court decision in the 1990 case of *Searle v. City of Berkeley Rent Stabilization Board*, which held that under vacancy control an indexing system for net operating income and expenses must be in place. Such a system could be potentially more costly to tenants as well as very expensive to administer.

Although these threats to rent stabilization in its current form appear unlikely to materialize, they need to be considered in the light of the changing real estate environment. By 1994, it had become evident that conditions in the housing market had worsened for both tenants and owners. Rising rent-to-income ratios, increases in overcrowding, and evidence that more households were living in substandard accommodations, such as garages, suggested that there was, indeed, an affordability crisis for the city's low-income population. The conclusion of the 1994 study that rent stabilization could do little to ameliorate these problems does not mean that it will not be pressed into service if there is the political will to do so. In fact, there is some evidence that the historic balance within the city council may have shifted to the left, even though the city elected a Republican mayor in 1993 to replace the retiring long-term Democratic mayor. The council and the now renamed Housing Department have become increasingly concerned with habitability issues, and have been edging toward tightened regulation. As the financial profitability of operating rental housing in Los Angeles declines, the confidence of owners and investors in the Los Angeles rental housing market may also drop, producing disinvestment and a possible cycle of intensified publicity and more stringent regulation. One of the few areas in which constant efforts have been made to modify the rent stabilization ordinance in recent years is in relocation assistance for no-fault evictions. Such payments have generally been expanding in scope and scale, suggesting that political pressures for change in rent stabilization may be growing. At this point, no one can say what is likely to be the next stage of development of rent stabilization, but a move toward a more stringent system cannot be ruled out.

In conclusion, one obvious point in favor of moderate rent control is simply that it has survived with only moderate change in a politically complex environment in Los Angeles. And it has survived in the face of enormous shifts in the larger economic and social character of the city. Rent stabilization has delivered financial benefit to some tenants and has increased the security of tenure of most. Tenants like it; the proportion of those surveyed who knew that they were living in a rent-stabilized unit grew from 55 percent in 1987 to 64 percent in 1993. When asked what they would be prepared to pay in order to avoid vacating their present unit, tenants universally valued the benefit of occupancy much higher than what was estimated in the study. Tenants also understand that the ordinance provides protection for them from eviction. However, their awareness of market reality is also evident. Whereas in 1984 tenants claimed they would be willing to pay up to an additional 25 percent of their current rent to keep their unit, by 1993 that hypothetical percentage had declined to 7 percent. Furthermore, for owners and investors, the system has not proven to be an excessive financial burden, although clearly they do not like it. Except in the adverse market of the past five years, rental housing has been profitable, and the construction of new rental housing has not been inhibited.

Skeptics would point to a different set of conclusions. Rent stabilization has not been able to prevent continuing increases in the housing cost burdens of poor tenants, who are now living in much more overcrowded conditions and paying higher rents than they were before the ordinance was enacted. The benefits are very unequally distributed, determined almost entirely by length of tenure and the degree of pressure in the housing market. Although benefits have shifted toward minority households recently, for most of the last two decades, these households have not gained much from the system. The vulnerability of the system to external conditions is similarly reflected in the varying outcomes for owners over time.

The *1994 Rental Housing Study* argues that rent stabilization has had very different consequences depending on whether the housing market was inflation driven (1979–84), demand driven (during the boom of 1984–1989), or recession driven (1989–1993) (Hamilton et al. 1994b, 246). But whether these varying outcomes have been disadvantageous or advantageous is debatable. In the current dire circumstances of the Los Angeles housing market, rent stabilization is probably best described as a marginal factor. Its greatest effect appears to have been in smoothing the impacts of housing market fluctuations on tenants in times of inflation without destroying owners' incentives to stay in business. At other times, it has also provided tenants with some security of tenure in the face of locally hot markets. Keeping it in place as an insurance mechanism against the inevitable return of pressure in the housing market may not be a bad idea.

Acknowledgments

I am grateful to many people for their insights about Los Angeles housing and rent control over the past years, especially Barbara Zeidman, James Fleck, Francine Rabinovitz, and Michael Smith-Heimer. Responsibility for any errors is mine alone.

Notes

1. New York City, which is larger than Los Angeles, also has a second-generation rent control system, but its structure is confounded by fifty years of conflict and change.

2. This discussion of the adoption of rent stabilization in Los Angeles is drawn from personal interviews, documents, and from an unpublished case (Chapman 1981).

3. As with all such ordinances, there were also a number of lesser exemptions that applied only to a small number of units. In Los Angeles, the "luxury" category was defined by a combination of rent level and number of bedrooms.

4. No precise count of the number of legally covered rental units existed then, nor does it exist now. The presence of rented condominium

units creates some degree of uncertainty, as does the failure of some owners to register. Nonetheless, the number of units outside the regulatory system is almost certainly quite small.

5. Actually, there were at least two earlier studies. A 1980 survey generated data, but did not evaluate rent stabilization (Clark et al. 1980). A 1981 study by Rand researchers developed an interesting model of impacts but had no data on the period of regulation (Rydell et al. 1981).

6. The actual adjustment mechanism uses the average change in the Los Angeles Consumer Price Index from October to September each year. Permissible new rent levels become effective on January 1 of the following year. Thus, there is substantial lag. In the first year only, there was a further minor adjustment.

KENNETH K. BAAR

10

New Jersey's
Rent Control Movement

INTRODUCTION

In New Jersey, approximately 120 cities, including all nine cities in the state with 70,000 or more inhabitants, have rent control ordinances. Most of these ordinances were adopted in the first half of the 1970s (Baar 1977). The rent-controlled cities contain about 70 percent of the state's one million rental units. Generally, the controls are very moderate, with provisions for vacancy decontrol and substantial annual increases.

BACKGROUND FOR THE EMERGENCE OF
RENT CONTROL IN NEW JERSEY

During the 1960s, a substantial number of large multifamily housing complexes were constructed in suburban New Jersey communities, as the state's population grew by 18 percent. Traditionally, such housing had been regarded as a way station to homeownership. However, as single-family home prices soared, middle-income households became locked into tenancy. Rapidly rising rents, which accompanied soaring house prices, were attributed primarily to housing shortages rather than to the cost of new construction or apartment operating cost increases (Marino 1975). Between 1960 and 1970, median rents increased by 64 percent, compared to a 33 percent increase in the CPI during the same period.[1]

142

In response to the substantial rent increases—which commonly ranged from 20 percent to 40 percent—and to decreasing maintenance, lower- and middle-income tenants in moderate-sized towns in the northeastern section of the state (suburbs of New York City) started to organize and strike (Kahn 1994, 80).

Tenant-organizing efforts were especially successful in large complexes where renters predominated. Strikes were a particularly safe and effective tactic under New Jersey law, because striking tenants who withheld their rent could not be evicted if they agreed to pay the rent when they appeared in court in response to an eviction suit.[2] Overall, the tenants' efforts received widespread publicity. In 1970, the New Jersey Tenants Organization (NJTO) was formed, and a business machine company president from Fort Lee was chosen to head the fledgling organization.

THE SPREAD OF LOCAL RENT CONTROL ORDINANCES

During 1970 and 1971, the NJTO pushed for statewide rent control legislation, since the state supreme court had ruled in 1957 (*Wagner v. City of Newark*) that municipalities did not have the power to adopt rent control ordinances. Although many legislators supported the NJTO's efforts, no action was taken. However, the tenants were able to obtain a legislative ban on retaliatory evictions, which afforded protection to tenant leaders.

After the state failed to act, the tenant organizers turned their attention on municipalities and tried to force them to take action, notwithstanding judicial precedent. In smaller cities, a concentration of middle-class tenants in large complexes, who were used to voting and having their demands met, could wield substantial political power by casting a significant portion of the votes in a local election. Since suburban communities were not plagued by other urban problems, rent control became a central campaign issue.

In 1972, a superior court ruled that municipalities could adopt rent control ordinances. The court concluded that although state legislation sixteen years earlier contained an intent to preempt the local rent laws, the legislation was not indicative of current legislative intent. In 1973, this decision was affirmed by the state supreme court (*Inganamort v. Borough of Fort Lee* 1973).

Federal price controls were also terminated in 1972. When it became clear that the state would not pass a rent control law, local controls were adopted in most cities that housed a significant number of rental units. By 1975, more than one hundred municipalities had adopted ordinances, most of them modeled after the Fort Lee ordinance. In general, these ordinances provided for annual rent increases tied to the Consumer Price Index (CPI), surcharges (pass-throughs) for property tax increases, hardship (fair return) increases, and capital improvement increases. Most did not provide for vacancy decontrol, however. The laws were administered by volunteer boards without staff and were called rent "leveling" rather than rent "control" ordinances, in order to distinguish them from the much maligned legislation in nearby New York City.

As the inflation rate soared in the mid-1970s (more than 9 percent per year), many cities amended their ordinances to limit annual increases to a portion of the increase in the CPI or a flat percentage. Interestingly, during this period, landlords started to support statewide rent control legislation in the hope of obtaining more favorable treatment. The NJTO opposed such a step. Although the state did not adopt rent control regulations, it did adopt the nation's only statewide "eviction except for cause" law, which limited the grounds for eviction to specified just causes.[3]

LEGAL CHALLENGES

Although the *Inganamort* decision in 1973 settled the local powers issue, a host of other constitutional issues remained regarding the specifics of rent control ordinances. Outside of New York, these issues had been addressed only within the context of war-era federal price controls, which were deemed "temporary emergency" measures. In 1975, the New Jersey Supreme Court issued three rent control decisions simultaneously, which covered the major legal challenges to the new ordinances. Specifically, the court ruled that:

1. The existence of an "emergency" was not a prerequisite to the validity of an ordinance (*Hutton Park Gardens v. West Orange*);
2. An ordinance did not have to provide for full CPI increases (*Brunetti v. Borough of New Milford*); and
3. An ordinance did not have to permit rent increases adequate to cover operating cost increases, since apartment owners may have been receiving excessive profits before the imposition of rent controls (*Troy Hills Village v. Township Council of Parsippany-Troy Hills*).

In addition, the court went to great lengths to address the issue of "fair return," which was a constitutional requirement. The principles enunciated in the ordinances were very general, often too vague to be useful, and/or totally impractical. The court rejected the view that a return based on value is appropriate in the context of rent regulation. It explained:

Rent control begins with the premise that rents are being unfairly inflated as a result of failure in the free operation of the rental housing market— e.g., housing shortages, monopoly power, etc. A standard of valuation which itself incorporates this failure will quickly defeat the purpose of rent control. Thus, valuation based on inflated rents would inevitably and erroneously lead the courts to the conclusion that a regulation which fails to permit such inflated rents is confiscatory. (*Troy Hills Village v. Township Council of Parsippany-Troy Hills* 1974, 44)

Rather than completely reject the return-on-value concept, however, the court developed an alternate concept of value—a form of equilibrium value—for the purpose of measuring fair return under rent regulations. This was defined as a value in a market "free of aberrant forces . . . in which the supply . . . is just adequate to meet the needs. . . ."

Hence we employ the term "value" in the present context to refer to the value of the property in a rental market free of the aberrant forces which led to the imposition of controls . . . [i.e.,] the worth of the property in the context of a hypothetical market in which the supply of available rental housing is just adequate to meet the needs of the various categories of persons actively desiring to rent apartments in the municipality. (*Troy Hills Village v. Township Council of Parsippany-Troy Hills* 1975, 44)

In regard to a fair rate of return, the ruling declared that the task of the courts was to determine the lowest constitutionally permissible rate, and that this rate was largely a determination of "fact." In order to ascertain this "fact," the court offered the following very general guidelines:

[A] rate of return must be high enough to encourage good management including adequate maintenance of services, to furnish a reward for effi- ciency, to discourage the flight of capital from the rental housing market, and to enable operators to maintain and support their credit. A just and reasonable return is one which is generally commensurate with returns on investments in other enterprises having corresponding risks. (*Troy Hills Village v. Township Council of Parsippany-Troy Hills* 1974, 47)

However, localities did not adopt the equilibrium value approach.

Three years later, apartment owners challenged a Fort Lee ordinance that limited annual across-the-board rent increases to 2.5 percent per year. This time the court concluded that the "value-based criterion" that it had proposed three years earlier "is practically unworkable" in a rent control context. Regarding the task of "estimating value in a hypothetical housing market where supply and demand are in equilibrium," the court observed that "none of the [expert] witnesses had performed such an analysis before; none knew of any recognized appraisal method for making hypothetical equilibrium valuations" (*Helmsley v. Borough of Fort Lee* 1978, 72).

The court introduced a different fair return concept, ruling that: "At some point, steady erosion of NOI (net operating income) becomes confiscatory." In other words, over the long run, rent controls should permit rent increases that are adequate to cover operating cost increases. With regard to return-on-investment formulas, the court gave mixed messages. On the one hand, it stated that formulas that discriminate based on financing terms serve no legitimate public purpose. In the same decision, however, it concluded that "there are no obvious theoretical obstacles to using an investment-based standard." In fact, investment formulas provided landlords with a specified rate of return on the cash investment, net of mortgage payments. Discrimination based on financing terms, therefore, is inherently part of the return-on-investment approach.

The 1975 decisions indicated that localities had broad discretion in setting the parameters of rent ordinances. In 1977 the state supreme court struck down a freeze on the rents of units occupied by low-income senior tenants. Under the ordinance in question, the municipality would pay up to, but not more than, an additional 10 percent of the rents for units occupied by seniors in the event that the landlord was entitled to additional rents after the rents of other units had been raised 15 percent. The court found that such a provision was an improper method of addressing the needs of low-income seniors; it deprived owners of a fair return and shifted onto them a subsidy role that was properly a public burden (*Property Owners Ass'n. v. Township of North Bergen* 1977). Subsequent legal challenges to rent controls have generally been rejected—for example, a challenge to the requirement that substantial code compliance be a precondition to rent increases (*Orange Taxpayers Council v. City of Orange* 1980); a claim that rent controls denied equal protection because units in smaller buildings were exempt (*AMN, Inc. v. South Brunswick Rent Leveling Board* 1983); and another fair return challenge (*Mayes v. Jackson Township* 1986).

THE PROPERTY TAX BURDEN ISSUE AND THE SPREAD OF VACANCY DECONTROLS

After failing in the state legislature and the courts, apartment owners shifted to an emphasis on exploitation of homeowners' fears about property tax increases. Apartment owners argued that rent controls reduced the value of apartments and, therefore, increased the share of the property tax burden that had to be covered by homeowners (Sternlieb and Hughes 1979). In the early 1980s, apartment owners organized publicity campaigns, funded studies on the issue (e.g., Harney 1980; Smith 1981), and filed tax appeals en masse. In some cities, they obtained millions of dollars in assessment reductions.

In fact, the interrelationships between homeowner property tax levels and rent controls were usually small and difficult to determine. In many communities with rent control ordinances, apartments constituted only a small portion of the tax base. A reduction in their value, therefore, had no significant impact on the tax burdens of single-family dwellings. But successful tax appeals were possible en masse because apartments, on average, were assessed at a higher ratio to value than single-family dwellings. The assessments, therefore, should have been reduced whether rents were controlled or not.

Measurement of possible connections between actual trends in assessments and rent controls was further confounded by the fact that the "coefficient of dispersion" (the average variation between market values and assessed values) was so high in New Jersey cities that shifts in assessments were as likely to reflect "refinements" (i.e., corrections) of assessments as to reflect changes in values. Before the adoption of rent controls, apartment owners commonly preferred to pass along tax increases rather than contest them. After rents were controlled, apartment owners began to file tax appeals, which yielded tax reductions for them and homeowner support for vacancy decontrol. (For a detailed discussion of the debate over the impact of rent controls on the property tax base, see Baar 1984.)

In response to concerns over the impact of rent control on the tax base, most rent-controlled cities adopted vacancy decontrols. Although apartment owners would have preferred to see the repeal of rent controls, the introduction of vacancy decontrols permitted market-rate increases in rents for many units, since the turnover rate of apartment tenants was very high. Data from the 1990 Census indicated that more than 25 percent of all tenants had moved into their units within the past fifteen months; two-thirds had moved in during the past five years. Vacancy decontrols were also politically more palatable to localities than the repeal of rent controls, because protections for current tenants were retained. Presently, about two-thirds of the ordinances in the state, including those that cover eight of the nine largest rent-controlled jurisdictions, contain vacancy decontrol provisions. In order to deter harassment of "sitting" tenants, a significant portion of these ordinances also require landlords to provide statements from departing tenants indicating that they have not been harassed, as a precondition for vacancy increases.

CONDOMINIUM CONVERSIONS

In the 1980s, a strong condominium market developed in New Jersey, and conversion of apartments to condominiums became widespread. In response to concern over the displacement of tenants as a result of the conversions, the state adopted legislation in 1981 that permitted conversions to continue but provided low- and moderate-income seniors with lifetime protection against evictions from converted buildings.[4] The act also specified that owners of the converted condominiums must wait at least three years before evicting non-senior tenants, and that any property tax increases associated with revaluations connected with conversions could not be passed through to tenants. In 1984, the U.S. Court of Appeals rejected a constitutional taking challenge to this law, based on the theory that the law authorized a physical taking of apartment owners' property by extending tenant occupancies (*Troy v. Renna* 1984). Ironically, the three-year-notice provision often benefited landlords by delaying sales in the first half of the 1980s, until after condominium values soared.

Between 1980 and 1987, 60,457 apartments (about 6 percent of the rental stock) were converted to condominiums. During that period, the volume of new apartment construction barely exceeded the number of apartments converted to condominiums. In some communities with an especially attractive condominium market, a substantial portion of all units were converted; in some counties there was even an overall loss of rental units between 1980 and 1990. In 1988, a state task force concluded that "the practicable limit of rent increases, even in the absence of controls . . . might be insufficient to meet investors' profitability goals; and conversion and withdrawals would remain a preferable investment option" (State of New Jersey 1988, 10). In other words, even market rents could not compete with the potential values associated with conversions. In Bergen County, where a sizable portion of the conversions took place, the median condominium value reached $167,000 by 1990. Additional incentives for conversions may also have been provided by the fact that some local ordinances exempted condominiums from rent controls. Since the late 1980s, the market for condominiums has weakened; as a result, the volume of conversions has been minimal.

STATEWIDE EXEMPTION OF NEW CONSTRUCTION FROM RENT CONTROLS

As in other jurisdictions with rent regulations, claims have been made that the rent controls in New Jersey have deterred new construction.[5] (For a contrary view, see Gilderbloom 1980.) Unlike the property tax burden issue, however, homeowners have not been particularly concerned with new apartment construction; indeed, they often oppose such construction. But the state government and the courts have undertaken substantial efforts to try to force localities to permit more apartment construction.

In 1987, despite NJTO opposition, the state adopted legislation that exempted newly constructed units from rent controls for thirty years or the period of amortization of the initial mortgage.[6] This legislation was touted as the route to overcoming insufficient apartment construction. In the past few years, however, multifamily construction levels have been even lower than before—in the range of only two to three thousand units per year, about one-quarter the level of the decade before the adoption of the new construction exemptions. (For construction data, see New Jersey Department of Community Affairs 1996, 13.)

CHARACTERISTICS OF CURRENT ORDINANCES

As noted earlier, approximately three-quarters of the New Jersey ordinances contain some type of vacancy decontrol provision. In a few cities, the vacancy decontrols are "permanent"—i.e., the units remain exempt from controls; they are not subject to new restrictions at the base levels established for the new tenants. A few jurisdictions have placed ceilings on vacancy increases, typically in the range of 15 to 35 percent; a few have restricted the frequency of vacancy increases to once every few years.

More than half of the ordinances allow for fixed annual percentage increases. These fixed amounts, usually in the range of 4 to 6 percent, have substantially exceeded the less than 4 percent average annual increases in the Consumer Price Index (CPI) for the past ten years. The ordinances that tie annual rent increases to the percentage increase in the CPI usually allow the landlords to capture the CPI increase in full. A few of the CPI standards have ceilings on the amount of the annual increase, typically about 5 percent. Under some of the ordinances, larger annual adjustments are allowed for units where the landlord pays for heat or all utilities.

About half the ordinances also allow for a pass-through of property tax increases, in addition to the annual general adjustments. Pursuant to state law, apartment owners must also pass through to their tenants any property tax reductions resulting from tax appeals. Buildings with a small number of units, usually between two and four, are typically exempt from the ordinances. Some of the ordinances limit such exemptions, however, to owner-occupied buildings. In the past decade, few changes have been made in the ordinances.

OVERVIEW

With vacancy decontrols and annual allowable increases generally equal to the rate of increase in the CPI, most New Jersey ordinances have not been a major constraint on the overall rate of rent increases. Indeed, median monthly rents in New Jersey rose 165 percent—from $223 to $592—between 1980 and 1990. By comparison, the CPI increased 59 percent, and the median income of renter households increased 112 percent during the same period. Nonetheless, the controls have provided significant protection, in the form of security of tenure, and have served as a ceiling on rents in areas where landlords could have commanded much higher rent increases.

Notes

1. A portion of this increase could be ascribed to new construction and the elimination of lower-rent units through demolition. During this decade, the new multifamily permits equaled about 15 percent of the multifamily stock.

2. 2A N.J.S.A. Ann., Sec.18-55.

3. N.J. Stat.Ann., Sec.2A:18-61.1 (1974).

4. N.J.S.A. Sec.2A:18-61.23.

5. As of 1990, 13 percent of all renter-occupied housing had been constructed since 1980.

6. N.J.S.A. 2A:42-84.3. (1987).

W. DENNIS KEATING

11

Rent Regulation in New York City:
A Protracted Saga

INTRODUCTION

New York City has had the greatest experience with rent regulation of any municipality in the United States. It has operated under some form of rent control—federal, state, or local—for more than half a century (1920–1929 and 1943–1998). These rent controls have been administered by public agencies, landlord self-regulation, and court-administered arbitration. During most of the 1920s and from the mid-1950s through the late 1960s, New York City stood alone as the only major U.S. city that controlled residential rents. Part of the reason for the persistence of controls is the very high percentage of New York residents who are tenants.

New York City's rent control policies have always been controversial, and landlord–tenant conflict has been a recurring feature of New York City politics, as well as a recurring subject in the city's courtrooms. Despite numerous studies, the impact of rent control on New York City's housing, tenants, and landlords remains in dispute.

THE COMPLEX HISTORY OF RENT CONTROL

Post-World War I (1920–1929)

New York City's first rent legislation, which was enacted in April 1920 (table 11.1), expanded tenants' rights by extending written leases and giving

151

tenants limited protection against arbitrary evictions. For the first time, tenants gained the right to defend themselves in court, based upon the presumption that a rent increase of 25 percent or more was "unjust, unreasonable, and oppressive."

The 1920 Rent Laws were passed in the politically charged atmosphere of the post-World War I "Red Scare." Tenant agitation for housing reform, led by the Socialist Party, began in 1917. Investigative committees appointed by the mayor and the state legislature confirmed the existence of emergency conditions (Drellich and Emery 1939). Just before adoption of this legislation, however, the state legislature expelled its Socialist members, who had been rent regulation's leading proponents (Spencer 1986). In this context, rent control can be seen as a temporary expedient designed to defuse social unrest and radical political agitation.

The laws placed administrative responsibility in the hands of the state judicial system rather than the city of New York. New York City's trial judges at the time were overwhelmed with massive numbers of eviction cases. The glut of cases, in fact, was one of the factors that led to the passage of the Emergency Rent Laws in September 1920. The new laws strengthened tenants' rights against eviction and instituted judicial arbitration to decide on the reasonableness of contested rent increases. Landlords had to submit evidence on their income and expenses. Over time, the courts developed allowable rent increase guidelines based on a fair rate of return for landlords of 8 percent of market value. Despite a conservative judicial climate, the New York Court of Appeals and the United States Supreme Court upheld the constitutionality of peacetime rent control as a temporary measure to address a housing crisis (Baar and Keating 1975).

Tenant organizing shifted from protest to representation of tenants in court, and organizers also began lobbying to preserve the rent legislation, which required renewal every two years. As the postwar housing crisis ebbed, tenants' political influence waned. The 1926 state renewal of the legislation exempted higher-priced apartments and limited rent control to only one year. The last state authorization legislation expired in June 1929. In the fall of that year, the New York City Council passed its own rent control ordinance, but this was ruled unconstitutional for lack of state authorization. As the Great Depression began, rent control ended in New York City.

The Great Depression and World War II (1930–1945)

With rents depressed and vacancies high during the 1930s, rent control was not a major concern. The Depression did result in considerable tenant

TABLE 11.1
Chronology of New York City Rent Regulation System

1920	*Rent laws preventing evictions and regulating rents are passed.*
1921	*United States Supreme Court upholds New York rent regulations.*
1929	*New York City's rent laws expire and are not renewed by the state legislature.*
1942	*President Franklin D. Roosevelt signs the Emergency Price Control Act, the enabling legislation establishing federal wartime rent controls.*
1943	*Federal rent control is administratively imposed in New York City.*
1947	*The Federal Housing and Rent Act of 1947 exempts apartments built after February 1947 from national rent control.*
1950	*The New York State legislature passes the Emergency Housing Act of 1950 that establishes the State Temporary Rent Commission to oversee New York State's rent control system.*
1962	*The Emergency Housing Act of 1962 gives New York City the responsibility of administering its rent control system.*
1969	*Rent stabilization begins in New York City. Rents in buildings built after 1947 and previously decontrolled units in buildings of six or more units are brought under rent stabilization. The Rent Guidelines Board, the Rent Stabilization Association, and the Conciliation and Appeals Board (CAB) are established to administer rent stabilization.*
1970	*New York City approves the Maximum Base Rent system, introducing the concept of economic rent to the city's rent-controlled stock.*
1971	*The Vacancy Decontrol Law of 1971 is imposed by the state, providing for the decontrol of all controlled and stabilized units after a change in tenancy.*
1974	*The Emergency Tenant Protection Act terminates vacancy decontrol for rent-stabilized apartments and requires that vacated rent-controlled units in buildings of six or more units come under rent stabilization after a free-market rent (subject to tenant challenge as excessive) is negotiated with the new tenant.*
1984	*New York State once again assumes full responsibility for administering New York City's rent regulation system. The CAB is eliminated.*
1993	*The Rent Regulation Reform Act extends the rent regulation system through 1997.*
1997	*Rent regulations renewed through 2003 (with minor reforms).*

organizing in New York City, however, and led to the formation in 1936 of the Citywide Tenants Council (Naison 1986).

With the advent of World War II and the imposition of federal rent control in selected defense areas elsewhere in the United States, the city's left and liberal housing groups lobbied Mayor Fiorella LaGuardia and President Roosevelt's Office of Price Administration (OPA) to freeze rents. Initially, OPA refused, claiming that the city's rental vacancy rate was too high to justify rent control. In the wake of an August 1943 Harlem riot and threatened rent strikes if landlords did not exercise voluntary restraints, however, OPA changed its mind and imposed a wartime rent freeze, beginning November 1, 1943, and retroactive to a "base" date of March 1, 1943 (Naison 1986; Tucker 1990). Thus began the longest continuing rent control saga in the United States.

For the remainder of the war, OPA, aided by volunteers from consumer groups, investigated complaints about illegal rents and issued eviction certificates. Weakened by the existence of OPA, the United Tenants League, the wartime successor of the Citywide Tenants Council, disappeared in 1945 (Schwartz 1986).

Post-World War II Federal Rent Control (1946–1950)

After 1945, the federal government temporarily extended wartime rent controls in order to deal with a continued housing shortage, which was aggravated by returning veterans. Rent control became a national political football in the partisan battle between liberal Democratic president Harry Truman and the conservative Republican Congress elected in 1946. In 1947, Congress weakened federal rent control by allowing 15 percent rent increases for vacated apartments and, when tenants voluntarily agreed, authorizing landlord hardship rent increases, exempting new construction, and ending OPA review of evictions.

These changes resulted in the approval of 250,000 lease extensions with voluntary rent increases in the second half of 1947 alone in New York City (Schwartz 1986, 43). Tenant fear of additional rent increases and eviction led to a revived tenant movement and the creation of a city rent commission to adjust hardship inequities and review evictions (Schwartz 1986).

NEW YORK STATE RENT CONTROL (1950–1962)

As federal rent control was phased out, the legislature of New York created a temporary agency, the State Housing Commission, to administer state rent control. A base date of March 1, 1950, was set, and a six-month moratorium was imposed on rent increases. State rent control was based on the existence of a housing emergency and required periodic findings of a continued emergency to justify renewal of the temporary legislation.

In 1950, New York City's rental vacancy rate was 1 percent, the lowest in its history. Whether this low vacancy rate continued to exist in New York City as time passed became the subject of intense debate between landlord and tenant groups, periodic studies by the state rent commission, review by the legislature, and litigation in the state and federal courts. Rent control could be terminated only when the rental vacancy rate reached 5 percent, which has never occurred. The most recent vacancy survey, conducted in 1996, found an overall rental vacancy rate of 4 percent (New York City Department of Housing Preservation and Development [NYCDHPD] 1997).

Under the state rent control system, all regulated units were required to be registered with the commission. Rent increases were allowed for voluntary lease renewals (15 percent maximum); increased operating costs and services; major capital improvements and/or substantial rehabilitation; and the establishment of a fair return (set at 4 percent of equalized assessed value plus a 2 percent depreciation allowance). Basing fair return upon assessed value determined under the city's byzantine assessment system complicated landlord appeals. Newly constructed apartments were exempt.

In 1953, an across-the-board rent increase of up to 15 percent over the World War II base level was permitted, and the return on assessed value was increased to 6 percent. In 1957, a limited luxury decontrol policy was initiated. State rent control policy has generally been described as one that encouraged rent increases, renovation, and gradual decontrol (Kristof 1970). As a result, rent control was somewhat weakened during the 1950s. However, what is more significant is that rent control survived at all. New York State was at that time the only area in the country where rent control continued to exist.

NEW YORK CITY MUNICIPAL RENT CONTROL (1962–1969)

In 1961, tenants and liberal reform Democrats were successful in strengthening the state rent control law during the New York City mayoral election campaign. Following the reelection of liberal Democratic mayor Robert Wagner, Republican governor Nelson Rockefeller in 1962 persuaded the state legislature to delegate the administration of rent control back to municipalities.

Generally, the city's rent control system was similar to the state's. The city's Rent and Rehabilitation Administration (RRA) emphasized neighborhood conservation and building rehabilitation. The Metropolitan Council on Housing (Met Council), formed in 1959, led the opposition to this policy on the ground that it would encourage gentrification and the displacement of poor tenants, especially minorities (Schwartz 1986).

According to 1960 Census data, 77 percent of New York City's rental housing stock (1,605,427 units) was rent-controlled. The rental vacancy rate was only 1.8 percent; the median gross monthly rent for rent-controlled units was $72, compared to $127 for units that were not controlled (e.g., newly constructed units) (RRA 1966). According to economist Frank Kristof, the rent controls administered by the city were overly restrictive and puni-tive, leading owners to cut back on maintenance and services (Kristof 1970). Kristof argued that rent controls, coupled with expanded tenant rights to withhold rent in substandard housing, led to the loss of approximately 100,000 units between 1965 and 1968, undercutting the city's rehabilitation policies.

The causal connection between rent control and abandonment has been much disputed. Substantial evidence exists that rent control alone does not cause abandonment, contrary to landlords' repeated claims. Instead, the age, condition, and location of a building, the financial situation of owners and tenants, the incidence of amateur landlord speculative invest-ments and mismanagement, and tenants' dependency upon welfare assis-tance to pay rent are all important contributing factors (Bartelt and Lawson 1982a; Marcuse 1981). Housing abandonment in New York City was con-centrated in the most distressed neighborhoods, where absentee landlords "milked" slum buildings. This pattern was similar to abandonment in other cities, like Cleveland and St. Louis, which had never enacted rent control.

In urging the relaxation of rent control, landlords have argued that middle- and upper-income tenants could afford to pay higher rents. No rent control system has ever been means-tested, however. Kristof estimated that during the 1960s, rent-controlled landlords were providing subsidies amounting to $220 million annually to tenants with yearly incomes of $8,000 or more. Other economists have similarly argued that the benefits of rent control were not equitably distributed, because upper- and middle-income tenants benefited disproportionately (Gyourko and Linneman 1985; Linneman 1987; Roistacher 1972). Tucker (1990) and others have provided anecdotal evidence to dramatize this argument.

Rent control critics have also argued that rent control restricts tenant mobility. In New York City, since landlords were entitled to a vacancy al-lowance of 15 percent and were eager to capture it, they claimed that rent control made tenants reluctant to move, thus limiting apartment turnover and leading, eventually, to underutilization of space by long-term tenants (Fisher 1966).

More data emerged from a study of rent-controlled landlords conducted by Rutgers University economist George Sternlieb (1972). Sternlieb's study of 9,863 rent-controlled buildings concluded that the majority of owners of the older buildings were not real estate professionals, that they typically owned between one and three buildings, were undercapitalized, had difficulty obtaining "conventional" mortgage financing, and could not adequately maintain their buildings at controlled rent levels and realize a reasonable return on their investment.

Sternlieb's report was reinforced by a companion study conducted by the New York City Rand Institute (New York City Rand Institute 1970). The Rand study concluded that rent increases averaging 2.4 percent annually between 1962 and 1969 had not kept pace with the increased costs of providing well-maintained housing. Keeping pace would have required annual rent increases averaging almost 6 percent. When incumbent liberal Republican mayor John Lindsay sought reelection in 1969 as a "fusion" reform candidate, housing became a campaign issue. Landlords, citing Kristof and the Rand and Sternlieb reports, demanded that the rent control system be revamped to allow for higher rents to improve maintenance and profitability.

Additionally, the owners of post-World War II rental housing that had been exempted from rent control threatened major rent increases, and the largely middle-class tenants of the 365,000 units built since 1947 demanded protection. These tenant demands could not be ignored by the embattled mayor. However, Lindsay was committed to rent control reform and opposed its extension to the unregulated rental stock. During 1969 and 1970, this commitment led to two major changes in New York City's rent regulation policies, as Lindsay won a second term in a hotly contested three-way race.

NEW YORK CITY MUNICIPAL RENT CONTROL (1969–1983)

Rent Control Reform: Maximum Base Rents (1970)

Based on the Rand and Sternlieb studies, the Lindsay administration recommended implementation of Maximum Base Rent (MBR), the first major change in the post-World War II rent control system. Rents were to be increased across the board, in amounts determined by the individual operating costs of landlords. In order to receive rent increases sufficient to cover operating and maintenance costs and provide a fair return on investment, landlords were required to certify that major housing code violations had been removed. Compliance required considerable paperwork and assumed greatly expanded data processing and code enforcement capability on the part of the City. To appease tenant opposition and protect those with lower incomes, MBR rent increases were not to exceed 7.5 percent annually for "sitting" tenants. Low-income elderly tenants were to receive special protection through grants of tax abatements to their landlords in return for lower rent increases. Rents for vacated apartments could be increased to full MBR rents immediately.

The MBR compromise legislation was adopted in 1970, and was to take full effect in 1972 once landlords had supplied the necessary data concerning rents, operating and maintenance costs, building conditions, and code compliance. MBR represented an attempt to rationalize graduated rent increases, increase code compliance, encourage rehabilitation, and protect tenants against steep rent increases.

However, MBR was hampered by numerous problems. Many landlords did not attain the code compliance required for eligibility for rent increases. The city ran into difficulty processing and reviewing landlord requests for rent increases and was not able to conduct the necessary code inspections to determine the extent of compliance (Hsia 1974). The complexity of the MBR system made it extremely difficult to administer and left both landlords and tenants dissatisfied. The MBR system also had much less impact than envisioned, because in 1974 a large portion of the rent-controlled housing stock was transferred to the newly formulated rent stabilization system (see following section). Whereas in 1970 there were 1,265,000 rent-controlled units eligible for MBR (Sternlieb 1972), by 1993 only 102,000 occupied rent-controlled units remained eligible (Lopez 1995). By 1996, this had dwindled to only 71,000 units (NYCDHPD 1997).

Rent Stabilization (1969–1973)

The concept of rent stabilization was introduced during the summer of 1969, as the Lindsay administration sought to negotiate a new form of rent regulation for post-World War II rental housing. This housing was newer, more expensive, and denser than the older rent-controlled housing stock, and it was mostly owned and managed by professional landlords and developers. In light of these distinguishing characteristics, a mayoral advisory committee and the real estate industry jointly created a system for landlord self-regulation.

This rent stabilization system had four important features. Regulated landlords (those owning six or more units) formed a Rent Stabilization Association (RSA), which developed a self-governing code. The RSA had the power to investigate tenant complaints and to discipline member landlords for violating its code. A Conciliation and Appeals Board (CAB) was appointed to resolve landlord-tenant disputes. RSA membership dues funded the CAB. An appointed Rent Guidelines Board (RGB) met annually to determine rent increases for lease renewals (ranging from one to three years) and vacancy leases (up to one year). The RGB's decisions were based in part on an annual survey of landlords' operating and maintenance costs. The city's Housing and Development Administration (HDA) was in charge of overseeing the RSA and its code. HDA could punish landlords who did not belong to the RSA or who did not comply with its code by placing their buildings under rent control (Keating 1987).

Rent stabilization differed significantly from rent control. First, landlords had a dominant influence over policy. Second, tenant influence was intentionally minimized. Third, rents were not registered; landlords were to inform their tenants of the legal rent. Fourth, the RSA dues were modest and the city's regulatory role was limited. Finally, landlords were guaranteed annual rent increases tied to operating and maintenance costs (Keating 1987).

During its initial term of five years, rent stabilization overcame its first two hurdles. The city forced the RSA to revise its code and successfully defended the constitutionality of landlord self-regulation against a landlord lawsuit. The RGB's rent increase guidelines covered operating and maintenance cost increases and also included a vacancy bonus and an allowance for increased mortgage interest. The small CAB staff disposed of tenant complaints and a handful of landlord hardship appeals. From the landlords' perspective, rent stabilization was a success, at least compared to the alternative of rent control. The landlords encountered little conflict with tenants; the annual rent increases exceeded increased operating and maintenance costs; and the public oversight of the RSA was negligible.

Vacancy Decontrol (1971–1973)

In 1971, Republican governor Nelson Rockefeller persuaded the state legislature to intervene in rent regulation in New York City for the first time since it had delegated this authority to the city in 1962. Despite the city's opposition, the legislature permanently decontrolled all vacated rent-controlled and rent-stabilized apartments. A companion law prohibited New York City from passing any rent control legislation stronger than that which already existed. Rockefeller's stated reasons for mandating vacancy decontrol were to arrest the deterioration of the rental housing stock said to result from rent control and to provide the incentive necessary for developers to build new housing which would not be regulated (Lawson 1986).

The passage of these twin laws at the state level seemed to spell eventual doom for rent regulation in New York City. Although the attrition process would be gradual, apartment turnover guaranteed that most units would eventually return to market rent levels. Whereas "sitting" tenants would be protected against displacement, future tenants would have to pay much higher rents. Politically, this was the most palatable approach for landlords; it prevented tenants from claiming that they were about to be evicted wholesale or had suffered massive across-the-board rent increases.

Two events quickly nullified the impact of Rockefeller's intervention, however. First, Republican president Richard Nixon unexpectedly imposed temporary federal wage and price controls in August 1971. These superseded New York State's vacancy decontrol regulations. The federal rent controls continued until January 1973. Upon their expiration, tenants headed to Albany for relief. Their hopes were raised by the resignation in December 1973 of Governor Rockefeller, who became President Gerald Ford's vice president.

Emergency Tenant Protection Act (1974)

In 1974, tenant lobbying led by the newly formed New York State Tenants and Neighbors Coalition (NYSTNC) and the Met Council prevailed over landlord opposition. In successfully arguing for repeal of vacancy decontrol, tenant advocates cited the enormous rent increases in decontrolled units that had taken place without improved maintenance; they also cited widespread illegal landlord harassment of tenants to force vacancies. However, the state's preemption of stricter rent regulation laws in New York City remained in place.

This complex compromise was known as the Emergency Tenant Protection Act (ETPA). Henceforth, the units that were deregulated between 1971 and 1974 were once again to be placed under regulation. They were not to be subject to strict rent control, however. Instead, largely because of the administrative problems with the MBR system, the units were incorporated into the rent stabilization system, originally intended only for post–1947 apartment buildings. In addition, all units built after 1969, which had been exempt, were now subject to rent stabilization. Landlords and tenants were charged with determining the appropriate regulated rent for the more than 500,000 deregulated units; the CAB was to calculate a fair market rent when landlords and tenants disagreed. ETPA was also applied to several New York City suburban counties where the state Division of Housing and Community Renewal (DHCR) was to administer rent stabilization.

ETPA was especially noteworthy for several reasons. For the first time, tenant lobbying in Albany achieved a more tangible result than simply blocking landlord efforts to weaken rent control. Nonetheless, the ETPA compromise spelled the eventual demise of the rent control system, since vacancy turnover would eventually place all the rent-controlled housing under the rent stabilization system. The incorporation of the older rent-controlled housing into the rent stabilization program would also contribute to the demise of landlord self-regulation.

Landlord Self-Regulation (1974–1983)

The addition of the older, smaller, and more substandard units previously under rent control to the rent stabilization system made the process of issuing rent guidelines, setting rents, responding to tenants' complaints, and ensuring landlord compliance much more complex. During the mid-1970s, the energy crisis and rising inflation (which translated into higher RGB guidelines), coupled with declining tenant income, led to increasing landlord–tenant conflict over regulated rents. With the city in the throes of a fiscal crisis and more conservative federal housing policies in effect, low- and moderate-income renters foresaw little prospect of relief.

Largely as a result, both landlords and tenants of rent-stabilized units became more politicized. The veneer of impartiality that was designed to shield the RGB and the CAB from political and public pressure, especially tenant pressure, was pierced and then collapsed utterly as the board's policies were subjected to criticism and legal attack from both sides. The 1977 election of neoconservative mayor Ed Koch added to the conflict. Koch, who had sponsored rent stabilization as a city council member, unabashedly favored the interests of landlords and developers. His favoritism was reflected in his appointments to the RGB and CAB, appointments the NYSTNC heartily opposed.

Tenant groups led by the NYSTNC and the Met Council launched an attack on landlord self-regulation based on:

◻ Nonrepresentation of tenant groups in Mayor Koch's selection of tenant representatives to the RGB and CAB.

◻ The failure of the CAB to process tenant complaints efficiently; the CAB's favoritism toward landlords; and the lax treatment by the CAB of landlords who were found to violate the RSA code (e.g., those who imposed illegal rent overcharges).

◻ The failure of the city to intervene to curtail RSA abuses (e.g., lobbying to end rent stabilization).

The RSA, dominated after 1978 by the owners of the old rent-controlled housing, also attacked rent stabilization, complaining primarily of the alleged inadequacy of the RGB's rent increases. The RSA lobbied to repeal rent stabilization or at least reintroduce vacancy decontrol. The RSA also initiated the first lawsuit that overturned an RGB rent increase order.

THE RETURN TO STATE-ADMINISTERED RENT REGULATION (1983–1997)

The RSA and tenant groups battled in both New York City and Albany. Finally, in 1983, the NYSTNC won a partial victory with the passage of the Omnibus Housing Act. The Act curtailed the authority of the CAB, ceding it instead to the New York State Division of Housing and Community Renewal (DHCR). After two decades, administration of rent regulation in New York City was returned to the state of New York. The most significant change that ensued was a new requirement that stabilized rents be registered. This change, together with the imposition of more severe penalties, was designed to eliminate allegedly widespread overcharging. The RGB was still authorized to set rent guidelines, however, and the RSA was authorized to continue its activities.

By 1985, DHCR had registered almost one million units, but the state's assumption of administrative responsibility was beset by serious problems. The state had inherited a backlog of 100,000 complaints, including thousands of tenant complaints of illegal landlord overcharges. DHCR took several years to resolve this massive backlog; meanwhile, the NYSTNC accused it of simply dismissing many tenant complaints without cause.

By 1987, the RSA's oversight role had been eliminated, leaving the RGB as the only administrative body established by the original 1969 legislation still in existence. Landlord and tenant groups continued to challenge its annual orders, and controversies continued. In 1994, the RGB, for the first time, added a surcharge ($15 monthly) to low-rent units (those with monthly rents of $400 or less) in small buildings (defined as having thirty or fewer units). The RGB also considered other policies to increase rents in "distressed" buildings. Vacancy allowances continued.

With inflation lower in the early 1990s, the annual rent increases were also generally lower than in the 1980s. Nevertheless, tenant groups continued to oppose the RGB guidelines. In 1993, the state legislature renewed rent regulations for four years (through June 1997) but conditioned this renewal on the introduction of luxury decontrol. Beginning in October 1993, apartments with a monthly rent of $2,000 or more were decontrolled upon vacancy, or if still occupied, were subject to decontrol if the tenants earned more than $250,000 annually. Although this stipulation affected only a tiny number of the 979,000 occupied rent-stabilized apartments in 1993, tenant advocates worried that another attempt might be made to expand this regulation to total vacancy decontrol. Their fears were well founded. In 1993, New York City elected a Republican mayor, and in 1994 New York State elected a Republican governor; both replaced liberal Democrats.

In December 1996, the Republican majority leader of the state senate, Joseph Bruno, announced that he would not allow an extension of the rent regulation laws upon their expiration in June 1997 unless they were to be totally terminated by 1999. Bruno indicated, however, that he favored continuation of protection in some form for elderly and disabled tenants. Since the Republicans commanded a five-vote majority in the state senate, this announcement triggered the most dramatic public debate over rent control in New York in years. A landlord-sponsored study projected average rent increases of 13 percent in New York City after decontrol, with much higher increases in certain locations and given certain tenant characteristics. Tenant advocates countered that most tenants and the neighborhoods in which they lived would be negatively affected (Kolbert 1997).

Although landlord organizations had poured large contributions into the coffers of Republican legislators during the period 1992–1996 (Dreier 1997; Perez-Pena 1997), Republican politicians had mixed views on rent control. For example, New York City's mayor, Rudy Giuliani, up for reelection in November 1997, opposed changing rent regulation legislation, while Governor George Pataki, up for reelection in 1998, favored gradual rent decontrol. Several key Republican senators with large tenant constituencies held pivotal votes. The Democratic speaker of the New York state assembly, Sheldon Silver, held fast against weakening the rent laws and attacked leading Republicans for favoring landlords over tenants.

For six months, public debate raged. Landlords ran a very expensive advertising campaign in favor of rent decontrol. Tenant organizations, led by the NYSTNC, organized tenants to pressure pivotal Republican senators and staged well-publicized rallies in Albany and New York City (Dreier 1997). A June 1997 *New York Times* poll of the city's residents showed that 80 percent opposed termination of rent controls, including two-thirds of homeowners (Firestone 1997).

With pressure growing for a compromise, Governor Pataki proposed vacancy decontrol, which if accepted would have reinstated Rockefeller's 1971 reform, leading to eventual termination by attrition. Democrats in the state legislature, led by Speaker Silver, opposed vacancy decontrol, however. A compromise did not emerge until after midnight on June 15, 1997, the expiration date of the existing laws. Instead of termination or vacancy decontrol, landlords were guaranteed vacancy bonuses of 20 percent for two-year leases when a tenant vacated. Luxury decontrol was expanded to include apartments occupied by tenants with annual household incomes of $175,000 or more, whose monthly rent amounted to $2,000 or more. And tenant succession rights were limited to one generation only. With these relatively minor changes, the legislature then extended rent control for six years, into the next millennium (Dao 1997).

THE DEBATE OVER RENT CONTROL AND ITS IMPACT

Despite the voluminous data generated by triennial housing and vacancy surveys and major studies by such organizations as the Rand Corporation and well-known housing experts like Peter Marcuse, George Sternlieb, and Michael Stegman, disagreement about the impact of rent control abounds. No one claims that rent regulation, whatever its form or implementation, has solved New York City's rental housing problems. Instead, the debate has centered on whether rent control is part of the solution or part of the problem.

Tenant advocates have argued that rent control policy has been unduly influenced by real estate interests to the detriment of tenants, especially lower-income tenants. They point to rising rent-to-income ratios of tenants, especially those with very low incomes. They decry the levels of rent increases allowed by the RGB. They complain about the inadequacy of the city's code enforcement efforts.

Yet, despite these flaws, tenants defend rent control as an essential protection against the threat of widespread tenant displacement if decontrol were to occur. With massive waiting lists for public housing, cutbacks in federal and state housing-subsidy programs, and a limit to the amount of subsidized housing that the city of New York can itself finance, rent regulation provides a form of protection against arbitrary evictions and steep rent increases.

Conversely, landlord organizations, their consultants, and academic critics argue that rent control has reduced the supply of available housing and its quality because regulated rents have not provided sufficient income to operate and maintain rental housing and yield a fair return on investment (A. D. Little 1985; Salins and Mildner 1992). They decry the inefficient administration of rent control and argue that its benefits are inequitably distributed, with better-off tenants—those least in need of protection—benefiting disproportionately (A. D. Little 1985; Linneman 1987).

The claim has been made that rent control has destroyed much of the rental housing market and resulted in the city of New York owning hundreds of thousands of units abandoned by landlords and taken over by the city in lieu of delinquent property taxes (Starr 1985). This claim has been disputed (Marcuse 1981, 1986). In the face of such contrasting conclusions, Stegman (1985) has observed that rent control's impact is muddled and mixed due to its long history of policy changes and politics.

THE POLITICS OF RENT CONTROL

New York City's rent control system was born amid political conflict. That conflict, involving organized landlords and tenants, the governments of New York City and New York State, and, on occasion, the federal government as well as political parties, has waxed and waned but nonetheless persisted since the 1920s. Tenants initially organized to enact rent control as protection against high rents and eviction. Later, tenants remained organized to enforce rent control and to lobby against landlord attempts to weaken the regulations. Landlords organized initially to defeat the enactment of rent control, then to repeal or weaken it. On both sides, rent control has at times become an ideological issue. Radical left organizers and groups have seen housing as a basic necessity whose price should be controlled, with housing treated as a public utility. Some have promoted rent control as a stepping stone toward the conversion of privately owned rental housing into limited-equity cooperatives. At the other end of the political spectrum, conservatives have seen rent control as a frontal assault on private property and the right of landlords to control and profit from their apartments without government oversight.

The political left has often been at the forefront of tenant organizing. Beginning with the Socialist Party during World War I, continuing with the Communist Party and the American Labor Party during and immediately after World War II, political radicals have supported rent control. With the demise of these parties, tenant organizers joined forces with the labor movement and often became leaders in the housing reform movement. A good example of this evolution was the Metropolitan Council on Housing. In the 1970s, however, the Met Council split into two separate organizations. One branch became the New York State Tenants Legislative Coalition (NYSTLC), an organization much more pragmatic in its orientation than its parent (Lawson 1986).

The leverage of the tenants' movement on local and state politicians has been most effective during electoral campaigns when tenants can be mobilized to support or oppose politicians based on their position on rent control. Rent control and its application to the unregulated rental sector were pivotal issues in the 1969 mayoral election, for example.

Landlords, on the other hand, have generally been more effective in influencing public policy and electoral politics through campaign contributions. Although most elected representatives in New York City publicly support rent regulation, not all of them endorse the positions of tenant organizations. In practice, the administration of rent control has been undercut on occasion by political appointees more sympathetic to the views of landlords than to those of tenants (Dobkin 1989). The real estate industry has regularly mounted media campaigns attacking rent control and hired consultants to produce studies that invariably indict rent control as a failure.

In the 1970s, a split developed within the ranks of landlords. The major real estate owners and operators in New York City formed the Rent Stabilization Association (RSA). The RSA was a self-regulatory body that preferred to stay out of the public limelight. But the smaller owners, whose units were then covered by rent control, became a very public presence. They formed the Community Housing Improvement Program (CHIP), which demanded an end to rent regulation. CHIP engaged in protest and litigation in pursuit of this goal. These political differences among landlords culminated in the takeover of the RSA in 1978 by the smaller owners; a CHIP slate won control of the board of directors. The RSA then became more publicly militant in demanding changes in the rent stabilization system (RSA 1980).

For almost four decades, tenant and landlord groups have engaged in this recurring public debate, often in the form of demonstrations and lobbying at New York City Hall and at the State Capitol in Albany, arguing over the extension and reform of rent regulation. The annual RGB hearings on rent increases have become organized shouting matches between tenant and landlord groups.

Overall, this long-standing political conflict has resulted in a stalemate. When landlords won the MBR reform of rent control in 1970, tenant opposition blunted its impact. After landlords won state vacancy decontrol in 1971, tenants won its repeal in 1974. After tenants succeeded in limiting landlord self-regulation in 1983, landlords prevented broader reforms. In 1997, tenants prevented a return to vacancy decontrol, while landlords won some minor concessions. Overall, while tenants have succeeded in keeping rent control alive for more than four decades, they have enjoyed little success in winning reforms to strengthen it. While landlords have defeated far-reaching tenant regulatory proposals, they have never been able to repeal rent control.

Still, most conflicts have been between individual landlords and their tenants (sometimes numbering in the thousands in large housing projects). These conflicts are over building conditions, as well as rent levels, and have resulted in tenant organizations conducting rent strikes, landlords abandoning buildings, and considerable litigation in the courts. A sizable part of the rental sector is currently exempt from the city's rent regulations. In 1993, this sector included 174,000 city-operated public housing units, 79,000 units of state-assisted housing, and 643,000 other units. The last category included city-owned property taken in foreclosure for nonpayment of property taxes and rental units in condominium and cooperative buildings.

RENT REGULATION IN THE COURTS

Landlords have repeatedly challenged the constitutionality of rent control, claiming that it violates state and federal constitutional guarantees of contract, due process, and equal protection, and that it represents a taking of private property without just compensation. Landlords have also regularly challenged the government's use of "police power" to regulate rents in the absence of a housing emergency. But beginning with its initial decision in 1920, the New York Court of Appeals (the highest state appellate court) has upheld the right of the state to control rents in the face of a legislatively defined housing emergency. Its decision has been further upheld by the United States Supreme Court. Despite repeated attempts by landlords to convince the courts that an emergency no longer exists in New York City, the courts have permitted rent control to continue based on the legislative findings of an emergency (Baar and Keating 1975).

Most of the litigation over rent control concerns four issues. First, there is the question of whether an apartment is subject to regulation. Second, quite often the courts are asked to determine procedurally whether administrative guidelines, statutory mandates, or due process requirements have been met in the treatment of landlords and tenants. Third, tenants contest evictions on numerous grounds related to the legal requirement for just cause for eviction. These eviction cases usually do not involve nonpayment by tenants, but rather involve conflicts over a tenant's legal status or a landlord's behavior or motivation. Fourth, many individual tenants contest rent increases on the ground that they are either unauthorized or excessive. In addition, both landlord and tenant groups have challenged the validity of the annual rent guidelines approved by the Rent Guidelines Board (Keating 1987).

CONCLUSION

What can be learned from this saga? From a tenant perspective, rent control, although flawed in its design and all too often in its implementation, has nevertheless kept much of New York City's rental housing affordable to millions of tenants who otherwise would have been denied housing, been displaced, or forced to pay a higher percentage of their income for rent. Low- and moderate-income tenants unable to secure federal- or state-subsidized housing have benefited in particular.

From a landlord perspective, New York City's various forms of rent regulation have all failed to maintain housing quality, increase the supply of rental units, or provide landlords with rents sufficiently high to accomplish these goals. Landlords cite horror stories about an underground market where so-called key money is necessary to obtain access to controlled units, where illegal subletting by tenants takes place, and where a mismatch exists between those tenants in occupancy and those most in need, whether by reason of income or household size.

Given the enormous complexity of New York City's rent regulation systems, the recurring political twists and turns of rent regulation, the size of the rental market, and the disagreement among those who have analyzed the regulated market and the impact of rent control (compared to many other factors) on the supply, quality, and price of rental housing, it is difficult to give any definitive answer as to whether New York City's rent controls have worked. However, although no rent regulation adopted in New York has ever been termed permanent, "temporary" rent control—whether municipal, state, or federal—has now been in effect for forty-five consecutive years. Its future seems destined to be as controversial as ever.

CATHERINE NASH AND ANDREJS SKABURSKIS

12

Toronto's Changing Rent Control Policy

INTRODUCTION

In the fall of 1975, Ontario's minority Conservative government reluctantly bowed to public pressure to enact temporary rent regulation legislation. Not surprisingly, rent control proved substantially easier to enact than to remove, even when the initial reasons for the policy no longer existed. Over the next two decades, rent regulation became a permanent fixture of the rental housing market; its application was expanded and strengthened. But the Conservative government, which was reelected as a majority government in 1995, now stands poised to dismantle the rent regulation system that took twenty years to build. This chapter traces the implementation of rent controls in 1975 and the adjustments made to the legislation over the next two decades. It concludes by showing that the policy was successful in reducing the amplitude of the price cycle while leaving long-run price trends unaffected.

FACTORS LEADING TO THE ADOPTION OF RENT CONTROLS IN 1975

Rent "Gouging" and Low Vacancy Rates

In the late 1960s, a national debate raged over the viability and success of the Canadian federal government's housing strategy; many lower- and middle-income households were perceived to have inadequate housing and to pay unaffordable rents. Many thought that the private market could not be entrusted with a service as important as housing and that government intervention was required on a large scale to deal with the growing housing problems. The issues were hotly contested by the housing industry, economists, and others. The debates added momentum to calls for a devolution in the responsibility for housing from the federal to the provincial governments. It was within this context that the move toward rent regulation was fostered.

Economic conditions in Canada changed rapidly in the mid–1970s, with rising unemployment, falling growth in per capita income, and double-digit inflation. The Consumer Price Index (CPI) for food rose 7.6 percent in 1972, 14.6 percent in 1973, and 16.3 percent in 1974. Energy costs increased at a similar rate, as did the cost of owning a home, but rental housing costs lagged behind. Figure 12.1 shows the Toronto CPI for homeownership rising by 40 percent over the five years before rent controls were imposed, just about in step with the CPI for all items. Meanwhile, the city's new house price index rose by 50 percent during the two-year period 1972–1973. Rents during the period 1970–1975, however, increased only 20 percent; it was this very stability in a world defined by record inflation that made almost half of Toronto's residents foresee massive income transfers to their landlords. The anticipated rise in rents was expected to make most people's current housing unaffordable, at the same time that access to alternative housing was becoming more difficult in both the homeownership and rental markets.[1] Vacancy rates dropped from 3.3 percent in 1971 to 1 percent in 1975 (about the same level as in the mid–1960s); as a result, adjustments in housing consumption were very difficult to make. The recent price increases in new houses had eliminated the ownership option for most renters. Since smaller rental units were simply not available, Toronto's large tenant population, faced with a major rent hike, chose to try to check the rent rise through political action.

A series of newspaper stories in late 1974 and early 1975 publicized cases of individual hardship; they told of poor people receiving notices of 50 percent rent increases. The public saw all tenants at risk of having their quality of life reduced. Because rent "gouging" by some landlords promised lifestyle change for all tenants, rent control emerged as a leading issue in the provincial election campaign of 1975.[2]

THE 1975 ELECTION CAMPAIGN

Potential rent increases became a particularly "hot" issue in Toronto, where local tenants groups and landlords looked to their city councils for

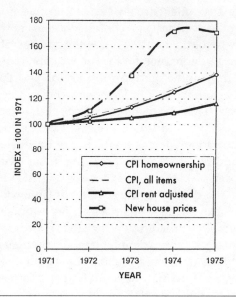

FIGURE 12.1

Changes in price indexes in Toronto before rent controls

Source: Canadian Census Public Use Microdata files

solutions. The Urban Development Institute (UDI), representing the developers, individual landlords, and their organizations, argued that rents had lagged behind the price of other goods and services and that some increases should be expected as part of a normal market adjustment. Furthermore, the UDI maintained, any apparent rent "gouging" was due either to a few "bad apples" or to a landlord's legitimate need to bring rents in line with rising operating costs. Still, even the proponents of free enterprise spoke of "unconscionable" rent increases—as though morality has anything to do with price setting in a competitive market.

The low vacancy rate in Toronto and media reports about gouging sparked wide public concern, which in turn led Toronto's city council to conclude that rent controls were necessary. Resolutions passed by the city council on March 19 and 20, 1975, asked the province for legislation that would allow the city to place a cap on rent increases of 5 percent a year and establish a rent review tribunal to review gouging complaints. By forwarding this request, the city of Toronto formally drew the provincial government into the rent regulation debate.

Most rent control opponents relied heavily on traditional economic arguments outlining the many adverse consequences of controls. They predicted the deterioration of the housing stock, the creation of a permanent housing shortage, and a depression for the construction industry. This position was supported by numerous North American and European studies, and largely as a result, the provincial government did not support any sort of direct intervention into the rental housing market. In fact, on April 19, 1974, Housing Minister Donald Irving promised the legislature that the Tories would not support any form of rent control whatever. The Deputy Minister of Housing, Michael Warren, proclaimed that rent controls had not worked in the past; he claimed that they would instead drive private builders out of the market and force the government into providing public housing for the less fortunate. In keeping with this position, the Conservative government formally turned down the city of Toronto's request for enabling rent control legislation, arguing that the government should not deal with rent controls in a piecemeal fashion but should look for solutions on a provincewide basis. Thus, the impending housing problem was placed in a larger context that would be enlarged again. Interestingly, this contextual shift would later allow the Conservative government to save face when it reversed its opposition to rent controls.

Although Toronto's bid for provincial legislation was denied, the public debate on housing issues and the perception of widespread rent gouging continued to put considerable pressure on the government to "do something." In addition, both the New Democratic Party (NDP) and the Liberal party had proposed their own form of rent control through private member bills. The Liberals saw the housing problem as created by an inadequate supply of affordable housing; they believed that the long-term solution was to build more housing units in both the rental and homeownership sectors. However, they argued that tenants needed immediate protection from rent gouging for a short-term period, while vacancy rates were low, until supply-side adjustments could ease market pressures. The leader of the Liberal party recognized that, over time, rigid rent controls would discourage new residential construction. Therefore, rent regulations needed to be a temporary measure—one that would be revoked at a later point in time.

The NDP took a much stronger position, arguing that housing was a basic human need and that anyone profiting unduly by fulfilling that need was "unconscionable." The NDP thought not only that immediate controls were needed to prevent rent gouging but that long-term controls were required to address the ongoing problems that low-income households face in finding suitable and affordable accommodation. In addition, the NDP

argued that it did not believe the "hoary mythology" espoused by the Tories that controls would reduce new residential construction. The party
proposed that properly drafted legislation could provide landlords with a
reasonable return on their investment. The NDP, however, also called for
vigorous government activity in the construction of public or socially assisted housing to expand the supply of lower-priced housing.

In response to these popular proposals, the Tories announced plans to
establish rent review boards in cities that had a serious shortage of rental
accommodation. The review boards would have no authority to roll back
rents but could use publicity to "shame" landlords into reducing their rents.
In addition, the Conservative government proposed amendments to the
existing landlord and tenant legislation that would improve the security of
tenure. The proposals were branded by the opposition as "window dress-
ing"—intended to help the Conservatives in the upcoming election, not
solve the impending housing problem. The developers' organization, UDI,
and landlord groups expressed their general approval of the Tory plan;
they all thought that review boards (without authority) were a good idea.
In approving the idea of review boards, however, all three political parties
were now committed to some form of rent regulation, and the escalating
rhetoric would eventually force the Conservatives to reconsider their position and come up with more effective proposals.

The NDP was successful in turning rent regulation into a high-profile
issue, in part by the timely release to the media of specific instances of rent
"gouging."[3] Many of these cases involved elderly households, single parents, or disadvantaged people living on fixed incomes during a period of
very high inflation. The publicized hardships of vulnerable people generated calls for government action from a broad spectrum of the electorate.
As a result, the 1975 Ontario election was fought, in part, as a "bidding
war" for tenant votes. Each party upped the ante in response to another
party's initiative on rent regulation. The Tories wound up swinging from
complete opposition to rent controls to a promise of some form of substantive rent review.

THE MINORITY GOVERNMENT OF 1975

Even after the Conservatives were reelected in the fall of 1975 with a minority government, rent control remained a major public issue. The Liberal
and NDP opposition forced the government to make major changes to its
proposed rent review legislation. Tenant groups and other social advocates
continued to lobby vigorously, and both opposition parties continued to
publicize hardship cases.[4] The minority government of William Davis

struggled through the fall of 1975 to defuse the housing issue and avoid rent controls. However, on October 13, 1975, Liberal prime minister Trudeau, as part of an overall anti-inflation policy, sought the cooperation of the provincial governments in the enactment of provincial rent controls and recommended a policy that would fix a statutory rent percentage increase per annum (after an exemption for new construction) for five years. A provision for landlords to recoup justifiable costs through rental increases in excess of the statutory minimum was also included. This introduction of controls provided the Ontario Tories with an opportunity to save face and do a turnabout on rent control. The Ontario Tories, in announcing the draft legislation enacting rent controls, argued that the policy was a necessary part of a broader national strategy to reduce inflation and that the controls were to be a temporary measure only. However, although the wage and price controls enforced by the federal government were subsequently repealed, the provincial rent regulation was not. What's more, the Ontario legislation, a compromise bill forged by a minority government and two strong opposition parties, contained relatively strong controls.

The draft legislation was sent to the select committee for public hearings between November 24 and December 8, 1975. Almost all of the sixty individuals who appeared at the hearings were landlords or their representatives, and most of the 108 briefs submitted opposed controls. Despite this opposition, the minority Conservative government implemented rent controls in December 1975.

The government was well aware of the possible side effects of rent control; these side effects had formed an integral part of the debates leading up to the 1975 policy. However, rent regulation was presented as a temporary measure, designed to "smooth out" price cycles or increase the time over which large increases in prices were to be experienced by renters. By arguing that controls were a temporary measure, the advocates of regulation could say that the predicted longer-term consequences (reduction in maintenance and repair, lower vacancy rates, and a reduction in the supply of rental housing) would not be realized. Even if the consequences did materialize, the Conservatives could deflect criticism over their responsibility for the policy by arguing that they were forced to comply with the controls, which were a part of the larger federal government strategy to fight inflation. The Conservatives could further argue that, as a minority government, they had to bow to political pressure from the opposition parties to avoid a vote of nonconfidence, which would force a new election. In the meantime, the NDP had clearly stated that it did not believe the existing research that pointed to the detrimental effects of rent regulation. Along with the Liberals, the NDP thought that properly drafted legislation could avoid the pitfalls.

THE ADMINISTRATION OF RENT CONTROLS: 1975–1986

Although the 1975 rent control legislation was enacted as a temporary measure to address specific conditions, after these problems ceased to exist, rent regulation, rather than being repealed, was considerably strengthened. Successive governments amended the legislation to address loopholes and inequities in the system, including administrative glitches. The first rent control legislation froze rents at the July 29, 1975, level and imposed an annual allowable statutory rent increase. Greater increases could be achieved, following reviews of specific problems. The result was a cost pass-through method of accounting, based on a dual system of rent control and rent review. Rental increases could be granted, for example, if necessary to prevent the landlord from sustaining a financial loss, or when the rent review officer was satisfied that the higher operating costs and capital expenses were justified. This system did not take into account the tenant's ability to pay, nor did it consider the landlord's return on equity.

The initial legislation exempted rental units constructed after January 1975 and did not apply to nonprofit or cooperative rental units, government-built housing, social housing projects, mobile homes, or home sites not occupied by rental units before January 1, 1976. The government also enacted complementary amendments to the Landlord and Tenant Act in 1979 to ensure that landlords could not evict tenants for noneconomic reasons, such as renovation or demolition. Other amendments, although incidental to rent control, also strengthened the tenants' position; one amendment, for example, increased the notice provisions required for termination of a tenancy. In effect, the 1979 amendments rendered rent regulation a permanent fixture of the housing market in Ontario. Under the 1975 legislation, tenants had the ability to require landlords to justify the *statutory* increase as well as any increase above that amount. This provision was removed in the 1979 Act. The 1979 legislation required whole-building review rather than unit-by-unit review. The 1979 legislation also exempted units renting for more than $750 a month, but this "luxury" decontrol was repealed in November 1984.

The 1979 Act introduced a new provision permitting rental increases to offset landlord "hardship." When the total rental increase allowable under the Act led to a loss, the review board could sanction a rent increase that would raise the gross revenue to a level 2 percent above costs. In addition, financial losses other than those incurred on the purchase and sale of property could be offset by a series of rent increases aimed at placing the landlord in a break-even position in five years.

In response to a perceived crisis involving the sale and resale of 11,000 rental units in the Toronto area, the 1979 Act was again amended in 1981 to address rent increases experienced by tenants after the sale of a rental property. Due to increased financing costs, tenants in several Toronto buildings faced substantial rental increases after the buildings were sold. The 1981 amendments prescribed the formula by which landlords could convert the new financing costs into rent increases, limiting the increase to 5 percent in the first year and allowing the recovery of these costs to be spread over more than five years.[5]

The Thom Commission

On November 26, 1982, the Tory government appointed Stuart Thom to head a major inquiry into rent regulation. His committee's first task was to consider the "operation of the existing system of rent regulation under the current legislation" and to consider changes designed to "provide for the fair and equitable treatment of landlords and tenants," including ways to make the system more expeditious and effective.[6] Public hearings were held, research studies commissioned, and detailed submissions made by numerous individuals and groups.

Largely as a result of this investigation, new amendments were adopted in 1986 in an effort to address landlord difficulties. These amendments substantially changed the rent regulation system in Ontario. Permitted rental increases, for example, were now to be calculated annually by a prescribed formula rather than established by regulation. The guideline increase was now to be based on the Residential Complex Cost Index, which was calculated as 2 percent or 2 percent plus two-thirds of the percentage increase in the three-year moving average of the Building Operating Cost Index. The Building Operating Cost Index included items related to the cost of maintaining a building, and the new method of calculation was intended to ensure that the permitted statutory increases more closely reflected actual increases in building operating costs experienced by landlords.

Perhaps the most significant amendment enacted in 1986, however, was the removal of the exemption for units constructed after 1975; new construction now became subject to rent controls. This move had long been anticipated, and many industry analysts argued that this expectation explained the mid-1980s decline in new rental construction. The Act contained provisions, however, ensuring that landlords could recover economic losses for buildings constructed after 1975; it allowed rent increases to cover debt costs and to yield a specified rate of return on equity—10 percent for buildings built before 1987 and 12.3 percent for buildings built in 1988. The Act also offered relief for owners of buildings constructed before 1976 where rents were determined to be "chronically" depressed. Rents in these buildings could be increased by more than the guideline amount, if the return on the landlord's equity was less than 10 percent and if the rent was determined to be, chronically, at least 20 percent below the rent for similar units in the city.

In 1986, a rent registry system was also established, requiring that the maximum legal rents for all buildings with more than six units be recorded. This information was needed so that rent control provisions preventing landlords from illegally raising rents could be enforced. The Rental Housing Protection Act, also enacted in 1986, prevented any conversion, demolition, or renovation that required vacant possession of rental units in buildings with four or more rental units, without the specific approval of the municipal authority. Conversion of rental units to condominiums was also controlled in all buildings, including those with four or fewer units. Many groups, both in favor of and in opposition to rent control, had argued that controls would drive landlords to remove rental units from the market through conversion to other uses. Although it was unclear how many substantial conversions had actually taken place, the government sought to forestall any conversion activity, concerned that it could seriously reduce the supply of rental units in Toronto.

The Thom Commission Findings: 1987

The second task of the Thom Commission was to consider whether other forms of rent regulation would treat landlords and tenants in a more equitable manner. The Commission was charged with considering the broad objectives of rent regulation and any possible alternative policies. Included in the Commission's mandate, for example, was a directive to consider any measures *in addition to* rent review that might "assist in providing rental accommodation at fair rents." Hearings on this subject began in 1984, and the findings (Thom Commission Report, Vol. 2) were submitted in April 1987.

The very nature of the Commission's mandate clearly indicated that the Tory government intended rent controls to continue. The purpose of the inquiry was to determine the difficulties and problems experienced in the existing system and to recommend solutions. Volume 1 of the Thom Commission report had contained a number of specific recommendations that were implemented in the 1986 amendments, but the crux of the Thom Commission's findings was summarized in Volume 2:

> RENTS HAVE BEEN REDUCED TO BELOW MARKET LEVELS WITH MOST OF THE SPECIFIC BENEFIT GOING TO TENANTS WHO COULD HAVE PAID MARKET RENTS. Private investors who might have invested in the

rental housing stayed out of the market with the result that the supply of new housing is inadequate. Those who are in the market have actively sought to disinvest by demolishing and converting their properties and reducing service. Vacancies have fallen to a low level and have become almost non-existent in some areas. . . . The government has been called upon in lieu of private sector involvement to invest heavily in rental housing for the benefit of low and middle income tenants; but the demand is not nearly satisfied. (Vol. 2, xx)

The Commission had considered the original intentions of the legislation and had sought to determine whether these intentions had been successfully met. The Commission's findings addressed the predictions made by the opponents of rent regulation ten years earlier and developed a number of interesting conclusions, which are presented below:

1. *Effects on the Return on Equity*

   The Thom Commission noted that the original intention of the 1975 legislation had been to implement temporary controls to fight inflation, as part of the federal government's Anti-Inflation Program. The two main thrusts had been, first, to keep rents from rising as fast as they might otherwise, and second, to protect tenants from sudden sharp rent increases. As such, the 1975 Act provided for rent increases only to the extent that they covered a landlord's increased operating costs and any capital expenditures incurred (including financing costs). The Commission concluded that this simplistic and straightforward "cost pass-through" mechanism of the original Act was appropriate in the short run only. Over the long run, the Commission argued, because the cost pass-through method did not take into account the landlord's return on equity, landlords' willingness to maintain the existing rental stock or build new rental housing would deteriorate. Under the existing regulations, landlords had tried to indirectly increase their return on equity, but the government and tenant groups had moved to close any avenues they perceived as "loopholes." The 1986 amendments were designed to partially address this issue by including economic loss provisions for post-1975 buildings that provided an explicit calculation for return on equity.

2. *Effects on Average Rent Levels*

   The Thom Commission tried to calculate the specific effects of rent regulation—e.g., it tried to measure how much less rent tenants in controlled units paid than they would have paid absent controls. Calculating this amount exactly proved to be a difficult exercise. Using several different methods, the Commission concluded that the savings was anywhere from 20 to 33 percent. One study the Commission reviewed placed that amount at only between 7.5 and 11 percent.[7] However, the Commission noted that even this low estimate represented a gross loss of revenue for landlords of "several hundred million dollars annually, extending for a period of more than a decade" (Thom Commission Report 1987, Vol. 2, 17).[8]

3. *Variation in Rent Increases*

One of the purposes of the 1975 legislation was to avoid sharp increases in rent. To that end, the regulations stipulated the statutory maximum amount by which landlords were permitted to raise rents. In practice, however, rent increases had varied widely, and it was difficult to keep track of the average price rises. Some landlords, for example, chose not to raise their rents the full amount permitted under the statutes; in such cases, the rents were not subject to rent review. It was also difficult to determine whether the rise in rents was greater than it would have been in the absence of regulation, since no system was in place to determine what would have happened in a free market. The Commission concluded, therefore, that there was no way of knowing how often large increases in rent would have occurred in the absence of regulation. For tenants who had experienced large rental increases, it was impossible to determine if those increases were in line with the market or not.

4. *Effects on Affordable Housing*

The Commission noted that one of the presumed effects of reduced rents was that rental housing would become more affordable. However, the Commission concluded that most of the benefits from reduced rents had gone to households with incomes well above the low to moderate levels; in other words, the benefits had gone to people who did not have an affordability problem in the first place.[9] Landlords seemed to select their tenants on the assumption that households with higher incomes, with few or no children, and/or those whose household head was single and professional make the best tenants. Poorer households with children were forced to find housing in the noncontrolled sector, and as a result, forced to pay higher rents. The Commission concluded, therefore, that rent regulation did not benefit the people it was intended to benefit.

5. *Reduced Return on Investment and Capital Value*

As noted earlier, the Commission determined that since 1975, rent regulations had reduced rents significantly, at the very least by some 7.5 to 11 percent. As a result, according to the Commission, landlords' return on equity was less, on average, than the return earned on alternative investments with similar risk. Moreover, the Commission deduced, this reduction in earnings had been accompanied by a decline in the value of the rental property, and the decline both in return on equity and in the value of rental property had several important consequences.

6. *Reduction in the Supply of Rental Housing*

The Commission noted that, in theory, a decline in return on equity should lead to a reduction in the supply of unsubsidized rental housing. And in fact, its review of the supply of rental housing in Ontario in the decade after the implementation of controls showed that the supply of new unsubsidized rental housing had been reduced.[10] However, the Commission pointed out that other factors were probably also at work. For example, the decline in rental housing starts began in 1974, one year before the implementation of controls. Many argued that the over-building of rental units in the early 1970s had held rents below market rates and was largely responsible for the decline in rental housing starts.[11] In addition, there had been a significant decline in household formation between 1976 and 1985, coupled with rising interest rates, increasing unemployment, and declining per capita income. All of these factors presumably had also played a role. Indeed, some studies reviewed by the Thom Commission argued that increases in financing and construction costs and higher interest rates had been more significant factors in the reduction of the rental housing supply than the existence of rent regulation.[12] However, almost all of the commissioned studies concluded that rent regulation was at least a contributing factor in the reduction in the supply of rental housing.

7. *Effects on Demolition and Conversion*

The Commission found very little evidence concerning the effect of rent controls on the demolition or conversion of rental properties to other uses. The statistical information available suggested that some conversions had taken place, but it was difficult to tell what the "usual" level of conversion in the rental market was, and whether rent controls had affected this level. The Commission did not offer any conclusions.

8. *Effects on Vacancy Rates*

The Commission reviewed the existing statistics on vacancy rates in Ontario and again noted the difficulties in drawing any conclusions. However, after reviewing regional vacancy rates for ten CMAs (Consolidated Metropolitan Areas), the Commission concluded that vacancy rates were "extraordinarily low from a historical perspective." Although any number of factors had acted to slow the growth of both supply and demand for rental housing, the Commission concluded that "Ontario's system of rent regulation is responsible for creating this crisis in rental housing availability" (Thom Commission Report 1987, Vol. 2, 35). Little or no evidence was presented to support this conclusion, however. The Commission seemed to rely on the standard theoretical arguments put forward by the opponents of rent regulation to explain the low vacancy rate.

One study undertaken for the Commission also argued that low vacancy rates had affected mobility, in that tenants in controlled units were generally reluctant to move and lose the benefit of possession of their controlled unit. Relocation for employment or because of changing housing services needs, therefore, had been curtailed. Another study prepared for the Commission, however, clearly demonstrated that tenants did not appear to be experiencing decreased mobility.

The Commission argued that the low vacancy rate could also lead landlords and tenants to charge a premium, or "key money," for controlled units; but again, the Commission had to acknowledge that evidence of this practice was hard to come by.

9. *Higher Rents for Uncontrolled Units*

Traditional theory argues that landlords who construct uncontrolled units in an area where vacancy rates for controlled units are low should be able to charge excessive rents. However, the Commission argued that the threat that regulations might extend to *all* units had reduced new construction of rental units, making this impact difficult to quantify. Furthermore, the Commission stressed that the uncertainty created by the possibility that the legislation might be extended ensured that the rents in the uncontrolled sector remained unnaturally high. The Commission referred to a review of several studies that "attempted to quantify the extent to which rents for uncontrolled units have increased as a consequence of rent regulation."[13] Based on the findings, the Commission concluded that rents for uncontrolled units in 1984 appeared to have been 9 to 10 percent higher on average than they would have been in the absence of regulation.

10. *Deterioration in the Housing Stock*

The Commission examined the theoretical argument that rent regulation leads to a decline in repair and maintenance of rental properties. Again, the Commission was forced to acknowledge that the data necessary to demonstrate this claim empirically were not available. The studies available to the Commission that pointed to undermaintenance of the stock were found to have serious methodological flaws. Landlords and property managers argued that their reduced revenues made it impossible for them to maintain and repair properties at precontrol levels. However, because rent regulation had reduced the vacancy rate, these same landlords had no difficulty in renting deteriorated units. Moreover, their current tenants were unlikely to move even in the face of reduced maintenance, given the difficulty of finding similarly priced units elsewhere.

In the end, regardless of data problems, the Thom Commission found that the rental housing stock in Ontario had depreciated more rapidly due to rent controls:

> Despite the evidence in the surveys, the combined weight of the *logical consequences* of reduced rent flows and the evidence of experienced property managers . . . indicates there is a problem of maintenance deterioration which is currently not pressing but . . . could become significant. (Emphasis added.) (Thom Commission Report 1987, Vol. 2, 41-42).

In other words, the Commission, when faced with insufficient data, fell back on the traditional economic arguments. The Commission argued that there was a maintenance problem because it expected to find one, and because landlords said they could no longer afford to maintain their buildings as they once had.

11. *The Distributive Effect of Rent Regulation*

The Commission considered the distribution of costs and benefits under rent control and concluded that the effect of rent regulation had been "mildly progressive" in distributing benefits among tenants. Lower-income households received greater benefit as a percentage of household income than did higher-income households. However, the Commission noted, this did not mean that the actual dollar value was less for higher-income households. Moreover, since not all unit rents were held down to the same degree, some tenants received more of a benefit than others.

The Commission also pointed out that there was no substantive evidence to support the idea that landlords of certain types of buildings had lower incomes than investors generally, although some anecdotal evidence suggested that this was the case. For both landlords and tenants, therefore, the rent regulation system contained components of unequal treatment.

In sum, the Thom Commission saw its task of assessing the rent regulation system as complicated by the "complete failure to compile statistics which would reveal the impact of regulation on the operation of the whole market" (p. 49). Regardless, the Commission concluded that the predicted detrimental effects of rent regulation had come to pass. Vacancy rates in several areas had reached their lowest levels ever; investment in existing buildings and construction of new rental housing had been greatly reduced; the "wrong" tenants had benefited; and landlords had suffered reduced returns on equity and declining property values. In many cases, these conclusions were not supported by evidence; in some cases, the prevailing economic theory was used to blame rent regulation.

THE SECOND DECADE: 1986–1990

Before the general election was held in May 1985, all three parties voiced their support of rent controls but differed in their recommendations for the stringency and duration of such controls. The Tories, for example, promised to keep rent regulation in place for the next four years, with the statutory rate of increase reduced from 6 percent to 4 percent. In future years, the Tories said, the statutory rate would be tied to wage and cost increases and would reflect the need for a fair return on investment. As noted earlier, this recommendation had been suggested by the Thom Commission. The Tories also promised to implement several other changes recommended by the Thom Commission, including the establishment of a rent registry to track base rents and rental increases, and the permanent implementation of the 1982 Act provision limiting rental increases to cover refinancing costs when a property was sold. The Thom Commission believed that some provision was required for "hardship relief" for landlords in certain cases; the Tories promised to address this issue as well. Finally, to confront the growing concern that owners of rental buildings were removing rental housing stock from the market through conversions, demolitions, and major renovations, the Tory government promised legislation to require landlords to maintain properties and pledged to remove the incentives to convert rental properties to luxury accommodations.

Both the Liberals and the NDP questioned the Tories' commitment to rent review, given the Tories' previous reluctance to implement controls. Both opposition parties argued that the Tories really intended to end controls. By contrast, both the Liberals and the NDP promised to extend rent controls to rental units occupied after January 1, 1975; these units had hitherto been exempt.

The Tories were reelected on May 2, 1985, with a minority government, but two months later they were defeated on a vote of nonconfidence. The opposition parties had reached an agreement whereby the Liberals would form the next government with the support of the NDP. As part of the agreement, the NDP would refrain from forcing a nonconfidence vote for two years. The Liberals would likewise refrain from requesting dissolution of the legislature for that same period. The agreement spelled out a number of specific policies the Liberals would implement, including major changes in the rent regulation legislation. The plan called for the establishment of a rent registry to record the "legal" rent for units as of July 1, 1985. It also called for a 4 percent statutory rent increase guideline, extension of rent regulation to units constructed or reconstructed after 1976, and legislative delegation of demolition control to local municipalities. The Liberal party implemented these promises; they are reflected in the 1986 amendments to the rent legislation, along with many of the Thom Commission's recommendations.[14]

The Liberals were reelected in September 1987 and remained in power until October 1990, when they were defeated by the NDP. By then, the continuing difficulties in administering rent regulations had brought about calls for a total overhaul of the legislation. Studies were undertaken by both the Liberal and NDP governments. The NDP finally repealed the 1986 Act and passed instead the Rent Control Act of 1991. This new legislation applied to all rental units and limited rent increases to an annual guideline set by the government. The guideline specified a 2 percent increase to cover major maintenance costs. Any increase above 2 percent required a formal review; an upper limit was set at 3 percent. Increases were permitted if there had been increases in heat, hydro, water, or property taxes—or if there had been an increase in interest rates upon refinancing. An increase could also be granted if a capital expenditure of the kind defined in the legislation had been made or if work had been done inside a tenant's unit with the consent of the tenant. An additional amount of up to 3 percent each year for two years could be approved by a rent review officer.

The NDP also extended the provisions of the rent control legislation to cover rooming and boarding houses and mobile homes. Pursuant to the Resident's Rights Act, rent control applied to the "accommodation" portion of the fee charged by any "care" facility, such as a drug or alcohol abuse treatment center, a rehabilitation center, or any other therapeutic facility. In addition, the NDP enacted legislation to legalize apartment units that had been created in single-family houses, if the units complied with fire and building code standards. Table 12.1 contrasts the features of this act with preceding legislation.

THE FUTURE OF CONTROLS IN ONTARIO

The Tories were reinstated in the spring of 1995 with a majority government. Never an ardent advocate of rent regulation, the Conservative government proposed a partial decontrol to take place in the spring of 1997. In the Conservatives' view, rent regulation was responsible for the deterioration in the rental housing stock and for the lack of new rental construction. The government argued that although rent legislation has smoothed out the impact of inflation on rental increases, it has at the same time discouraged new rental construction, forcing tenants to live in deteriorating conditions with ever-diminishing opportunities to find new and better accommodation. Vacancy rates have continued to decline in Toronto.

While preserving the existing guideline formula, which allows for rental increases to cover increases in capital expenditures and extraordinary increases in operating costs, municipal taxes, or utilities, the government plans to let landlords negotiate rents on vacant apartments without restrictions. Once a new rent is established, the rent guidelines will again apply. Rent guidelines will not apply to new construction, however, and the rent registry will be eliminated with maximum rents frozen at current levels. The

TABLE 12.1

Features of the Ontario Rent Regulation Legislation, 1975 to 1996

	1975 Act	1979 Act	1982 Act	1986 Act
1. Method of Regulation				
a. Control	Yes	Yes	Yes	Yes
b. Review	Yes	Yes	Yes	Yes
2. Expiry Date	December 1978	Permanent	Permanent	Permanent
3. Exemptions				
a. New construction	Yes	Yes	Yes	No
b. Public housing	Yes	Yes	Yes	Yes
c. Nonprofit and co-op units	Yes	Yes	Yes	Yes
d. Units < $750/month	No	Yes	No	No
4. Rent Increase Permitted				
a. Statutory	Once per year 8%	Once per year 6%	Once per year 6%	Once per year 4%
b. On review				
• Cost pass-through	Yes	Yes	Yes	Yes
• Economic loss (pre-1976)	No	No	No	Yes
• Return on equity (post-1975)	No	No	No	Yes
• Cash flow loss (CFL)	No	No	No	Yes
• Cash flow loss (financing)	No	Yes	Yes	Yes
• Hardship	No	Yes	Yes	Yes
5. Administration				
a. Rent registry	Yes	Yes	No	Universal registry
b. Mediation	Yes	Yes	Yes	Yes
c. Tribunal	Yes	Yes	Yes	Yes
6. Conversions/Demolition Control	No	No	No	Yes

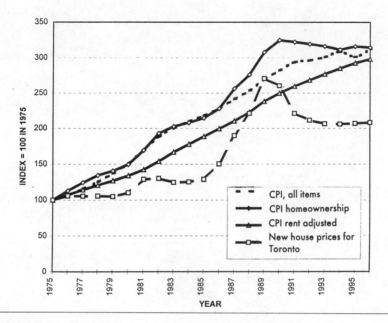

FIGURE 12.2
Changes in Toronto's price indexes, 1975 to 1996

legislation preventing the conversion of rental buildings to other uses (e.g., condominiums, co-ops, or demolition) will also be amended to remove the need for municipal approval. The government's primary strategy is to encourage new construction of dwelling units. The focus, therefore, is on protecting "sitting" tenants, rather than protecting the units themselves.

The Price Effects: 1976–1996

At least one question can now be answered in regard to the consequences of rent control. Figure 12.2 shows the changes in the major price indexes over the twenty years since the passage of rent controls and illustrates the potential volatility of housing prices. It shows rents rising in a steady manner after rent controls were in place, while the price of new housing more than doubled between 1986 and 1990. Figure 12.3 contrasts the average rent of a two-bedroom unit built before 1976 (and therefore subject to rent control) with the average rent for a unit built January 1, 1976 or after (these units were exempt for a while but were subsequently subject to controls). As figure 12.3 shows, the average price of a post-1975 two-bedroom unit is higher than the hypothetical price that would have prevailed

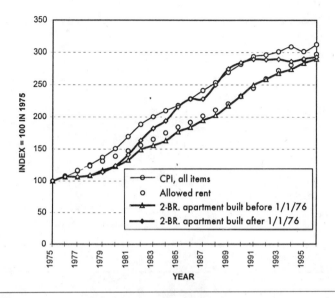

FIGURE 12.3
Comparison of rent levels for apartment buildings constructed before and after January 1, 1976
Source: Canada Mortgage and Housing Corporation

in the absence of rent controls.[15] This is because landlords generally insist on compensation for the lost opportunity to raise rents fully in the future. These data can also be used to estimate the maximum price effect that can possibly be attributed to rent controls.

Figure 12.4 shows price ratios for the housing stock built before and after January 1, 1976, deflated by Toronto's CPI for all items. It shows that the rent on the newer units generally followed price movements in the other goods and services. The top line, which tracks the ratio of the average price of units built before and after January 1, 1976, is greater than one for at least three reasons:

1. Rent controls depressed the price in the old stock
2. Depreciation reduced the value of the old stock
3. Tenure discounts are more prevalent in old stock by virtue of its age

Figure 12.4 also shows that the average price difference between the units built before January 1, 1976 and those constructed after that date rose through the first decade of rent regulation, and then fell back to its initial level during the next decade. Rent controls appear to have smoothed out the cycle and redistributed the potential income landlords might have gained to

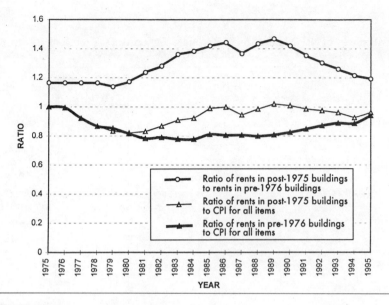

FIGURE 12.4

Ratio of rents for two-bedroom apartments built before and after January 1, 1976
  Source: Canada Mortgage and Housing Corporation

the tenants, who gained lower than "free market" rents. The maximum redistributions occurred during the 1984–1990 period, when the rent on the post-1975 stock was 40 percent higher than that on the pre-1976 units. This differential is in line with the Thom Commission's findings of the price difference attributable to rent controls. However, not all of the difference can reasonably be attributed to rent control alone. The price difference also reflects quality differences due to depreciation and the inevitable differences in tenure discounts due to the amount of time the stock has been in existence.

A simple way to estimate the price effect of Toronto's rent control policy can be developed on the assumption that depreciation rates and tenure discounts in Vancouver would have been similar to those in Toronto were it not for rent control. In 1986 and 1991, the housing markets in the two cities had the same level of activity, even though Vancouver dropped its rent controls in 1981.

We propose the following simple model. Rents are to be a function of the number of rooms in a dwelling and of the building type. People who moved in the last year will pay higher rents than people living in similar units, due to tenure discounts. People who moved within the last five years will pay higher rents than longer-term residents for the same reason. Any

TABLE 12.2

Estimates of the Maximum Differences in Rents Due to Rent Control
1986 and 1991

Variable	1986 Coefficient	t-statistic	1991 Coefficient	t-statistic
INTERCEPT	217.33	22.66	181.19	17.92
TORONTO	−31.61	−6.71	15.51	2.93
POST1976	26.57	3.51	34.16	4.10
TORONTO.POST1976	68.51	7.22	102.61	9.95
MOVE>1 YEAR	n.a.	n.a.	62.57	12.76
MOVE>5 YEARS	64.97	15.64	87.64	17.90
ROOM COUNT	37.53	29.15	60.68	42.49
S.F. DETACHED	27.38	3.48	88.40	11.42
APT.1–4 FLOORS	−6.45	−1.02	−14.14	−2.19
APT.5+ FLOORS	−32.14	−4.94	−24.52	−3.73
INCOME.NONGOV ($1,000)	3.39	35.24	3.75	48.52
INCOME.GOV ($1,000)	2.24	3.57	2.44	6.43
n-cases	7,305		19,031	
Dep-Mean	486.77		690.21	
C.V.	32.31		40.17	
R.squared	40.82		37.67	

n.a. = not applicable

two units of the same vintage, room number, and building type will command different rents depending on their quality; quality is to be proxied here by tenant income. Higher-income tenants will pay more than others for higher levels of quality, and the owners of higher quality rental units will be more successful in siphoning off the more reliable tenants. Units in social housing projects will be proxied by identifying household income received through government transfers.

Three variables are needed in this model to estimate the price effect of rent controls in Toronto: a categorical variable to identify the Toronto units; another variable to identify the units built in either Toronto or Vancouver after the date rent controls were introduced in Toronto; and a third variable to identify the Toronto units built after rent control was implemented. A regression of rents against all but the last variable will describe the effects of building age (post-1975 and pre-1976), unit quality (as proxied by the tenant's income), unit size, building type, and the overall difference in market conditions prevailing in the two cities. The coefficient for the variable identifying only the post-1975 Toronto buildings will measure the unique effect of rent control in Toronto, because the other relevant factors have been controlled for.

Table 12.2 shows the estimated coefficients using the 1986 and 1991 Census Public Use Microdata files. Overall, it shows that rents in Toronto were $32.11 lower than in Vancouver in 1986 but were $15.51 *above* Vancouver rents in 1991. This is an across-the-board difference, not attributable to the age differences in the stock. The difference between the pre-1976 and post-1975 stock is a modest $26.57 and $34.16, respectively, during the two time periods, with the newer stock the higher priced. The unique difference that can be attributed to rent controls during the two time periods is $68.51 and $102.61, respectively. Since the difference due to inflation is about 30 percent, the estimates using the two independent data sets yield about the same dollar value in real terms and show that, at the very most, the price difference attributable to rent controls in Toronto was $102.61 in 1991 dollars. In other words, rent regulation depressed Toronto rents in controlled units an average of 15 percent during the time its bite was the most severe.

CONCLUSIONS

This case study illustrates the importance of stability in rents and shows how price expectations can lead to rent control policy. The Ontario controls eliminated the price cycle in Toronto, but they did not create the massive distributional consequences that might justify lobbying for new legislation at a later date. The redistributions from landlords to tenants in the form of depressed rents were below 15 percent during the height of the cycle, and they were much smaller for most of the time the controls were in effect.

This case study also shows the peculiar political situation that forced a Conservative government to implement and tighten rent controls. A workable system evolved through a decade of legislative effort and institution building, but as this chapter is being written in 1997, the legislation is about to be seriously modified for largely ideological reasons. This too will create costs; it will also re-create the opportunity to implement more stringent rent controls in the future, when business booms again and when landlords try to boost rents to levels the market deems "unconscionable."

Notes

1. Social Planning Council of Metropolitan Toronto (SPC), Ministry Publications.

2. See "A growing trend in Metro rentals has law makers, tenants alarmed," *Toronto Star*, May 10, 1975; "Pensioners' rent up $215; Alderman calls it 'gouging,'" *Toronto Star*, May 5, 1975; "Seniors hit by 23–59 percent Metro rises," *Toronto Star*, May 6, 1975, as cited in Stanbury and Thain (1986).

3. Stanbury and Thain (1986).

4. The SPC issued its study entitled *Rent Controls: Why We Need Them, What Kind? How Long?* in October 1975. The city of Toronto Task Force on the Status of Tenants made its report public on September 6, 1975.

5. The "hardship" allowances would not be granted to landlords until after the financial loss pass-through has been completed. The Act also modified the method for apportioning the total rental increase allowed on whole-building review.

6. Order in Council #3092, as amended by #2504/83.

7. Slack (1987).

8. Our estimates are in line with the lower figures and are presented at the end of this chapter.

9. See, for example, Miron and Cullingsworth (1983); Steele and Miron (1984); Stanbury and Vertinsky (1986).

10. According to Stanbury and Vertinsky (1986), citing various studies and reports, in 1969 72.2 percent of rental starts were unsubsidized. Between 1975 and 1980, the proportion fell to 37.8 percent. The Ministry of Municipal Affairs and Housing (MOMAH; 1983) states that direct government subsidies were a factor in 75 percent of all rental unit starts between 1976 and 1981.

11. Stanbury and Vertinsky (1986).

12. See, for example, Clayton Research Group (1984) and the Social Planning Council of Metropolitan Toronto (1985).

13. Slack (1987, 20).

14. The establishment of a rent registry to record rental units and base rents created a serious backlog in the administration of rent controls. In addition, numerous economic regulations were passed detailing the specific method of calculating "chronically depressed" rents, economic loss, and hardship. Those making applications for rent review found the system ad hoc, constantly changing, complex, and severely backlogged.

15. Data on the post-1975 stock is available only for October 1978 and later. The 1976 and 1977 figures are interpolated using the Consumer Price Index.

KENNETH K. BAAR

13

Controlling "Im"Mobile Home
Space Rents

INTRODUCTION

The regulation of rents charged for mobile home park spaces constitutes a special category of rent control. In the United States, more than
two million households live in mobile homes situated on land in mobile
home parks that is rented from the park owners. Florida alone has more
than 400,000 mobile home park spaces, and California has approximately
375,000 park spaces.[1] Parks typically contain between fifty and several hundred spaces. The average cost of a new mobile home, not including transportation or setup, has risen from $15,000 in the 1960s and 1970s to $35,000
in the 1990s. (For a discussion of mobile home ownership and its history,
see Baar 1992; Bernhardt 1980; Drury 1972; Morris and Woods 1971; Nutt-
Powell 1982; and Wallis 1991.)

Due to the peculiar nature of the landlord–tenant relationship, special
laws have been adopted for mobile home space rentals that are not applicable to apartment rentals. The California Civil Code states why mobile
home owners need this special protection:

> The legislature finds and declares that, because of the high cost of moving
> mobile homes, the potential damage resulting therefrom, the requirements
> relating to the installation of mobile homes, and the cost of landscaping or
> lot preparation, it is necessary that the owners of the mobile homes . . . be
> provided with the unique protection from actual or constructive eviction.
> (Civil Code Sec. 798.55(a))

193

Nearly every state that has a substantial number of mobile home park spaces has laws specifically governing their rental practices and evictions from them (Sheldon and Simpson 1991). The laws commonly require just cause for evictions and prohibit fees for transferring the ownership of a mobile home. Some laws also guarantee the right of an owner to sell a mobile home in place; limit utility charges to utility costs; specify minimum notice periods for rent increases, typically ranging from sixty to ninety days (as opposed to the thirty-day notice requirement for rent increases for apartments); require that mobile home owners be offered one-year leases; and/or prohibit "tying" arrangements, which require that mobile home owners purchase their mobile homes or other services from the park owner. Under the laws of some states (e.g., Florida, New Jersey, and Vermont), park residents have a first right of refusal when a park is offered for sale; some states also stipulate that relocation benefits be paid in the event that a park is closed. (For a discussion of these laws, see Baar 1997.)

None of the state laws regulate space rent increases, however, except for the Florida mobile home park law, which addresses this issue by authorizing courts to refuse to enforce rent increases that are "unreasonable," taking into account the CPI, increases in operating costs, and other factors (Fla. Stat. Sec. 723.033).

Mobile homes are really prefabricated dwellings and typically range in size from five hundred to fifteen hundred square feet. A majority of the mobile homes constructed in the past few decades have been "double-wide," i.e., they consist of two prefabricated sections that have a combined area of more than one thousand square feet. Once a mobile home is moved to a site, its "mobility" drastically decreases. The wheels are generally removed and the home is placed on a simple foundation. Typically, improvements such as steps, landscaping, garages, and/or sheds also accompany the installation. The cost of moving and setting up a mobile home ranges from a few thousand to ten thousand dollars. In desirable urban areas, the mobility of mobile homes is further diminished by the limited number of vacant pads for rent, and by the fact that most parks will not accept mobile homes that are more than a few years old. In recognition of the immobility of mobile homes, federal law has substituted the term "manufactured" housing for "mobile home"; however, the term "mobile home" still predominates in everyday usage. In reality, mobile home owners are captive tenants who have a substantial investment in their homes.

Mobile homes are generally sold in place. As a result, the rent of the mobile home space becomes a principal determinant of the value of a mobile home. Rent increases can effectively convert mobile home values into land values for park owners. In parks where particularly steep rent increases have been imposed (e.g., on the order of several hundred dollars per month), mobile homes have been rendered worthless. On the other hand, where rent regulations are in effect, mobile home values may have increased.

The legitimacy of rent controls has always been in question in the United States on ideological and policy grounds. However, mobile home space rent controls have generally been considered more legitimate than apartment rent controls, due to the captive nature of mobile home tenancies and the large investments by the tenants (mobile home owners). Furthermore, because a substantial portion of park residents are senior citizens, they are typically seen as more deserving of protections than are apartment dwellers. As of 1997, approximately one hundred California jurisdictions had mobile home space rent control ordinances, compared to only twelve with apartment rent regulations. These California localities contain about 150,000 mobile home park spaces. In New Jersey, roughly ten jurisdictions have mobile home space rent ordinances. In Massachusetts, about twenty-five cities have mobile home rent ordinances.

MOBILE HOME RENT CONTROLS IN CALIFORNIA

Two-thirds of California's 375,000 mobile home park spaces are located in the 1,297 parks that contain one hundred or more spaces. Fourteen percent are in the 130 parks that contain three hundred or more spaces. Mobile home park construction was widespread in California in the 1960s and during the first half of the 1970s. Most of the parks were built on the fringes of metropolitan areas where land was cheap and overall development costs, including land costs, were in the range of $3,000 to $6,000 per space. In the second half of the 1970s, however, as land prices increased and opposition to park developments grew as the suburbs expanded, mobile home park construction drastically declined and substantial rent increases were widespread.

A few years after Los Angeles, San Francisco, Oakland, and San Jose adopted apartment rent control laws in 1978 and 1979, mobile home space rent ordinances were also enacted. In addition, cities passed measures that regulated the closing of mobile home parks by park owners and conversion of the underlying land to other uses. Typically the park owners were required to give their tenants relocation assistance.

Under some ordinances, any increase is legal unless the residents petition for a hearing. Under most of the laws, annual rent increases ranging from 50 to 100 percent of the increase in the Consumer Price Index are permitted. Often, the annual increase provisions have a floor and/or ceiling on the amount; a ceiling of 5 percent is typical. All of the ordinances, however, allow owners to petition for greater increases in order to obtain a fair return. The criteria for evaluating proposed increases under fair return standards often consist of merely a list of factors without any formula; however, specific maintenance of base period net operating income standards is also common. Hearings on petitions are adjudicated by an appointed mobile home commission, city council, or arbitrator.

The mobile home space rent controls in California differ from apartment rent ordinances in some critical aspects. A majority of the ordinances, for example, do not contain vacancy decontrols that permit increases upon changes of ownership of a mobile home. About a quarter of the ordinances do not provide for automatic annual increases. Under ordinances without annual increase provisions, either all increases—or alternatively, only increases that are opposed by a majority of the residents of a park—become subject to review by a board. Consideration of increases on a park-by-park basis is administratively feasible because ownership is concentrated in a relatively small number of park owners (i.e., five to forty parks within most cities).

The adoption of mobile home space rent controls has pitted large-scale investors against well-organized residents. From the outset, lengthy hearings and legal challenges have been common, and trial courts have ruled against cities on a number of issues. In addition, park owners and residents have constantly sought to obtain state legislation to override local measures.

Legal Issues under California Regulations

In 1984, in the first mobile home rent control case reviewed by the California Supreme Court, the Court ruled that mobile home rent ordinances did not have to contain an annual across-the-board rent increase provision, as long as applications for increases were to be ruled on within a reasonable period of time (in this case 105 days) (*Carson Mobile Home Park Owners Ass'n v. City of Carson* 1983). The Court also held that an ordinance did not have to contain a specific fair return formula. In several mobile home and apartment rent control cases, appellate courts rejected the claim that park owners were entitled to a fair return on the "value" of their parks. Courts did uphold fair return formulas based on maintenance of net operating income, however. Such formulas define fair return as pre–rent control (base period) net operating income adjusted by a percentage of the increase in the Consumer Price Index (e.g., *Oceanside Mobile Home Park Owners' Ass'n v. City of Oceanside* (1984) and *Fisher v. City of Berkeley* (1984).

In 1986, however, in *Hall v. City of Santa Barbara*, a U.S. Circuit Court of Appeals ruled that mobile home space rent controls were unconstitutional unless they contained vacancy decontrols that permitted rents to be adjusted every time there was an "in-place" sale of a mobile home. The author of this opinion was a judge who was strongly opposed to economic regulation. He reasoned that the combination of the rent control and the right to sell a mobile home in place constituted a permanent "physical occupation" of the park owner's land by the mobile home owner. The rent control ordinance, the judge said, created a transferable possessory interest that had a "market value," and this possessory interest distinguished the mobile home rent control scheme from conventional apartment rent controls. The apartment rent controls, which had consistently been held to be constitutional by the courts, did not create occupancy rights that were transferable. Therefore, the judge ruled that under the mobile home regulations "tenants were reaping a *monetary windfall*." He concluded that the regulatory scheme resulted in a *physical* taking of the park owner's property—a key distinction, because physical takings are considered takings per se under contemporary judicial doctrine, whereas "regulatory" laws are considered takings only if they take away all economically viable use of a property.

Although this opinion, which affected many cities and thousands of mobile home owners, seemed clearly contrary to judicial precedent, a petition for review was rejected by the U.S. Supreme Court. In subsequent cases, California appellate courts concluded that the federal court of appeals decision was in error and that they were not bound by its opinion (*Yee v. City of Escondido* 1992; *Casella v. City of Morgan Hill* 1991). In response to the uncertainties about potential municipal liability created by the *Hall* decision, however, many California cities introduced vacancy decontrol provisions into their rent ordinances during the next few years. As a result, mobile home values fell because of the potential for unlimited land rent increases upon changes in ownership. In the interim, a federal court of appeals in New Jersey adopted the theories of the *Hall* opinion (*Pinewood Estates v. Barnegat Township Rent Leveling Board* 1990).

In 1992, in the face of conflicting federal and state opinions, the United States Supreme Court finally addressed the issues raised by the *Hall* opinion. In *Yee v. City of Escondido*, it ruled that mobile home space rent controls without vacancy decontrol did not constitute a physical taking. The Court distinguished between the mobile home rent regulations without vacancy decontrol and physical taking cases on the basis that the park owners voluntarily entered into the rental agreements authorizing occupation of their land by the mobile home owners, and that neither state nor city law compels park owners to continuously rent their spaces. The Court rejected the view that a transfer of wealth resulting from rent controls constituted a taking. However, it is important to note that the Court stated that a different case would have been presented if the regulations had prohibited conversions of mobile home parks to other uses, thereby "compelling" continuing rental of mobile home park spaces.

Although the *Yee* decision ended claims that vacancy decontrols were constitutionally required, before the decision was handed down, California adopted legislation exempting leases with a term of more than one year from rent control, provided that the exemption created by the lease was fully disclosed (California Civil Code Sec. 798.17). In response, park owners commonly require potential mobile home owners to enter into "exempt" leases as a condition of approving a purchase of a mobile home in their park. This practice effectively created across-the-board vacancy decontrols, notwithstanding provisions in local ordinances. Some jurisdictions responded by adopting ordinances that prohibited park owners from requiring prospective tenants to execute "exempt" leases; these ordinances in turn led to legal disputes about whether state law preempted local legislation in this area. In 1990, the state adopted an amendment to the exemption legislation that appeared to permit park owners to require prospective tenants to enter such leases (California Statutes 1990, ch. 1046); however, this amendment was repealed the next year (California Statutes 1991, ch. 24, sec.1).

The question of "fair return" has been another pivotal issue in the administration of mobile home rent controls. The absence of annual across-the-board increase standards under some ordinances and the magnitude of the investments in mobile home parks have led to frequent fair return hearings and appeals to courts—a much higher relative volume, in fact, than the volume of fair return appeals under apartment rent controls. In some cases, the mobile home fair return cases have developed into lengthy and expensive processes, as administrative boards and courts have tried to navigate through the sea of judicial uncertainty surrounding what constitutes a fair return. Although the courts have concluded that any one of several fair return standards (formulas) is facially constitutional (*Fisher v. City of Berkeley* 1984), the courts have also held that the standard must be constitutional as applied to a particular case, without setting forth a specific constitutional standard.

Most commonly, park purchasers have claimed that they are not obtaining a fair return because the rents are not adequate to cover their mortgage interest expenses and provide a reasonable return on their investment.

Alternatively, some park owners have claimed that their overall rate of return (net operating income ÷ purchase price) is less than a fair return. The reality is that in a competitive market there is no standard rate of return; in fact, rates of return on real estate investments vary enormously from low or negative levels at the time of purchase to high levels after lengthy periods of ownership.

In the past decade, maintenance of net operating income approaches have become the most widely used measures of fair return. Fair net operating income is defined as base period net operating income adjusted by a portion or all of the percentage increase in the Consumer Price Index since the base date. In one case, an appellate court indicated that the review board must also consider whether an owner is obtaining a fair return, independent of whether net operating income has been maintained (e.g., *Kirkpatrick v. City of Oceanside* 1991), notwithstanding the absence of any consensus (or possibility of any consensus) or declarations by the courts on what return would be fair under an alternate methodology.

In the last few years, another legal issue has been raised by the same justice who authored the *Hall* opinion. In *Sierra Lake Reserve v. City of Rocklin* (1991), the U.S. Circuit Court of Appeals ruled that "every dollar the landlord puts into the property by way of capital improvements constitutes an investment in the property for which a 'fair and reasonable' return must be allowed." Until that decision, issues related to capital improvements under rent controls had not been subject to judicial consideration. A subsequent federal trial court decision included language that has been interpreted to indicate that capital improvements must be considered independently of other expenses and income from a property. However, on appeal, that decision was ruled moot on procedural grounds. In 1997, the California Supreme Court rejected the concept that courts are required to examine individual aspects of a rate-making scheme without looking at the overall scheme (*Kavanau v. Santa Monica Rent Control Board* 1997).

The Cost of Administering California Regulations

Although localities are sympathetic to the plight of mobile home owners, public expenditures on rent control programs do not have much political legitimacy. Proposals for local ordinances are generally met with exaggerated horror stories about the expenditures in other jurisdictions. At the same time, mobile home owners often oppose requirements that they pay registration fees to finance the regulatory programs, even though these fees are small compared to the savings and benefits of the programs.

A survey of FY 1993–94 program expenditures in California revealed that the average net expenditures for programs have been less than $1.00 per mobile home space per month, and usually less than 0.1 percent of the municipal budget (Baar 1995). When viewed as a cost of maintaining affordable housing units, these expenditures are tiny compared to the costs of other housing programs.

Most cities with budgets for mobile home rent controls over $25,000 finance their programs through registration fees, ranging from $1.00 to $5.00 per month per mobile home space. Varying proportions of the fee can be passed through by park owners to their tenants.

Most of the local expenditures on mobile home rent programs have been concentrated in only a few jurisdictions. The great majority of jurisdictions have made only minimal expenditures and held few or no hearings. Two-thirds of the programs, in fact, have either been self-financing or had net expenditures of less than $10,000. In a few cities, however, the expenditures have been more than $200,000 per year.

Proposition 199

In 1995, a group of park owners placed a statewide referendum, known as Proposition 199, on the California ballot. The goal of Proposition 199 was to permanently exempt mobile home spaces from rent controls upon changes in the ownership of the mobile home. The measure was labeled the Mobile Home Fairness and Rental Assistance Act. The "assistance," which was to flow to mobile home owners, consisted of a 10 percent rent reduction for 10 percent of the tenants in return for permanent exemptions. The rent reduction was to be calculated using the rent levels set by the park owner. In their ballot arguments and campaign publicity, the park owners claimed that mobile home rent controls were costing localities $45 million per year. A court required the authors to amend this "argument" to state "a few million dollars," however, on the basis that the $45 million figure was false and misleading.

Proponents of Proposition 199 further claimed that:

1. Rent controls discourage production of new mobile home parks and therefore exacerbate rather than resolve mobile home owners problems.
2. Households that owned a mobile home when rent controls were first adopted received a "windfall" as a consequence of the regulations.

3. Households that purchased mobile homes after the adoption of rent regulations received no similar benefit, because they had to pay a "premium" for their purchase that incorporated the benefits of the rent protections.

(For a discussion of these issues—one that is sharply critical of mobile home rent controls—see Hirsch and Hirsch 1988.)

In retrospect, the average voter probably had little interest in encouraging new park production. Instead, the voters were more concerned about the prospect of seniors being driven into poverty as a result of unconscionable rent increases than about claims about windfalls for mobile home owners. The press, which sympathized with the plight of the mobile home owners, was highly critical of the park owners' misleading claims that the purpose of the new measure was to aid mobile home owners. As a result, the referendum was soundly defeated by a margin of 62 to 38 percent.

THE IMPACT OF RENT CONTROLS ON THE SUPPLY OF PARK SPACES

Since 1990, state law has exempted all newly constructed parks from rent controls (California Civil Code, Sec. 798.45). Available data on park construction dates are seriously limited. However, it appears that land-use restrictions have had a much greater dampening effect on park construction than have rent control regulations. The spread of land-use restrictions to the outer parts of urban areas, for example, seriously curbed park construction starting in the 1970s. Local laws commonly contain large minimum acreage requirements for mobile home parks, restrictions of density to one-half the level allowed for apartments, and/or discretionary use permit requirements with vague standards. At the same time, alternative land uses have become more profitable as land values and house prices have soared. Land that could have been purchased for a few thousand dollars per mobile home space in the 1960s and early 1970s rose in price to $20,000–$30,000 in the 1980s, as builders of condominiums and single-family dwellings vied for land to build on.

Whose "Windfall"?

Although it is true that many mobile home owners have benefited as a result of the passage of mobile home space rent regulations, by and large the park owners have realized far greater appreciation in their investments than the mobile home owners. The original costs of a mobile home far exceeded the original per-space cost of the park land and improvements in the park. Today, park values are several hundred percent higher than the original land and construction costs, while current mobile home values are about the same as their original cost plus installation.

Reports and surveys indicate that average park costs in California were about $6,000 per pad in the 1970s. A 1974 report by the Western Mobilehome Association estimated that the total cost of on-site improvements averaged $2,600 to $4,000 per lot, exclusive of land (Western Mobilehome Association 1973, 4). This same report projected land costs in the range of $5,000 to $25,000 per acre, with permitted densities of eight and a half spaces per acre; this translated into land costs of $3,000 to $7,000 per space, or total costs of $5,600 to $11,000 per space. A 1984 study by the City of Los Angeles found that park owners had paid about $6,000 per mobile home pad, and estimated that the current value of the parks was about $18,000 per pad (Rent Stabilization Division 1985, 33). Currently, most park values range from $15,000 to $45,000 per pad, with averages in the range of $20,000 to $32,000 per pad.[2]

Statewide, in 1994, the average resale price of a mobile home in a park was $24,162.[3] Two-thirds of the mobile homes were manufactured in the 1960s and 1970s; one-quarter were manufactured in the 1980s. The mobile homes that were resold had an average of 1,091 square feet; approximately two-thirds were double-wide. The average original price of the resold mobile homes was $19,443. These data seem to indicate that the resale prices of the mobile homes do not substantially exceed their original costs plus installation and improvement costs.

THE FUTURE OF MOBILE HOME SPACE RENT REGULATIONS

It is difficult to predict whether mobile home space rent protections will contract or spread outside of California and Florida in future years. The lack of mobility faced by mobile home owners is not unique to those states; pressure for controls by mobile home owners could build. However, at least twelve states have laws that prohibit all forms of rent control.

Park owners, like other classes of people, oppose regulation of their profits. But ironically, because the viability of mobile home ownership in parks depends on the predictability and reasonability of rent increases, the future of parks as economic enterprises may hinge on regulations that secure the viability of investments in mobile homes placed in the parks. Conversely, if competition for land use steps up as urban areas expand, park owners may view mobile homes and rent controls as obstacles that prevent them from converting their land to more profitable uses. At the same time, in expanding urban areas, the likelihood of pressure for rent regulation and other protections is also greater.

Notes

1. One study estimated that there were 1.6 million spaces in mobile home parks in 1974 (Bernhardt 1980). Data for the 1990s for California, Florida, Michigan, and Ohio indicate that these states have nearly one million spaces—50 percent more than estimated in the 1974 study (Baar 1992, 157).

2. The estimate in this section is based on the author's review of data contained in several hundred park sales reports of the CompData service (San Diego).

3. Sales data compiled by Berlin Research Corp., San Luis Obispo, California. The data are based on 19,774 sales.

W. Dennis Keating, Michael B. Teitz, and
Andrejs Skaburskis

14

Conclusion

In this book we have reviewed both the evidence and the debate over rent control. The case studies provide a rich history of various types of rent control in the United States and Canada, primarily the second-generation rent control systems that emerged in 1969 and have continued through the 1990s. As the chapters on the economic, political, and legal contexts of rent control explain, the debate over rent control and its impact on tenants, landlords, and the rental housing market has often been vitriolic, and heavily influenced by the ideology of the participants. However, the more moderate versions of second-generation rent control in California and New Jersey have gained broad acceptance as a means of addressing rental housing problems. The varying degrees of success of rent control programs underscore the need to consider carefully the type of rent regulation enacted, the way it is implemented, and, to the extent known, its actual impact rather than hypothetical speculation about its results. In addition, before any new regulations are enacted, both proponents and opponents should identify and explain the viable alternatives to rent control.

In an era marked by the growing dominance and political preeminence of market ideology, rent control might seem to be an anomaly. Yet, like other regulatory policies that survive, rent control can be regarded as a social response to a perceived social problem. Since it has not been adopted as a national policy in the United States or Canada, its utility is limited to circumstances where localized conditions in housing markets have generated political support for governmental intervention. No unique and identifiable set of housing market conditions invariably results in support for such intervention. The evidence in the literature and in our case studies suggests that very rapid fluctuations in rent levels in markets with large proportions of renters are preconditions making it likely that rent control will reach the political agenda. Whether regulation will, in fact, occur cannot be predicted. What is predictable, however, is the likelihood that once rent control is in place, it will not easily be repealed—assuming that decision is left up to the local electorate.

What is the impact of rental regulation? At the conservative end of the spectrum, the prevailing view continues to be that, at best, rent control distorts the regulated housing market, causing far more problems, especially in the long run, than benefits, mostly in the short run, for tenants. (This view is analyzed in chapter 4.)

In the past, apocalyptic results have sometimes been ascribed to rent control (e.g., Walker 1975). Anti-rent control hyperbole has often reached a fever pitch during electoral campaigns in California. In New York City, the long-running debate over rent control has also frequently turned shrill. More grounded arguments take into account other factors affecting housing supply, pricing, and distribution—including land-use controls, mortgage-financing arrangements, tenant income, and landlords' managerial capabilities.

What would replace a regulated housing supply in the most troubled rental housing markets? Salins and Mildner (1992), who argue for total deregulation of controlled units in New York City, call for relaxed land-use controls, liquidation of city-owned, tax-foreclosed housing by auction or sale, privatization of publicly assisted middle-income housing, and rationalization of the property tax system. They claim such measures would lead to a great increase in the construction of unsubsidized new housing and a more equitable allocation of existing unregulated housing. They concede, however, that this unregulated market would be more expensive for most New York City renters (outside of public housing). They also concede that the allocation of space determined by market prices would not eliminate all inequity.

Advocates of strong rent controls take two approaches. As long as serious housing problems remain and absent any other viable policy, they argue that rent regulation is needed to subsidize housing for those whose rent burdens are unfairly high. (And they advocate not just on behalf of poor tenants but also on behalf of moderate- and middle-income tenants.) A more radical approach (mentioned in chapter 7) favors the conversion of much of the regulated rental housing in North America to permanent nonprofit status, e.g., to limited-equity cooperatives (Gilderbloom and Appelbaum 1988, chapter 9).

A less ideological view of rent control has also been propounded, in which its possible utility is recognized, depending upon the regulation's design and the circumstances. Arnott (1994), for example, points out that economists no longer reject rent control out of hand as a regulatory policy that cannot succeed. Niebanck (1985) calls for a reasoned analysis of controls. He notes that: "The rent control field requires the application of research approaches that have an unusual capacity for close observation and critical reflection" (p. 122). The chapters in the present book on Berkeley (chapter 7), the District of Columbia (chapter 8), and Los Angeles (chapter 9) all refer to empirical rent control evaluations that have identified rent control's positive effects while recognizing its limitations and possible negative impacts. Dueling experts and the conflicting conclusions from their studies are referred to in these chapters.

As discussed in chapter 5, the future of rent control and its reputation as a regulatory policy are strongly influenced by politics. Politics have often overshadowed economic, social, and legal factors in determining the fate of rent control. Whenever rent control becomes a political issue, landlord and tenant groups clash; often homeowners play a key role.

The most recent adoption of rent control by federal, state, provincial, and municipal governments in North America appears to have peaked in the 1970s. In the 1990s, rent control receded as regulatory policy. This recession can be explained by two important factors: a lower rate of inflation in housing costs and a more conservative political climate. These factors have overshadowed declining tenant incomes and the continuing shortage of decent, affordable housing for lower-income renters—the result of cutbacks in the 1980s in federal housing subsidy programs in Canada and the United States. However, given its history, rent control may once again come to the fore, should rapid rent inflation return, and with it, awakened tenant political organizing.

Several lessons can be drawn from this book's extensive review and analysis of rental regulation in North America. First, rent control is public regulation. Debates about its adoption, modification, or termination are therefore bound to be political and imply different potential outcomes for the groups involved. As with other forms of regulation, good public policy requires that the implications be understood, to the extent possible, by all the participants, so that they may argue from fact rather than ideology. A factual basis will not guarantee that better policy decisions will be made, but at least the decisions will not be made entirely in ignorance of reality.

The second lesson to be drawn, we would argue, is that rent control is not best described by the simple, rigid model made familiar by generations of economics textbooks. The emergence of second-generation controls, in response to both market and constitutional concerns, has created a much more subtle landscape of regulation in rental housing. There is little evidence to suggest that such regulation does significant harm to housing markets. By the same token, the benefits to tenants are modest also. Whether the apparatus of regulation is worthwhile in this circumstance is reasonably debatable.

The third lesson, in consequence of the previous point, is that rent control, in the form that is constitutionally permissible in the United States, cannot solve the problems of the poor in urban housing markets. If there is any lesson to be learned from the politics of rental regulation, it may be that such an enormous expenditure of effort could be used in more constructive ways to address the problem of low-income housing. The growth of an effective nonprofit housing sector in many markets is an encouraging sign that the problem is being tackled in other ways, though the seemingly permanent lack of resources in the nonprofit sector hampers its role. Still, if rent control is not the answer, neither is it the primary problem, and that fact, too, needs to be recognized. Ultimately, housing in the United States will continue to be delivered through the private market. Finding ways to build alliances that could support moderate regulation while relaxing constraints on development might make more sense than fighting the same wars over and over.

Fourth, the possibilities of further innovation in rental regulation are probably not exhausted. The burst of change in the 1970s showed clearly that learning in this policy area is both possible and useful. Since the 1970s, few innovations have been introduced, despite the social, political, and market changes in many of the places with rent control. Now may be a good time to rethink the possibilities of regulation, to see how it could be made more socially useful, instead of simply seeking to make controls more stringent or to abolish them.

These are not the conclusions that advocates on either side of the rent control debate want to hear. Nonetheless, they are probably more practical than the prescriptions put forward by either side. One thing is sure: Rent control will continue to be advocated and opposed. Our hope is that this book will help inform and guide future discussions of the role of rent regulation in addressing complex housing problems.

Bibliography

A. D. Little, Inc. 1985. *New York: how well is it housed?* New York: Rent Stabilization Association of New York City.

Abraham, J. M., and P. H. Hendershott. 1996. Bubbles in metropolitan housing markets. *Journal of Housing Research* 7: 191–207.

Adams, E. B.; P. Ing; J. Ortved; and M. J. Park. 1986. *Government intervention in housing markets: an overview.* Commission of Inquiry into Residential Tenancies, Research Study No. 29. Toronto: Queen's Printer.

Adams, E. B.; P. Ing; and J. Pringle. 1985. *A review of the literature relevant to rent regulation.* Commission of Inquiry into Residential Tenancies, Research Study No. 28. Toronto: Queen's Printer.

Albon, R., and D. C. Stafford. 1987. *Rent control.* London: Croom Helm.

Alston, R. M.; J. R. Kearl; and M. B. Vaughan. 1992. Is there a consensus among economists in the 1990s? *American Economic Review* 82: 203–209.

Anas, A., and R. J. Arnott. 1993. Technological progress in a model of the housing-land cycle. *Journal of Urban Economics* 34: 186–206.

Anas, A., and J. R. Cho. 1988. A dynamic, policy-oriented model of the regulated housing market: the Swedish prototype. *Regional Science and Urban Economics* 18: 201–231.

Appelbaum, R. P.; M. Dolny; P. Dreier; and J. I. Gilderbloom. 1992. Sham rent control: a further reply. *Journal of the American Planning Association* 58 (Spring): 220-224.

_____. 1995. Scapegoating rent control: masking the causes of homelessness. *Journal of the American Planning Association* 57 (Spring): 153-164.

208

Arnott, R. 1979. Rent controls and housing maintenance. Mimeo. Queen's University, Kingston, Ontario, Canada.

_____. 1981. *Rent control and options for decontrol in Ontario.* Ontario: Ontario Economic Council.

_____. 1987. Economic theory and housing. In E. S. Mills, ed., *Handbook of regional and urban economics.* Vol. II. Amsterdam: North-Holland, 959–988.

_____. 1989. Housing vacancies, thin markets, and idiosyncratic tastes. *Journal of Real Estate Finance and Economics* 2: 5–30.

_____. 1994. Rent control: A contemporary perspective. Preliminary draft, Department of Economics, Boston College, Boston, Massachusetts.

_____. 1995. Rent control: a contemporary perspective. *Journal of Economic Perspectives* 9, 1: 99–120.

Arnott, R.; R. Davidson; and D. Pines. 1983. Housing quality, maintenance, and rehabilitation. *Review of Economic Studies* 50: 467–494.

Arnott, R., and N. Johnston. 1981. *Rent control and options for decontrol in Ontario.* Toronto: Ontario Economic Council.

Arnott, R., and J. M. Mintz, eds. 1987a. *Policy forum on rent controls in Ontario.* Kingston, Ontario: Queen's University, John Deutch Institute for the Study of Economic Policy.

_____. 1987b. *Rent controls: the international experience.* Kingston, Ontario: Queen's University, John Deutch Institute for the Study of Economic Policy.

Atlantic Marketing Research and Cambridge Economic Research. 1998. *Cambridge rental housing study: impacts of the termination of rent control on population, housing costs, and housing stock.* Cambridge Community Development Department.

Atlas, J., and P. Dreier. 1986. The tenants movement and American politics. In R. G. Bratt, C. Hartman, and A. Meyerson, eds., *Critical perspectives on housing.* Philadelphia: Temple University Press.

Audain, M., and C. Bradshaw. 1971. *Tenants' rights in Canada.* Ottawa: Canadian Council on Social Development.

Baar, K. 1977. Rent control in the 1970s: the case of the New Jersey tenants movement. *Hastings Law Journal* 28: 631–683.

_____. 1983. Guidelines for drafting rent control laws: lessons of a decade. *Rutgers Law Review* 35: 721–885.

_____. 1984a. Rent control: an issue marked by heated politics, complex choices, and a contradictory legal history. *Western City* 61: 47.

_____. 1984b. Rent controls and the property tax base: the political economic relationship. *Property Tax Journal* 3: 1–20.

_____. 1986. Facts and fallacies in the rental housing market. *Western City* 63.

_____. 1987. Peacetime municipal rent control laws in the United States: local design issues and ideological policy debates. In W. Van Vliet, H. Choldin, W. Michaelson, and D. Popenoe, eds., *Housing and neighborhoods: theoretical and empirical contributions.* New York: Greenwood Press.

_____. 1992. The right to sell the "im"mobile manufactured home in its rent controlled space in the "im"mobile home park: Valid regulation or unconstitutional taking? *Urban Lawyer* 24: 157–221.

_____. 1995a. The cost of mobilehome rent control programs in California. Unpublished report, commissioned by the Golden State Mobilehome Owners League.

_____. 1995b. *Issues and options for rent increase standards under Berkeley's rent stabilization ordinance.* Berkeley, CA: Berkeley Rent Stabilization Board.

_____. 1997. Laws protecting mobilehome park residents. *Land Use and Zoning Digest* 49: 3–7. November.

Baar, K., and W. D. Keating. 1975. The last stand of economic substantive due process—the housing emergency requirement for rent control. *Urban Lawyer* 7: 447–511.

_____. 1981a. *Fair return standards and hardship appeal procedures: a guide for New Jersey rent leveling boards.* Berkeley, CA: National Housing Law Project.

_____. 1981b. Controlling rent control. *New Jersey Reporter* 11.

Baar, K., and R. LeGates. 1982. Rent control and abandonment: a second look at the evidence. *Journal of Urban Affairs* 4: 49–64.

Baar, K.; F. Leigh; M. Gellen; and W. D. Keating. 1984. *Berkeley rent stabilized properties operating costs and debt service.* Berkeley, CA: Berkeley Rent Stabilization Board.

Ball, M.; M. Harloe; and M. Martens. 1988. *Housing and social change in Europe and the USA.* London: Routledge.

Bartelt, D., and R. Lawson. 1982a. Rent control and abandonment in New York City: a look at the evidence. In R. G. Bratt, C. Hartman, and A. Meyerson, eds., *Critical perspectives on housing.* Philadelphia: Temple University Press.

_____. 1982b. Rent control and abandonment in New York City: a second look at the evidence. *Journal of Urban Affairs* 4, 4: 49–64.

Barton, S. 1985. Property rights and democracy: the beliefs of San Francisco neighborhood leaders and the American liberal tradition. Ph.D. dissertation, Department of City and Regional Planning, University of California, Berkeley.

_____. 1996. Social housing versus housing allowances: choosing between two forms of housing subsidy at the local level. *Journal of the American Planning Association* 62, 1 (Winter): 108–119. On-line at http://www.asu.edu/caed/proceedings97

_____. 1997. Property, community, democracy: barriers to social democracy in the beliefs of San Francisco neighborhood leaders. Working Paper, *COMM-ORG, the On-Line Conference on Community Organizing and Development*. On-line at http://uac.rdp.utoledo.edu/docs/comm-org/papers97/barton.htm.

Bay Area Economics (BAE). 1988. *Berkeley rent control 1988: historically low rents and tenant and housing profile*. Berkeley, CA: BAE.

_____. 1989. *Berkeley rent control 1988: historically low rents and tenant and housing profile—technical appendices*. Berkeley, CA: BAE.

Bernhardt, A.D. 1980. *Building tomorrow: the mobile/manufacturing housing industry*. Cambridge, MA: MIT Press.

Block, W., and E. Olsen, eds. 1981. *Rent controls: myths and realities*. Vancouver, BC: Fraser Institute.

Börsch-Supan, A. 1984. The demand for housing in West Germany and the States: A discrete choice analysis. Ph.D. dissertation, Massachusetts Institute of Technology.

_____. 1986. On the West German tenant's protection legislation. *Journal of Institutional and Theoretical Economics* 142: 380–404.

Breyer, S. G. 1982. *Regulation and its reform*. Cambridge, MA: Harvard University Press.

Brooks, J. 1990. Mobilehome park development: can it still happen in Southern California? *WMA Reporter* 16, 19.

California Department of Housing and Community Development. 1986. *Incentives for family mobilehome parks*.

_____. 1990. *Manufactured housing for families: innovative land use and design*.

California Public Interest Research Group (CALPIRG). 1979. *The impact of and rate of compliance with Measure I: the Berkeley renter property tax relief ordinance*. Berkeley, CA: CALPIRG.

_____. 1981. *Berkeley tenant survey*. Berkeley, CA: CALPIRG.

Canadian Council on Social Development. 1973. Background papers and proceedings of the Canadian Council on Social Development seminar on rent policy, "Is There a Case for Rent Control?" Ottawa.

Cantor, P. 1995. Massachusetts defeats rent control. *Shelterforce* 28, 2: 6–10.

Capozza, D. R., and R. W. Helsley. 1989. The fundamentals of land prices and urban growth. *Journal of Urban Economics* 26: 295–306.

Carroll, B. W. 1989. Post-war trends in Canadian Housing Policy. *Urban History Review* 18: 64–74. June.

Case, K. E., and R. J. Shiller. 1985. The efficiency of the market for single-family homes. *American Economic Review* 79: 125–137.

Chapman, Jeffrey T. 1981. *Rent control in Los Angeles: a response to Proposition 13.* Boston, MA: Intercollegiate Case Clearing House.

Chinloy, P. 1979. The estimation of net depreciation rates on housing. *Journal of Urban Economics* 6: 432–443.

_____. 1980. The effect of maintenance expenditures on the measurement of depreciation in housing. *Journal of Urban Economics* 8: 86–107.

_____. 1996. Real estate cycles: theory and empirical evident. *Journal of Housing Research* 7: 173-190.

City of Berkeley, California. 1983, 1984. *The rent stabilization program.*

_____. 1984. *The rent stabilization program: a supplemental report.*

_____, City Planning Department. 1973. *Building condition and household surveys: technical report.*

_____, Community Development Department. 1994. Rent control in the city of Berkeley, 1978 to 1994. December 20.

Clark, W. A. V., and A. Heskin. 1982. The impact of rent control on tenure discounts and residential mobility. *Land Economics* 58, 1: 109–117.

_____, and L. Manuel. 1980. *The Los Angeles rental housing market.* Los Angeles: Institute for Social Science Research, University of California, Los Angeles.

Clayton Research Group. 1984. *Rent regulation and rental market problems.* Research Study No. 10. Toronto: Commission of Inquiry into Residential Tenancies.

Congressional Budget Office (CBO), Congress of the United States. 1994. *The challenges facing federal rental assistance programs.* Washington, DC: CBO.

Cooper, C. 1976. The house as symbol of the self. In W. H. Ittelson and L. G. Rivlin, eds., *Environmental psychology: people and their physical setting.* New York: Holt, Rinehart and Winston.

Dahl, R. A. 1967. *Dilemmas of pluralist democracy: autonomy vs. control.* New Haven: Yale University Press.

Dahl, R. A., and C. E. Lindblom. 1953. *Politics, economics, and welfare.* New York: Harper.

Dao, J. 1996. Hot issues make for a lively '97 in Albany. *New York Times,* November 11: B12.

_____. 1997. Differences split: rent melodrama is another version of longest running show in Albany. *New York Times,* June 17: A16.

Davis, M. 1992. *City of quartz.* New York: Vintage Books.

deLeeuw, F., and R. J. Struyk. 1975. *The web of urban housing: analyzing policy with a simulation model.* Washington, DC: Urban Institute.

Dennis, M., and S. Fish. 1972. *Programs in search of a policy.* Toronto: A. M. Harkert.

Denton, F., et al. 1994. *Testing hypothesis about rent controls.* Prepared for Canada Mortgage and Housing, Ottawa.

DeParle, J. 1996. The year that housing died. *New York Times,* October 20: Sec. 6, 52–57, 68, 94, 105.

Devine, R. J. 1973. Institutional mortgages in an area of racial transition: Bronx County, 1969–1970. Ph.D. dissertation, New York University.

_____. 1986. *Who benefits from rent control?* Oakland, CA: Center for Community Change.

Diner, S. J. 1983. The regulation of housing in the District of Columbia: an historical analysis of policy issues. In S. J. Diner, J. S. Paige, I. Richter, and M. M. Reuss, eds., *Housing Washington's people: public policy in retrospect.* Washington, DC: Department of Urban Studies, University of District of Columbia.

Dobkin, S. 1989. Confiscating reality: the illusion of controls in the Big Apple. *Brooklyn Law Review* 54: 1249–1266.

Donnison, D. 1967. *The government of housing.* Harmondsworth, Middlesex, England: Penguin Books.

Dowell, D. 1984. *The suburban squeeze: land conversion and regulation in the San Francisco Bay Area.* Berkeley, CA: University of California Press.

Downs, A. 1957. *An economic theory of democracy.* New York: Harper.

_____. 1988. *Residential rent controls: an evaluation.* Washington, DC: Urban Land Institute.

_____. 1989. Residential rent controls. *Urban Land* 48, 2: 16–20.

Dreier, P. 1979. The politics of rent control. *Working Papers for a New Society* 6: 55-63.

_____. 1997. The landlords stage a rent strike. *Nation* 264, 24:17–22.

Dreier, P., and D. Hulchanski. 1993. The role of nonprofit housing in Canada and the United States: some comparisons. *Housing Policy Debate* 4: 43–80.

Drellich, E. B., and A. Emery. 1939. *Rent control in war and peace.* New York: National Municipal League.

Drobak, J. N. 1986. Constitutional limits on price and rent control: the lessons of utility regulation. *Washington University Law Quarterly* 64: 107–150.

Drury, M. J. 1972. *Mobile homes: the unrecognized revolution in American housing.* New York: Praeger.

Epstein, R. A. 1985. *Takings: private property and the power of eminent domain.* Cambridge, MA: Harvard University Press.

_____. 1988. Rent control and the theory of efficient regulation. *Brooklyn Law Review* 54: 741–780.

Evans, A. E. 1995. The property market: ninety percent efficient? *Urban Studies* 32: 5–30.

Fallis, G. 1984. *Possible rationales for rent control*. Research Study No. 5. Toronto: Commission of Inquiry into Residential Tenancies.

_____. 1988. Rent control: the citizen, the market, and the state. *Journal of Real Estate Finance and Economics* 1: 309–318.

Fallis, G., and A. Murray. 1990. *Housing the homeless and poor*. Toronto: University of Toronto Press.Firestone, D. 1997. Poll finds strong support for New York rent laws. *New York Times*, June 11: A22.

Firestone, D. 1997. Poll finds strong support for New York rent laws. *New York Times* (June 11): A22.

Fischel, W. 1991. Comment on Anthony Downs. *Housing Policy Debate* 2, 4: 1139–1160.

Fisher, E. M. 1966. Twenty years of rent control in New York City. In *Essays in urban land economics*. Los Angeles: Real Estate Research Program, University of California, Los Angeles.

Follain, J. R., and S. Malpezzi. 1979. Dissecting housing value and rent: estimates of hedonic indexes for thirty-nine large SMSAs. Washington, DC: Urban Institute.

Foucault, M. 1977. *Discipline and punish*. New York: Pantheon.

Frankena, M. 1975. Alternative methods of rent control. *Urban Studies* 12: 303–308.

Fried, J. P. 1976. City's rent rises outpace tenant income increases. *New York Times*, January 19: A-1.

Friedman, L. M. 1968. *Government and slum housing: a century of frustration*. New York: Rand McNally.

Friedman, L. S. 1984. *Microeconomics policy analysis*. New York: McGraw-Hill.

George, H. 1992 [1879]. *Progress and poverty*. New York: Robert Schalkenbach Foundation.

Gilderbloom, J. I. 1980. *Moderate rent control: the experience of U.S. cities*. Washington DC: Conference on Alternative State and Local Policies.

_____. 1983. The impact of moderate rent control in New Jersey: an empirical analysis of 26 rent-controlled cities. *Urban Analysis* 7: 135–154.

_____. 1986. The impact of moderate rent control on rents in New Jersey communities. *Sociology and Social Research* 71: 11–14.

Gilderbloom, J. I., and R. C. Appelbaum. 1988. *Rethinking rental housing*. Philadelphia: Temple University Press.

Glaeser, M. G. 1957. *Public utilities in American capitalism*. New York: MacMillan.

Goodman, A. C., and T. Thibodeau. 1995. Age-related heteroskedasticity in hedonic house price functions. *Journal of Housing Research* 6, 1: 25–42.

Gould, J. R., and S. G. B. Henry. 1967. The effects of price control on a related market. *Economica* 34: 42-49.

Grampp, W. D. 1950. Some effects of rent control. *Southern Economic Journal* 16: 425–447.

Gyourko, J., and P. Linneman. 1985. Equity and efficiency aspects of rent control: an empirical study of New York City. *Journal of Urban Economics* 26: 54–74.

Hamilton, Rabinovitz & Alschuler. 1988. *1988 Rent stabilization review*. Los Angeles: City of Los Angeles, Community Development Department, Rent Stabilization Division.

_____. 1991a. *Defining "fair rate of return" in Berkeley rent regulation in the aftermath of the Searle decision*. Los Angeles, CA.

_____. 1991b. *Inflation indexing in Berkeley rent regulation in the aftermath of the Searle decision*. Los Angeles, CA.

_____. 1994a. *The 1994 rental housing study: summary report on issues and options*. Los Angeles: City of Los Angeles, Housing Department, Rent Stabilization Division.

_____. 1994b. *The 1994 rental housing study: technical report on issues and policy options*. Los Angeles: City of Los Angeles, Housing Department, Rent Stabilization Division.

Hamilton, Rabinovitz, Szanton & Alschuler. 1985a. *The Los Angeles rent stabilization system: impacts and alternatives*. Los Angeles: City of Los Angeles, Community Development Department.

_____. 1985b. *1984 rental housing study: executive summary*. Los Angeles: City of Los Angeles, Community Development Department.

Harney, D. 1980. *The invisible tax: what homeowners pay to support local rent controls*. Washington, DC: National Apartment Association.

Hartle, D. G. 1984. *The political economy of rent control in Ontario*. Research Study No. 12. Toronto: Commission of Inquiry into Residential Tenancies.

Hartman, C. 1984. *The transformation of San Francisco*. Totowa, NJ: Rowman and Allanheld.

Haurin, D. P.; P. Hendershott; and D. Kim. 1990. *Real rents and household formation: the effects of the 1986 Tax Reform Act*. National Bureau of Economic Research, Report No. 3309.

Hawley, P. K. 1978. *Housing in the public domain: the only solution*. New York: Metropolitan Council on Housing.

Heidegger, M. 1968. *What is a thing?* Chicago: H. Rugnery Co.

Heskin, A. 1983. *Tenants and the American dream*. New York: Praeger.

Heskin, A.; N. Levine; and M. Garrett. 1995. *Rent control without vacancy decontrol: a spatial analysis of four California cities*. Paper presented at ACSP Conference, Detroit.

Hirsch, W. Z. 1987. *Rental housing database*. Sacramento, CA: California Department of Real Estate.

Hirsch, W. Z., and J. G. Hirsch. 1988. Legal–economic analysis of rent controls in a mobile home context: placement values and vacancy decontrol. *UCLA Law Review* 35: 399–466.

Housing Preservation and Production Department. 1991. *Comprehensive housing affordability strategy (CHAS)*. Los Angeles: City of Los Angeles, Housing Preservation and Production Department.

Hsia, R. C. 1974. The ABCs of MBR: how to spell trouble in landlord/tenant relations (up against the crumbling walls). *Columbia Journal of Law and Social Problems* 10: 113–176.

Hubert, F. 1990a. Long-term rental contracts. Working paper, Freie Universitat Berlin.

_____. 1990b. Tenure security for tenants. Working Paper, Freie Universitat Berlin.

_____. 1991. The regulation of rental contracts in the housing market. Frankfurt am main: Peter Lang.

Igarashi, M., and R. Arnott. 1994. Rent control, mismatch costs, and search efficiency.

Illing, W. 1969. The rising cost of housing and problems of financing. In M. Wheeler, ed., *The right to housing*. Montreal: Harvest House.

Joint Center for Housing Studies. 1989. *The state of the nation's housing*. Cambridge, MA: Harvard University.

Jones, L. D. 1989. Current wealth and tenure choice. *Journal of the American Real Estate and Urban Economics Association* 17: 17–40.

Kahn, M. 1994. Organizing for structural reform: the case of the New Jersey Tenants Organization. *Journal of Community Practice* 1, 2: 87–110.

Kain, J., and J. Quigley. 1970. Measuring the value of housing quality. *Journal of the American Statistical Association* 65: 532–548.

Kalymon, B. A. 1981. Apartment shortages and rent control. In W. Block and E. Olsen, eds., *Rent control: myths and realities*. British Columbia: Fraser Institute.

Kann, M. E. 1986. *Middle-class radicalism in Santa Monica*. Philadelphia: Temple University Press.

Keating, W. D. 1983. *Rent control in California: responding to the housing crisis*. Berkeley: Institute of Governmental Studies, University of California, Berkeley.

_____. 1985. Dispersion and adaptation: the California experience. In P. L. Niebanck, ed., *The rent control debate*. Chapel Hill, NC: University of North Carolina Press: 57–73.

_____. 1987. Landlord self-regulation: New York City's rent stabilization system (1969–1985). *Journal of Urban and Contemporary Law* 31: 77–134.

Keynes, J. M. 1965. *The general theory of employment, interest, and money.* New York: Harcourt, Brace & World, 149–150.

Kiefer, D. 1980. Housing deterioration, housing codes and rent control. *Urban Studies* 17: 53–62.

Kingdon, J. W. 1984. *Agendas, alternatives, and public policies.* Boston: Little Brown.

Kolbert, E. 1997. Sides sharply disagree about life after rent control. *New York Times,* April 6: A23.

Kolko, G. 1965. *Railroads and regulation.* Princeton, NJ: Princeton University Press.

Kristof, F. S. 1970. Housing: the economic facets of New York City's problems. In L. C. Fitch and A. M. H. Walsh, eds., *Agenda for a city.* New York: Institute of Public Administration.

Lawson, R. 1986. Tenant responses to the urban housing crisis, 1970-1984. In R. Lawson and M. Naison, eds., *The tenant movement in New York City, 1904–1984.* New Brunswick, NJ: Rutgers University Press.

Leigh, W. A. 1979. The estimation of tenure-specific depreciation/replacement rates using housing quantity measures for the U.S., 1950-1970. *The Quarterly Review of Economics and Business* 19: 49–59.

Levine, N.; J. E. Grigsby; and A. Heskin. 1990. Who benefits from rent control? *Journal of the American Planning Association* 56 (Spring): 140–152.

Lindbeck, A. 1971. *The political economy of the New Left: an outsider's view.* New York: Harper and Row.

Linneman, F. 1987. The effect of rent control on the distribution of income among New York City renters. *Journal of Urban Economics* 22: 14–34.

Lipsky, M. 1970. *Protest in city politics.* Chicago: Rand McNally.

Lithwick N. H. 1970. *Urban Canada: problems and prospects.* Report prepared for the Minister of Housing, Government of Canada. Ottawa: CMHC.

Lopez, V. J. 1995. *1995 rental housing study.* Albany, NY: New York State Assembly Housing Committee.

Los Angeles Rent Stabilization Division. 1985. *Rental housing study: mobilehome parks under rent stabilization.*

Lowry, I. S., ed. 1970a. *Rental housing in New York City, Vol. 1: confronting the crisis.* Research memo no. RM-6190-NYC. New York: Rand Institute.

_____. 1970b. Filtering and housing standards: a conceptual analysis. In A. Page and W. Seyfried, eds., *Urban analysis.* Glenview, IL: Scott, Foresman.

_____. 1985. *The financial performance of rental property under rent control: Berkeley, California, 1978–85.* California Housing Research Institute.

Malpezzi, S. 1996. *Interim bibliography on urban development: 1996 edition.* Madison, WI: Center for Land Economics Research, University of Wisconsin (Working Paper Series).

Malpezzi, S.; L. Ozanne; and T. Thibodeau. 1980. *Characteristic prices of housing in fifty-nine metropolitan areas.* Washington, DC: Urban Institute Press.

_____. 1987. Measuring and modeling spatial variation in rates of economic depreciation for residential real estate: a preliminary investigation. Working paper 87-2, Center for Research in Real Estate and Land Use Economics. Edwin, L. Cox School of Business, Southern Methodist University, Dallas, Texas.

Marcuse, P. 1975. Residential alienation, home ownership, and the limits of shelter policy. *Journal of Sociology and Social Welfare* 3: 181–203.

_____. 1981. *Housing abandonment: does rent control make a difference?* Washington, DC: Conference on Alternative State and Local Public Policies.

_____. 1986. *The uses and limits of rent regulation.* New York State, Division of Housing and Community Renewal.

Margolis, S. 1981. Depreciation and maintenance of houses. *Land Economics* 57: 91–105.

_____. 1992. Depreciation of housing: an empirical consideration of the filtering hypothesis. *Review of Economics and Statistics* 64: 90–96.

Marino, M. 1975. Rent leveling in New Jersey. Report prepared for New Jersey Department of Community Affairs, Bureau of Housing, Trenton, New Jersey. pp. 2–3. January.

Markusen, J. R. 1978. The timing of residential land development. *Journal of Urban Economics* 5: 411–424.

Markusen, J. R., and D. T. Scheffman. 1977. *Speculation and monopoly in urban development: an analytical foundation with evidence for Toronto.* Toronto: University of Toronto Press.

_____. 1978. The timing of residential land development. *Journal of Urban Economics* 5: 411–424.

Marks, D. 1987. Rent control and housing policy. In R. J. Arnott and J. M. Mintz, eds., *Policy forum on rent controls in Ontario.* Kingston, Ontario: Queen's University, John Deutch Institute for the Study of Economic Policy.

Mascall, M. 1985. *Report on the rental housing market.* Research Study No. 22. Toronto: Commission of Inquiry into Residential Tenancies.

Mayer, N. S. 1978. Determinants of landlord housing rehabilitation decisions. Ph.D. dissertation, University of California, Berkeley.

_____. 1981. Rehabilitation decisions in rental housing: an empirical analysis. *Journal of Urban Economics* 10: 76–94.

_____. 1984. Conserving rental housing. *Journal of the American Planning Association* 49 (Summer): 311–325.

McKinley, J. C. 1994. Council votes to lift controls on luxury rentals in future. *New York Times*, March 21: A-13.

Michelson, W. 1977. *Environmental choice, human behaviour, and residential satisfaction.* New York: Oxford Press.

Miron, J. 1990. Security of tenure, costly tenants and rent regulation. *Land Economics* 58: 109–117.

Miron, J., and J. B. Cullingsworth. 1983. *Rent control: impacts on income distribution, affordability and security of tenure.* Toronto: University of Toronto, Centre for Urban and Community Studies.

Mitgang, A. S. 1995. The power to regulate: an overview of the legal context of California's rental housing regulations. *San Francisco Law Review* 5: 17–48.

Mitnick, B. M. 1980. *The political economy of regulation: creating, designing, and removing regulatory forms.* New York: Columbia University Press.

Moe, T. M. 1984. The new economics of organization. *American Journal of Political Science* 28: 739–777.

Morris, E. W., and M. E. Woods, eds. 1971. *Housing crisis and response: the place of mobile homes in American life.* Ithaca, NY: Cornell University.

Muller, R. A. 1989. The experience with rent regulation in Canada. Research Report 244. Program for Quantitative Studies in Economics and Population, McMaster University, Hamilton, Ontario, Canada.

Murray, A. 1990. Homelessness: the people. In M. Fallis, ed., *Housing the homeless and poor.* Toronto: University of Toronto Press.

Murray, M. P., et al. 1991. Analyzing rent control: the case of Los Angeles. *Economic Inquiry* 29 (October): 601–625.

Muth, R. 1975. Numerical solution of urban residential land use models. *Journal of Urban Economics* 7, 4: 307–332.

_____. 1986. Expectations of house-price changes. *Papers of the Regional Science Association* 159: 45-55.

Naison, M. 1986. From eviction resistance to rent control: tenant activism in the Great Depression. In R. Lawson and M. Naison, eds., *The tenant movement in New York City, 1904–1984.* New Brunswick, NJ: Rutgers University Press.

Nesslein, T. S. 1992. The effects of rent control: an analytical reassessment and the experiences of Berkeley and Santa Monica, California, 1980-1990. Ph.D. dissertation, University of Washington.

New Jersey Department of Community Affairs. 1996. *New Jersey Construction Reporter* (June).

New York City Department of Housing Preservation and Development. 1997. *1996 New York City Housing and Vacancy Survey.* New York: Department of Housing Preservation and Development. Also on the World Wide Web at http://www.nycrgb.com

New York City Rand Institute. 1970. *Rental housing in New York City.* New York: New York City Rand Institute.

Niebanck, P. L. 1985. The politics and economics of rent control. In P. L. Niebanck, ed., *The rent control debate*. Chapel Hill, NC: University of North Carolina Press.

Noll, R. 1989. Economic perspectives on the politics of regulation. In R. Schmalensee and R. Willig, eds., *Handbook of industrial organization*. Amsterdam and New York: North-Holland.

Nutt-Powell, T. 1982. *Manufactured homes: making sense of a housing opportunity*. Boston, MA: Auburn House.

Olsen, E. O. 1969. A comparative theory of the housing market. *American Economic Review* 54: 612–621.

_____. 1972. An econometric analysis of rent control. *Journal of Political Economy* 80: 1081–1100.

_____. 1988. What do economists know about the effect of rent control on housing maintenance? *Journal of Finance and Economics* 1: 295–307.

Olson, M. 1965. *The logic of collective action*. Cambridge, MA: Harvard University Press.

Ontario Law Reform Commission. 1968. *Interim report on landlord and tenant law applicable to residential tenancies*. Department of the Attorney General.

Ontario Ministry of Government Services. 1985a. *Assured housing for Ontario: a position paper*. Toronto.

_____. 1985b. *Assured housing for Ontario: reforms to rent review*. Toronto.

Ontario Ministry of Housing. 1973. *Advisory task force on housing policy report*. Toronto: Queen's Printer.

_____. 1974. *Housing Ontario*. Toronto.

Ontario Welfare Council. 1973. *A study of housing policy in Ontario: a general report*. Toronto.

Ozanne, L., and S. Malpezzi. 1985. The efficacy of hedonic estimation with the Annual Housing Survey: evidence from the demand experiment. *Journal of Economic and Social Measurement* 13: 1533–172.

Pahl, R. E. 1969. *Whose city?* Harmondsworth, Middlesex, England: Penguin Books.

Patterson, J., and K. Watson. 1976. *Rent stabilization: a review of current policies in Canada*. Canadian Council on Social Development.

Perez-Pena, R. 1997. Landlords quietly raised donations in rent battle. *New York Times*, May 4: C20.

Pringle, J. 1986. *Ontario's residential tenancies: a statistical profile*. Commission of Inquiry into Residential Tenancies.

Putnam, Robert D. 1993. *Making democracy work*. Princeton, NJ: Princeton University Press.

Quigley, J. M. 1990. Does rent control cause homelessness? Taking the claim seriously. *Journal of Policy Analysis and Management* 9: 89–93.

Rabin, E. 1984. The revolution in residential landlord–tenant law: causes and consequences. *Cornell Law Review* 69: 517–683.

Radin, M. J. 1986. Residential rent control. *Philosophy and Public Affairs* 15: 350–380.

Rawls, John. 1971. *A theory of justice*. Cambridge, MA: Harvard University Press.

Rechlis, M. B., and A. Yezer. 1985. Urban location and housing price appreciation. *Papers of the Regional Science Association* 57: 155–164.

Rent and Rehabilitation Administration (RRA), City of New York. 1966. *City of New York: a study of some effects of two decades of rent control*. New York: RRA.

Rent Guidelines Board (RGB), City of New York. 1995. *Housing NYC: rents, markets and trends '95*. New York: RGB.

Rent Stabilization Association of New York City (RSA). 1980. *A rational approach to housing in the 1980s: preserving New York City's rental apartments*. New York.

Rent Stabilization Division. 1985. *Housing production and performance under rent stabilization*. Los Angeles: City of Los Angeles, Community Development Department, Rent Stabilization Division.

Rex, J., and R. Moore. 1967. *Race, community and conflict: a study of Sparkbrook*. London: Oxford University Press.

Roistacher, E. A. 1972. The distribution of tenant benefits under rent control. Ph.D. dissertation, University of Pennsylvania.

Rose, A. 1980. *Canadian housing policies, 1935–1980*. Ontario, Canada: Butterworth and Company.

Rothenberg, J.; G. C. Galster; R. V. Butler; and J. Pitkin. 1991. *The maze of urban housing markets: theory, evidence and policy*. Chicago: University of Chicago Press.

Rydell, C. P.; C. L. Barnett; C. E. Hillestad; M. P. Murray; K. Neels; and R. H. Sims. 1981. *The impact of rent control on the Los Angeles housing market*. Rand Note N-1747-LA. Santa Monica: Rand Corporation.

St. John, M. 1989. The effects of rent controls on property value: a test of the capitalization hypothesis. Ph.D. dissertation, University of California, Berkeley.

_____. 1993. *The distribution impact of restrictive rent control programs in Berkeley and Santa Monica, California*. Paper presented at the Western Economic Association.

Salins, P. D., and G. C. S. Mildner. 1992. *Scarcity by design: the legacy of New York City's housing policies*. Cambridge, MA: Harvard University Press.

Schaub, E. L. 1920. The regulation of rentals during the war period. *Journal of Political Economy* 1.

Schwartz, J. 1986. Tenant power in the liberal city, 1943–1971. In R. Lawson and M. Naison, eds., *The tenant movement in New York City, 1904–1984*. New Brunswick, NJ: Rutgers University Press.

Sheldon, J., and A. Simpson. 1991. *Manufactured housing park tenants: shifting the balance of power.*

Sheldon, S. S. 1981. Rethinking rent control: an analysis of "fair return." *Rutgers Law Journal* 12: 617–651.

Skaburskis, A. 1988. Speculation and housing prices: a study of Vancouver's boom–bust cycle. *Urban Affairs Quarterly* 23: 556–560.

_____. 1994. Determinants of Canadian headship rates. *Urban Studies* 31: 1377–1389.

Slack, E. 1987. Ontario's experience with rent regulation. In R. J. Arnott and J. M. Mintz, eds., *Policy forum on rent controls in Ontario*. Kingston, Ontario: Queen's University, John Deutch Institute for the Study of Economic Policy.

Smith. 1981. *Impact study on the effects of rent control upon community tax base.* Apartment House Council of New Jersey.

Smith, L. B. 1971. *Urban Canada—problems and prospects.* In *Housing in Canada*, Research Monograph 2. Ottawa: CMHC.

Smith, W. 1968. Quotation from lecture presented at the University of California, Berkeley.

Social Planning Council of Metropolitian Toronto. 1974. *The rent race*. Toronto.

_____. 1975. *Rent controls: why we need them. What kind? How long?* Toronto: Community Review and Research Group.

_____. 1979. *Brief to the Ontario Legislative Assembly, respecting Bill 163, an Act to reform the law respecting residential tenancies.* Toronto.

_____. 1985. *Brief to rental tenancies commission.*

Spencer, J. A. 1986. New York City: tenant organizations and the post-World War I housing crisis. In R. Lawson and M. Naison, eds., *The tenant movement in New York City, 1904–1984.* New Brunswick, NJ: Rutgers University Press.

Stanbury, W. T. 1985. *Normative bases of rent controls.* Research Study No. 15. Toronto: Commission of Inquiry into Residential Tenancies.

Stanbury, W. T., and P. Thain. 1986. *The origins of rent regulations in Canada.* Research Study No. 17. Toronto: Commission of Inquiry into Residential Tenancies.

Stanbury, W. T., and I. Vertinsky. 1986. *Rent regulation: design characteristics and effects.* Toronto: Commission of Inquiry into Residential Tenancies.

Starr, R. 1985. The *rise and fall of New York City*. New York: Basic Books.

State of New Jersey. 1988. Report of the Rental Housing Study Commission, Trenton, New Jersey.

Steele, M. 1993. Conversions, condominiums and capital gains: the transformation of the Ontario rental housing market. *Urban Studies* 30: 103–126.

Steele, M., and J. Miron. 1984. *Rent regulation, housing affordability problems, and market imperfections.* Research Study No. 9. Toronto: Commission of Inquiry into Residential Tenancies.

Stegman, M. A. 1985. *Housing in New York: study of a city, 1984.* New Brunswick, NJ: Center for Urban Policy Research, Rutgers University.

Sternlieb, G. 1972. *The urban housing dilemma: the dynamics of New York City's rent-controlled housing.* New York: New York City Housing and Development Administration.

Sternlieb, G., and J. W. Hughes. 1976. *Housing and economic reality: New York City 1976.* New Brunswick, NJ: Center for Urban Policy Research, Rutgers University.

_____. 1979. Rent control's impact on the community tax base. *Appraisal Journal* 47: 381.

Stone, M. E. 1993. *Shelter poverty: new ideas on housing affordability.* Philadelphia: Temple University Press.

Struyk, R.; M. Turner; and M. Ueno. 1989. *Future U.S. housing policy: meeting the demographic challenge.* Washington, DC: Urban Institute Press.

Sweeney, J. L. 1974a. A commodity hierarchy model of the rental housing market. *Journal of Urban Economics* 1: 288–323.

_____. 1974b. Quality, commodity, hierarchies, and housing markets. *Econometrica* 42: 147–167.

Teitz, Michael B. 1987. Rental housing regulation in California: What do we know? In L. Graymer, J. Dimento, and F. Schnidman, eds., *Rental housing in California: market forces and public policies.* Boston, MA: Oelgeschlager, Gunn and Hain.

Thom, S., Commissioner (Thom Commission Report). 1987. *Report of the Commission of Inquiry into Residential Tenancies.* 2 Vols. Toronto: Queen's Printer.

Tognoli, J. 1987. Residential environments. In D. Stokols and I. Altman, *Handbook of environmental psychology.* New York: Wiley Interscience Publishers.

Truman, D. B. 1960. *The governmental process: political interests and public opinion.* New York: Alfred Knopf.

Tucker, W. 1987. Where do the homeless come from? *The National Review* (September 25): 32–43.

_____. 1989. *America's homeless: victims of rent control. Backgrounder* 685. Washington, D.C.: The Heritage Foundation.

_____. 1990. *The excluded Americans.* Washington: Regnery Gateway.

_____. 1991. Scapegoating rent control: a reply. *Journal of the American Planning Association* 57 (Autumn): 485–489.

Turner, M. 1990. *Housing market impacts of rent control: the Washington, D.C. experience.* Washington, DC: Urban Institute Press.

Turner, M., and Edwards, J. 1993. Affordable rental housing in metropolitan neighborhoods. In G. Kingsley, and M. Turner, eds., *Housing markets and residential mobility.* Washington, DC: Urban Institute Press: 125–160.

U.S. Bureau of the Census. 1994. *1993 New York City housing and vacancy survey.* New York: U.S. Bureau of the Census.

U.S. Department of Housing and Urban Development (HUD). 1973. Abandoned housing research. Washington DC: Government Printing Office.

_____. 1976. *American housing survey for the Washington metropolitan area in 1974.* Washington, DC: HUD.

_____. 1995. *The national homeownership strategy: partners in the American dream.* Washington, DC: HUD.

_____. 1996. *Rental housing assistance at a crossroads: a report to Congress on worst case housing needs.* Washington, DC: HUD. March.

Urban Development Institute. 1974. *The case against rent controls.* Ontario.

Walker, J. 1988. Operation and administration of the District's rent control program. In *Rent control in the District of Columbia.* Washington, DC: Urban Institute.

Walker, M. A. 1975. What are the facts? In *Rent control: a popular paradox.* Vancouver, BC: Fraser Institute.

Wallis, A. D. 1991. *Wheel estate.* New York: Oxford University Press.

Weiss, M. A. 1987. *The rise of the community builders.* New York: Columbia University Press.

Western Mobilehome Association. 1973. *Mobilehome park development.*

Weston, R. R. 1972. The quality of housing in the United States, 1929–1970. Ph.D. dissertation, Department of Economics, Harvard University, Cambridge, Massachusetts.

Wheeler, M., ed. 1969. *The right to housing.* Montreal: Harvest House.

Wilensky, Harold. 1965. *Industrial society and social welfare.* New York: Free Press.

Wolfe, M. F. 1983. The actual and perceived profitability in rental housing: a disaggregate analysis. Ph.D. dissertation, University of California, Berkeley.

Law Cases

AMN, Inc. v. South Brunswick Rent Leveling Board, 93 N.J. 518, 461 A.2d 1138 (1983).

Benson Realty Corp. v. Beame, 431 N.Y. S.2d 475, 409 N.E.2d. 948 (1980).

Birkenfield v. City of Berkeley, 17 C.3d 129; 130 Cal.Rptr. 465, 550 P.2d 1001 (1976).

Block v. Hirsh, 256 U.S. 135 (1921).

Bowles v. Willingham, 321 U.S. 503 (1944).

Brunetti v. Borough of New Milford, 68 N.J.576, 350 A.2d 19 (1975).

Carson Mobile Home Park Owners Ass'n v. City of Carson, 35 Cal.3d 184 (1983).

Casella v. City of Morgan Hill, 280 Cal.Rptr. 876 (1991).

Chastleton v. Sinclair, 264 U.S. 543 (1924).

Clarendon Management Corp. v. State Div. of Housing & Community Renewal, 529 N.Y.S. 2d 692 (1988).

Fisher v. City of Berkeley, 37 Cal.3d 644, 693 P.2d 261 (1984) and 475 U.S. 460 (1986).

Fresh Pond Shopping Center v. Callahan, 464 U.S. 875 (1983).

Hall v. City of Santa Barbara, 833 F.2d 1270 (9th Cir. [1986]) cert. denied, 485 U.S. 940 (1988).

Helmsley v. Borough of Fort Lee, 78 N.J. 200, 394 A.2d 65 (1978).

Help Hoboken Housing v. City of Hoboken, 650 F.Supp. 793 (1986).

Hutton Park Gardens v. West Orange, 68 N.J. 543, 350 A.2d 1 (1975).

Inganamort v. Borough of Fort Lee, 62 N.J. 521, 303 A.2d 298 (1973).

Javidzad v. City of Santa Monica, 251 Cal.Rptr. 350 (1988).

Kavanauv v. Santa Monica Rent Control Board, 66 Cal. Rptr. 2d 672 (1997)

Kirkpatrick v. City of Oceanside, 232 Cal.App.3d 267 (1991).

Lindsey v. Normet, 405 U.S. 56 (1972).

Mayes v. Jackson Township, 103 N.J. 362, 511 A.2d 589 (N.J. 1986).

Nash v. City of Santa Monica, 207 Cal.Rptr. 285 (1984).

Oceanside Mobile Home Park Owners' Ass'n v. City of Oceanside, 157 Cal.App.3d 887 (1984).

Orange Taxpayers Council v. City of Orange, 83 N.J. 246, 416 A2d 353 (1980).

Parks v. Hazlet Township Rent Control Board, 107 N.J. 217, 526 A.2d 685 (1987).

Pennell v. City of San Jose, 485 U.S. 1 (1988).

Pinewood Estates v. Barnegat Township Rent Leveling Board, 898 F.2d 347 (3d. Cir 1990).

Property Owners Ass'n. v. Township of North Bergen, 74 N.J. 327, 378 A.2d 25 (1977).

Searle v. City of Berkeley Rent Stabilization Board, unpublished (Cal. App. Ct. 1990).

Seawall Associates v. City of New York, 542 N.E.2d 1059 (1989).

Sierra Lake Reserve v. City of Rocklin, 938 F.2d 951 (9th Cir. 1991).

Troy Hills Village v. Township Council of Parsippany-Troy Hills, 68 N.J. 604, 350 A.2d 34 (1975).

Troy v. Renna, 727 F.2d 287 (3d Cir. 1984).

Wagner v. City of Newark, 24 N.J. 467, 132 A.2d 794 (1957).

Yee v. City of Escondido, 503 U.S. 519 (1992).

Contributors

W. DENNIS KEATING is Professor of Urban Planning and Law, Chair of the Department of Urban Studies, and Associate Dean of the Levin College of Urban Affairs at Cleveland State University. His most recent books include *Revitalizing Urban Neighborhoods* (coeditor), University Press of Kansas 1996; *Cleveland: A Metropolitan Reader* (coeditor), Kent State University Press 1995; and *The Suburban Racial Dilemma: Housing and Neighborhoods,* Temple University Press 1994. Keating has written about rent control in California, rent stabilization in New York City, commercial rent control, and legal issues related to rent control. He has been a consultant on rent control in California, New Jersey, and Jamaica.

MICHAEL B. TEITZ is Director of Research at the Public Policy Institute of California and Professor Emeritus of City and Regional Planning at the University of California, Berkeley, where he taught from 1963 until 1998. He has written and consulted widely on housing economics and policy, working with the U.S. Department of Housing and Urban Development and the municipal governments of New York City, Los Angeles, and Berkeley, California, among others. His work on rent control began when he served as project leader for the Rand Corporation's studies of housing and rent control in New York City between 1968 and 1970. Subsequently, he was responsible for the specifications of a series of studies of rent stabilization in Los Angeles from 1984 to 1994. In addition, he has written about rent control in California and has studied its impacts in Berkeley. In 1988, he received a Guggenheim Fellowship for research on rent control.

ANDREJS SKABURSKIS is Professor in the School of Urban and Regional Planning at Queen's University in Kingston, Ontario. He received his Ph.D. in City and Regional Planning from the University of California at Berkeley and established a planning consulting firm before joining the Queen's University faculty in 1984. He has conducted considerable research on housing (specializing in applied economics) and has published in the *Journal of Architectural and Planning Research, Journal of Planning Education and Research, Journal of Regional Science, Canadian Journal of Regional Science, Environment and Planning A* and *C,* and *Urban Studies.*

227

KENNETH K. BAAR, an attorney and urban planner, received his doctorate from UCLA. He has served as a consultant to numerous California jurisdictions on apartment and mobile home rent controls. He has also served as an expert witness in rent control fair return cases. His extensive publications on rent control, which include the widely used work "Guidelines for Drafting Rent Control Laws: Lessons of a Decade" (*Rutgers Law Review* 35, 4 [1983]), have frequently been cited by state supreme and appellate courts. During the 1994–95 academic year, he was a Visiting Assistant Professor in the Graduate School of Architecture, Planning, and Preservation at Columbia University.

STEPHEN E. BARTON is coauthor of *Common Interest Communities: Private Governments and the Public Interest* (Institute of Governmental Studies Press 1994) and has published numerous articles on housing issues. He is currently a Senior Planner for the City of Berkeley. He received his Ph.D. in City and Regional Planning from the University of California at Berkeley and has taught courses in planning, research methods, and urban problems at the University of California, Berkeley, at San Francisco State University, and at New College of California.

CATHERINE NASH is a Ph.D. candidate in the Department of Geography at Queen's University. She completed her master's degree in City and Regional Planning at Queen's in 1995. Previously, she was a partner in a law firm specializing in municipal law and land development. She received her LL.B. from the University of Ottawa in 1983.

MARGERY AUSTIN TURNER is a Principal Research Associate at the Urban Institute in Washington, D.C., where she conducts research on spatial and racial dimensions of anti-poverty policies within urban regions. Ms. Turner served as Deputy Assistant Secretary for Research at the U.S. Department of Housing and Urban Development from 1993 through 1996, where she focused HUD's research agenda on the problems of racial discrimination, concentrated poverty, and economic opportunity in America's metropolitan areas. Prior to joining the Clinton administration at HUD, Ms. Turner directed the housing research program at the Urban Institute. She holds a master's degree in Urban and Regional Planning from George Washington University.

Index

Note: Page numbers in italics refer to tables.

F

fair return, 19–23, 31, 33, 144, 152, 155
  and mobile home rent controls, 198
  case law, 31–33
    rate of return, 32
    adjustment for inflation, 32–33
  doctrine, 30–31
  rent adjustments, 35
  standards, *20*
  variables considered in—formulas, *21*
Federal Housing and Rent Act, *153*
federal rent controls, 3, 6
  during the Great Depression, 8
  in Canada, 6
  wartime emergency measure, 4, 28
Fisher v. City of Berkeley, 33, 37, 93, 106, 196, 198
Florida, 193, 194, 202
Ford, Gerald, 160
Fort Lee, New Jersey, 143, 145
Fresh Pond Shopping Center v. Callahan, 36

G

Gann, Paul, 92, 126
George, Henry, 89
Germany, 80, 85
Giuliani, Rudy, 163
Great Depression, 8, 27, 63, 80, 86, 152

H

Hall v. City of Santa Barbara, 197, 199
Hayden, Tom, 127
Hayward, California, 107
Helmsley v. Borough of Fort Lee, 34, 146
Help Hoboken Housing v. City of Hoboken, 37
Heskin, Allan, 70–71
Historically Low Rent and Single Family Home Amendments of 1990, 104, 105, 106
history of rent control, 1–3
  origins and development, 3
    in Canada, 6–7

mobile home
  controlling space rents, 193–195
    impacts of rent regulation, 201–202
  rental regulation, xi, 5, 19, 24, 31
    future of, 202–203
    in California, 195–202
Mobile Home Fairness and Rental Assistance Act, 200
monopoly power, 47–49, 63, 65
Mortgage Bankers Association, 13

N

Nash v. City of Santa Monica, 36
National Apartment Association, 13
National Association of Home Builders, 13
National Association of Realtors, 13
National Multi-Housing Council, 13
National Realty Committee, 13
Netherlands, the, 85
net operating income (NOI), 20–22, 33, 106, 146
New Deal measures, 28
Newfoundland, Canada, 6
New Jersey, 2
  Bergen County, 148
  case study, 142–150
  condominium conversion legislation, 36, 148
  current ordinances, 149
  exemption of new construction, 148–149
  Fort Lee, 143, 145
  legal challenges, 143, 144–146
  local ordinances, 143–144
  mobile home space rent ordinances, 195, 197
  moderate rent control in, xi
  municipal rent control, 5
  preemption, 39, 143
  property tax, 146–147
  rent control in, 34, 69, 70, 142–143, 204
  rent regulation, 24
  Supreme Court, 34, 40, 143, 144
  Tenants Organization (NJTO), 70, 143, 144, 149
  vacancy decontrol, 18, 77, 142, 144, 146–147, 150
New York, 35
  administration of rent control, 25
  Court of Appeals, 37, 38, 40, 167

S

T

New Jersey, 18, 77, 142, 144, 146–147, 150
New York City, 18, *153*, 159–160
West Germany, 50
Vacancy Decontrol Law of 1971, *153*
Vancouver, Canada, 189, 190, 191
Veiller, Lawrence, 67
Vietnam conflict, 5, 28
volunteer boards, 24–25

W

Wagner, Robert, 155
Wagner v. City of Newark, 143
Warren, Michael, 172
Washington, D.C., 2, 206
   case study, 110–124
   first enacted in, 28, 69
   home rule government, 5
   housing production and availability, 120–123
   landlords, 112–113
   low-cost housing, 110, 113, 120, 122
   moderate rent control in, xi, 78, 110–112
   profitability and maintenance, 116–120
      perceptions among tenants and landlords, 112–113
   rents and housing affordability, 113–116
   temporary emergency controls, 4, 28
   tenants, 112–113
West German Tenants Protection legislation, 50
West Hollywood, California, 72
World War I, viii, 3, 28, 152, 155, 165
World War II, viii, 4, 6, 28, 33, 126, 154, 157, 158, 165

Y

Yee v. City of Escondido, 31, 197–198